"The beauty of *Gospel-Centered Marriage Counseli* theology with practical explanations and applications the actual counseling process. Dr. Kellemen is both a trained theologian and an experienced biblical counselor. In reading this book, you will be listening to words that are saturated with the gospel and characterized by case-specific wisdom. This will feel less like reading a book and more like watching an experienced biblical counselor in action, and then practicing the principles yourself under the direction of an experienced coach. Every pastor and biblical counselor should add this important work to their library."

Dr. Steve Viars, senior pastor, Faith Church, Lafayette, IN;
author of *Loving Your Community*

"Having served as a pastor and counselor for over thirty years now, I read marriage and counseling books like other people devour the sports page. So I can say with confidence that Dr. Kellemen has given us a book that addresses what has been missing for so long: *a biblical, practical, and seasoned step-by-step way forward*. As I read *Gospel-Centered Marriage Counseling*, I said, 'Finally! This what we've needed.' Bob has done the church and the biblical counseling world an enormous service in putting real feet on what marriage counseling looks like. He frames it up with hope and the gospel, and then provides clear and specific step-by-step guidance on how to do effective and biblical marriage counseling. If you've lost heart and felt overwhelmed at the prospect of marriage counseling, this is the book for you! Buy it. Read it. Tell others about it."

Brad Bigney, lead pastor of Grace Fellowship (EFCA);
author of *Gospel Treason: Betraying the Gospel with Hidden Idols*

"Marriage counseling presents some of the toughest situations that can be found. In *Gospel-Centered Marriage Counseling,* biblical counselors who desire to grow in their ability to provide help for marital issues will find what they have been searching for. This is not just another book on marriage counseling; it is a *training manual*. Bob's writing is practical and biblical; he provides a step-by-step process, built firmly upon the gospel of grace, for learning how to help struggling marriages. I am so excited for this book to be published! It will be valuable for novice and seasoned biblical counselors alike. I highly recommend everyone get a copy and begin to put these soulu-tions into practice!"

Dr. Julie Ganschow, author of *Living Beyond the Heart of Betrayal*;
coauthor of *A Biblical Counselor's Approach to Marital Abuse*

"If you are looking to be equipped in a discipleship-focused approach to marriage counseling, *Gospel-Centered Marriage Counseling* is what you're looking for. Few people have the heart, mind, and experience to write a book on marriage counseling for pastors and lay leaders as Dr. Bob Kellemen has done. I have long admired Bob's balanced emphasis on the need to address both sin and suffering in counseling. In *Gospel-Centered Marriage Counseling*, you will find a practical theology to address the hard things a couple faces (suffering) and the bad things a couple does (sin) with the hope of the gospel."

Brad Hambrick, ThM, EdD, pastor of counseling at The Summit Church, Durham, NC; author of *Romantic Conflict* and *Self-Centered Spouse*.

"There are many excellent biblical books about marriage, but Dr. Bob Kellemen makes a unique contribution as he goes beyond teaching *about* marriage to *equipping* counselors to *do* marriage counseling. Reading this book is like sitting in and watching an experienced master biblical counselor apply the gospel to broken marriages. Bob includes many instructive counseling dialogues (or 'trialogues') that serve as a model for counselors who want to get to root problems and then apply gospel truth. The strengths of *Gospel-Centered Marriage Counseling* include its faithful practical exposition of Scripture, a God-centered perspective on marriage, and a practical training manual for marriage counseling."

Dr. Jim Newheiser, director of the Christian counseling program and associate professor of pastoral theology at Reformed Theological Seminary, Charlotte, NC; executive director of IBCD

"I have to be honest, when I heard that another book on marriage was coming out, I had my doubts that it would add anything new to what currently exists. What a pleasant surprise *Gospel-Centered Marriage Counseling* turned out to be. Not only is the book easy to digest and implement in my counseling ministry, it is *one of a kind*, aimed at training pastors, counselors, students, and interns to become effective marriage counselors faithful to God's Word. Claiming that *Gospel-Centered Marriage Counseling* is a game-changing resource might sound cliché, but for those engaged in the practice of marriage counseling, as well as those training in the classroom, this resource does indeed offer what other marriage books simply cannot—comprehensive, practical, hands-on equipping."

Dr. Ben Marshall, pastor of counseling at Canyon Hills Community Church; board president of The Damascus House

GOSPEL-CENTERED
Marriage Counseling

An Equipping Guide
for Pastors and Counselors

ROBERT W. KELLEMEN, PhD

BakerBooks
a division of Baker Publishing Group
Grand Rapids, Michigan

© 2020 by Robert W. Kellemen

Published by Baker Books
a division of Baker Publishing Group
PO Box 6287, Grand Rapids, MI 49516-6287
www.bakerbooks.com

Printed in the United States of America

Library of Congress Cataloging-in-Publication Data
Names: Kellemen, Robert W., author.
Title: Gospel-centered marriage counseling : an equipping guide for pastors and counselors / Robert W. Kellemen, PhD.
Description: Grand Rapids, Michigan : Baker Books, [2020] | Series: The equipping marriage and family counselors series
Identifiers: LCCN 2020003207 | ISBN 9780801094347 (paperback)
Subjects: LCSH: Church work with married people—Handbooks, manuals, etc. | Marriage counseling—Religious aspects—Christianity—Handbooks, manuals, etc. | Pastoral counseling—Handbooks, manuals, etc. | Bible—Psychology—Handbooks, manuals, etc.
Classification: LCC BV4012.27 .K45 2020 | DDC 259/.14—dc23
LC record available at https://lccn.loc.gov/2020003207

In keeping with biblical principles of creation stewardship, Baker Publishing Group advocates the responsible use of our natural resources. As a member of the Green Press Initiative, our company uses recycled paper when possible. The text paper of this book is composed in part of post-consumer waste.

21 22 23 24 25 26   7 6 5 4 3 2

Contents

Acknowledgments

My motivation for writing *Gospel-Centered Marriage Counseling* began while I was serving as counseling pastor at Bethel Church in northwest Indiana. Many pastors, ministry leaders, and lay leaders from Bethel journeyed with me as we counseled, discipled, and shepherded many couples. I want to thank each of them for their co-ministry, encouragement, and friendship: Pastor Steve DeWitt, Pastor Brad Lagos, Pastor Mark Culton, Pastor Dexter Harris, Pastor Dan Jacobsen, Pastor Jared Bryant, Pastor Chris Whetstone, Pastor Gary Butler, Pastor Dustin Rouse, and ministry leaders/lay leaders Ken Barry, Lauri Mollema, Gail Morris, Skye Bryant, Jennifer Culton, Laura Sauerman, Caitlin Marsee, Joy Katts, Amanda Wilson, and Melissa Anderson.

Before, during, and after I wrote *Gospel-Centered Marriage Counseling*, I've been serving alongside the ministry team at Faith Bible Seminary in Lafayette, Indiana. Thank you for your ministry in my life: Pastor Steve Viars, Pastor Brent Aucoin, Pastor Rob Green, and Kirk Fatool.

Foreword

The book you're holding in your hands is unique—and uniquely helpful. As you read through its pages, you will find at least two ways *Gospel-Centered Marriage Counseling* is not typical, and neither is its author, Dr. Bob Kellemen.

First, this book is not typical in how it approaches marriage. So many marriage help books convey a view of marriage that doesn't include much beyond the couple's own interests in the relationship. They don't go any further than trying to offer solutions to the problems a couple is aware of. Yes, in this book you will find guidance for approaching the problems a couple presents to you in the counseling room. You will read suggestions for addressing the specific dynamic that exists between *this* couple, the history of their interactions, and the goals that they can set for their future. You will gain insight into the particular troubles that arise in marriages—anger, disappointment, self-pity, distance, loss, and pain unique to each spouse. But you will also find that Bob views these problems through a wider lens that takes in parts of the scene often left on the periphery.

In this wide-angle view, Bob equips us to see marriage according to the broader purposes of God and to address the couple in light of realities they're probably not considering when they first come for help. They are usually seeing marriage primarily as an arrangement that ought to balance the values they want—shared domestic labor, agreeable companionship, long-term security. If they are willing to go through the process of marital counseling, it's often because they recognize these values are worth the effort to trudge through the difficulties that brought them for help. In other words, the benefits of staying together are worth the annoyances, drawbacks, and pain.

This book will demonstrate that marriage counseling is about *helping them see their marriage from a larger set of eyes*. God tells us his perspective of marriage from the Bible's opening chapter in Genesis to its closing chapter in Revelation. It is a perspective that supersedes ours in every way—beckoning our small concerns for marriage upward into a larger epic. An epic that involves two people displaying in their little time and place the ancient love of the Almighty God—and even more specifically, the love of Jesus Christ for his bride, the church.

In *Gospel-Centered Marriage Counseling*, Bob insists that the epic purposes of God are the only true way a couple can see their own marriage correctly. Marriage is the uniting of two distinct persons into one flesh, where both spouses give of themselves for the magnification of the other. Such love can only happen through the transformative power of the Lord Jesus Christ. This is why the gospel is so central to the counseling process. Only by receiving the love of God through faith can a spouse act like Jesus to the other. As an experienced biblical counselor, Bob doesn't let you forget this throughout his book, even while he remains thoroughly practical.

Speaking of practical, that is the second way this book is unique. Bob offers a number of strategies for addressing different types of troubles in a marriage. Each provides a fresh angle of approach suitable to a number of different needs. Bob's experience in the counseling room and his desire to see marriages reflect the beauty of Jesus's love are strongly displayed.

These strategies involve different ways of helping couples reshape the way they see and respond in their marriage. Bob may surprise you in how he accomplishes this. For example, one of his strategic focuses is on resurrection—the truth that because Jesus died for the sins of his people and proved his victory over sin by being resurrected from the dead, Jesus therefore has authority to lend this victory to whoever would grab hold of it.

Jesus's resurrection power can change everything in a marriage, freeing each spouse to live not for themselves but for the wider purposes of God. Resurrected people don't act the same. The concerns that once preoccupied them fade into lesser importance. Tendencies that were once glaring don't stick out as much. Differences that once seemed insurmountable lose their threat. The couple suddenly becomes aware of goodness they'd been overlooking: hidden graces in the other, higher purposes in working through conflict, deeper joy in laboring through the bleak seasons.

Insight into those different seasons a marriage can go through is why this book will be so helpful to you. Some couples you counsel will need you to think carefully about *sustaining* their marriage—helping them to move from anger with each other to actually caring about and empathizing with each other. Others will need biblical *healing*—finding gospel hope *together* through Christ's grace and truth. Some will need the hard work of *reconciling*—repenting of sinful actions and attitudes and granting forgiveness to each other. Still others require the work of biblical *guiding*—leaning into Christ's resurrection power to put on new, Christlike ways of relating to each other.

A good counselor will meet a couple where they're at but won't let them stay there. In *Gospel-Centered Marriage Counseling*, Dr. Bob Kellemen will guide *you* as you guide *them*. I'd encourage you to follow along with him. His approach is not typical, and that's why it's so uniquely helpful in relating the gospel to the heart of the marriage relationship.

Jeremy Pierre, PhD, chair of the Department of Biblical Counseling and Family Ministry; Lawrence and Charlotte Hoover Associate Professor of Biblical Counseling, Southern Baptist Theological Seminary

Series Introduction

As an equipper of pastors and counselors, I hear all the time how intimidating marriage and family counseling is. Recently, an experienced pastor shared with me:

> Marriage counseling? I'm clueless. I feel like I'm standing in traffic on an expressway, with cars going both ways, half of them the wrong way, most of them swerving out of control. I have no idea how to move from my good theology of marriage to actually helping the troubled couple sitting in front of me.
>
> Family counseling? Don't even get me started on that. By the time family members get to me, they're so angry that they aren't listening to each other. And half the time they don't even want to listen to me!

The Purpose of This Two-Book Series: Filling the Gap

The contemporary Christian world churns out books—great books—on marriage and the family. Theory of marriage and family? Tons of books. Books for couples? Scores of books. Books on the family and parenting? Boatloads.

However, even in the biblical counseling world, we have next to nothing available about *procedures*—the how-to of counseling hurting couples and families. *Pastors and counselors desperately need help in relating their theology to marital messes and family chaos.* They need training manuals on the nuts and bolts of the procedures and processes of helping the couple or family sitting in front of them.

Gospel-Centered Marriage Counseling and *Gospel-Centered Family Counseling* step into this void. This two-book series of equipping guides provides practical, user-friendly training for pastors, counselors, lay leaders, educators, and students.

Not Your Parents' Counseling Books

These two books walk you as the reader through step-by-step training to develop your *skills and competencies* in marriage and family counseling. In fact, "reader" is the wrong word. "Participant" is better.

Gospel-Centered Marriage Counseling and *Gospel-Centered Family Counseling* are workbooks—think of them as working books or even workout books. Thus the subtitle *An Equipping Guide for Pastors and Counselors*. Chapter by chapter, skill by skill, as a participant you will use the questions, exercises, role-play directions, sample dialogues, and much more to develop your competency and increase your confidence as a biblical marriage and family counselor.

Introduction

I always enjoy radio interviews related to my books. Interviewers typically start by asking, "What motivated you to write this book?" For *Gospel-Centered Marriage Counseling*, my answer relates both to *me* and to *you*.

Like many biblical counselors and pastors, I have an adequate level of comfort, confidence, and competence as a counselor of *individuals*. I also have provided a good deal of marriage counseling, and for over two decades I have equipped pastors and counselors for marriage counseling. Still, I have experienced marriage counseling as exponentially more complex and messy than individual counseling. Where do you start? How do you sort through all the he said, she said? How do you help couples move forward when they are so focused on past hurts? How do you make headway when painful emotions are strewn everywhere?

But even the complexity of marriage counseling was not enough to motivate me to craft this manual. My motivation arose a year before this book project started. I was serving as a lead elder at our church when our counseling pastor informed the elder team that he wanted to move to part-time status. My fellow elders looked at me and said, "Why don't you do a job share, Bob? Counseling's in your blood." So I agreed.

I met with our counseling pastor so he could walk me through cases he wanted to transition to me. I'll never forget his words as he handed me three thick files: "In my forty years of pastoral ministry, these are three of the toughest marriage counseling situations I've ever worked with."

My first thought: "What have I gotten myself into?" My second, more arrogant thought: "I teach pastors how to do this marriage counseling stuff. These may be *his* most difficult marriage counseling cases, but I'm a pretty competent counselor . . ."

You know where I'm headed next. He was right. These three cases were among the most complex marriage counseling cases I had ever experienced in my three decades of ministry.

Two things started happening. First, I began admitting to myself and to God that I was an *incompetent* marriage counselor without Christ. For years, I had highlighted Romans 15:14 when equipping people to be competent counselors. But now there was something freeing about acknowledging my own incompetence and pursuing competence in Christ.

Second, not only did I start devouring the materials I had developed to equip others for biblical marriage counseling but I also started updating and upgrading those notes—scouring God's Word for wisdom.

What motivated me to write *Gospel-Centered Marriage Counseling*? I wrote this book first for *me*! I needed God's help and wisdom if I had any hope of being a competent marriage counselor for those three difficult marriages—and for any marriages.

How You Can Benefit from This Book

I also wrote this book for *you*. I'm picturing you—a *pastor*—who perhaps had one class on counseling and possibly zero classes on a gospel-centered, how-to approach to marriage counseling.

I am picturing you—a *trained biblical counselor*—who likely had one class on marriage counseling theory and theology but no lab class to specifically train you how to provide effective biblical marriage counseling.

I am picturing you—a *layperson* (a nonprofessional counselor who is not a vocational pastor)—who loves people and marriages but feels overwhelmed when trying to help a brokenhearted couple.

I am picturing you—*educators*—who teach pastors and counselors in a Christian college or seminary setting. When you search the evangelical publishing landscape, you can find hundreds of books about marriage. Yet, even with your level of academic awareness, you are likely at a loss to identify Christian books that equip your students with a biblical, practical, step-by-step process for learning how to help struggling marriages. You have to turn to the secular publishing landscape to find books with a hands-on focus for training in marital therapy. But you are not interested in a worldly way to help Christian marriages. Neither am I.

There is a reason I included the phrase *Gospel-Centered* in this book's title. This is *not* a secular marital therapy manual. I have examined Scripture and asked myself, What would a model of biblical marriage counseling look like that was built solely upon Christ's gospel of grace? This book is my answer to that question.

How You Can Use This Book

I have written *Gospel-Centered Marriage Counseling* to provide *hands-on* training in *biblical* marriage counseling. Think first about that word "biblical." Part 1 of this book offers a theological primer for biblical marriage counseling. Theology matters. Christ's gospel of grace makes a daily difference in our marriages. Christ's eternal story invades and impacts our daily story.

But how? How do we take theology, the gospel, and Christ's story and relate them to the troubled couple sitting in front of us? Think now of a second phrase: "hands-on." And consider the subtitle of this book: *An Equipping Guide for Pastors and Counselors*. This is not just a book *to read*. It is a training manual *to use*. After every section of every chapter you will find training exercises with the heading Maturing as a Biblical Marriage Counselor. Overall you will have the opportunity to engage in *hundreds* of such equipping exercises.

This is why part 2 of this book provides practical training for biblical marriage counselors by developing twenty-two marriage counseling relational competencies. See figure I.1 for a list of those gospel-centered counseling skills.

I have never been too wild about words like "skills" and "techniques" when used in conjunction with biblical counseling. A central verse that shepherds my counseling ministry is 1 Thessalonians 2:8: "Because we loved you so much, we were delighted to share with you not only the gospel of God but our lives as well."

Paul shares the gospel of God—he models gospel-centered ministry. He also is delighted to share his very own soul because he loves people so much and because they are so dear to him. Paul models truth and love, gospel and relationship. While "relational competency" is still not the greatest phrase in the world, I have chosen it to try to capture the combination of gospel and relationship that is central to biblical marriage counseling.

Throughout *Gospel-Centered Marriage Counseling* you will learn a step-by-step process for developing twenty-two marriage counseling relational competencies. You will learn how to relate Christ's eternal truth to messy, complex marriages today. For that to happen, please prioritize time for responding to the Maturing as a Biblical Marriage Counselor training exercises. You can use these individually. They are also ideal for small group lab usage—where you receive counseling training in a group setting.

You will quickly notice that many of the interactive questions relate to your own life. Maturing as a biblical counselor is never just about developing counseling competencies. It is also about growing in Christlike character.

When using *Gospel-Centered Marriage Counseling* in a small group lab setting:

- Read the assigned chapter *before* the lab meets. Do not use lab time for lecturing on the content. Interact briefly about how the content relates to the practice of marriage counseling, but reserve most of the lab time for the following suggested activities.

- Respond in writing to the Maturing as a Biblical Marriage Counselor questions *before* your small group meets.
- During your small group lab interact about the questions.

Figure I.1

Overview of Biblical Marriage Counseling
22 Gospel-Centered Marriage Counseling Relational Competencies

Infusing Hope

H Having Hope as a Marriage Counselor (chap. 5)

O Offering Hope to Hurting Couples (chap. 5)

P Promoting God's Perspective (chap. 5)

E Enlightening Couples (chap. 5)

Parakaletic Biblical Marriage Counseling for Suffering Spouses

- **Sustaining**: Like Christ, we care about each other's hurts.

    C Coupling with the Couple (chap. 6)

    A Assisting the Couple to Become Intimate Allies (chap. 6)

    R Renewing the Couple's Trust in the God of All Comfort (chap. 7)

    E Engaging the Couple through Empathetic Encouragement (chap. 7)

- **Healing**: Through Christ, it's possible for us to hope in God together.

    F Fighting Satan's Lying and Condemning Earthly Narrative (chap. 8)

    A Applying Christ's Truth and Grace Eternal Narrative (chap. 8)

    I Inviting Couples to Crop the Life of Christ into Their Marital Life (chap. 9)

    T Trialoguing about Christ's Truth and Grace Eternal Narrative (chap. 9)

    H Healing Individually and Together in Christ (chap. 9)

Nouthetic Biblical Marriage Counseling for Sinning Spouses

- **Reconciling**: It's horrible to sin against Christ and each other, but through Christ it's wonderful to be forgiven and to forgive.

    P Probing Theologically (chap. 10)

    E Exposing Marital Heart Sins (chap. 10)

    A Applying Truth Relationally (chap. 11)

    C Calming the Conscience with Grace (chap. 11)

    E Enlightening Couples about Biblical Marital Reconciliation (chap. 11)

- **Guiding**: It's supernatural to love each other like Christ, through Christ, for Christ.

    L Leaving the Past Behind (chap. 12)

    O Ongoing Gospel Growth (chap. 12)

    V Victorious Together through Christ (chap. 13)

    E Exalting Christ Together (chap. 13)

- The questions related to your life provide opportunities to counsel one another during your small group meeting. A premise of this book is that *we become effective biblical counselors by giving and receiving biblical counseling in community.*
- The questions related to marital counseling situations provide opportunities for role-playing marriage counseling. They also provide opportunity for real-life marriage counseling of each other if spouses are part of the training group or invited into parts of the group time.
- After role-play or real-life marriage counseling, offer feedback to one another so you can grow together as biblical marriage counselors.

My motivation to write this book is likely the same as your motivation to read it. We want to glorify God by growing as biblical marriage counselors who apply Christ's gospel of grace to help hurting and hurtful spouses to become Christlike and Christ-honoring spouses.

Maturing as a Biblical Marriage Counselor

1. Regarding the theory/theology of marriage:

   a. What reading have you done about married life—biblical teaching about roles in marriage, desires of husbands and wives, problems in marriage?

   b. How easy or hard has it been for you to translate those teachings into practical, relational ways to help the couple sitting in front of you?

2. Regarding the practice/methodology of marriage counseling:

   a. What reading have you done in marriage counseling practices or methods? To what extent have you been able to find biblical resources on the how-to of counseling couples?

   b. On a scale of 1 to 10 (1 = "Not prepared to do marriage counseling" and 10 = "I could teach marriage counseling"), currently how prepared are you to do marriage counseling?

3. I admitted to being incompetent to counsel without Christ.

   a. How does my admission impact your thoughts about using this book? Does it encourage you or discourage you? Why?

   b. If you have marriage counseling experience, as you reflect on your past counseling of couples, has marriage counseling been easier or harder than individual counseling? How competent or incompetent have you felt as a biblical marriage counselor?

   c. If you have not yet provided marriage counseling, as you think ahead to counseling couples, are you excited, intimidated, or both?

4. Through the Maturing as a Biblical Marriage Counselor component of this book, you will have the opportunity to engage in hundreds of training exercises.

   a. Some of those exercises will require you to take an honest, biblical look at your life. How willing are you to do that?

   b. If you are going through this material in a small group lab, how prepared are you to share about your life with those in your training group? What could your group do to make this training experience safe, encouraging, and mutually edifying?

PART 1

A Theological
Primer for
Biblical Marriage
Counseling

ONE

Marriage God's Way

Introduction: Solution Focused or Soul-u-tion Focused?

Picture Travis and Britney. They have been married for over a dozen years—at least ten of those years have been filled with communication difficulties and unresolved conflicts. They have seen several counselors, read a batch of marriage books, attended marriage conferences, and spent a weekend at a marriage restoration retreat center.

As you engage with Travis and Britney about the history of the work they have done on their marriage, you detect two common themes. They have concluded that:

- We fight because we miscommunicate with each other. We need better communication skills.
- We fight because we misunderstand each other. We need better teaching about roles and responsibilities in marriage.

You mentally file away those facts as the three of you begin interacting about Travis and Britney's latest eruption of conflict. As they each tell their story, you notice they could successfully teach a seminar on marital communication, roles in marriage, and spousal needs. But you detect something more significant—they each use their skills and knowledge in self-centered and self-sufficient ways. Travis tends to use his communication skills to manipulate and corner Britney—almost like a prosecuting attorney grilling a witness. Clearly there is a heart issue at work. Travis's training in communication skills has created *a more effective manipulator*.

Having been placed on the witness stand, Britney is quick to expose the myriad ways Travis fails to fulfill his roles and responsibilities and fails to meet her God-designed marital longings. She is even quicker to describe the ways she has applied biblical marriage principles—to no avail. As you listen, you wonder if you are hearing self-righteousness that seems to communicate, "I've done my part. I've been a good wife. Now it's up to God to fix Travis and for Travis to get his act together!" Britney's training in marital roles, responsibilities, and desires has created *a more self-sufficient sinner*.

Between meetings with Britney and Travis, you prayerfully review your notes. You scribble down, "How can such good tools like biblical communication principles and a biblical understanding of marital roles be so misused?" Then you jot down your summary. "Travis and Britney's self-diagnosis: We lack fulfillment in our marriage because of our miscommunication and misunderstanding. Their self-prescription: The solution to our marriage problems is to work harder at applying communication skills and good teaching."

Travis and Britney have a *solution*-focused approach to their marriage—which leads to self-centered goals. If we could discern the thoughts and intents of Travis's heart, this is what we might hear: "Marriage is about meeting *my* needs. If better communication gets Britney to meet my needs, then I'm all for that!"

Solution-focused marriage counseling also leads to self-sufficient efforts. Britney thinks, "Working on my marriage is a self-improvement project. If I become a good enough wife, then Travis will come around and meet my needs."

Travis and Britney have misdefined the ultimate purpose of marriage, misdiagnosed the core problem in their marriage, and misunderstood God's prescription for marital healing and health. They need marriage counseling that is *soul-u-tion* focused. They need to hear the heart of God about the heart of marriage. They must begin to grasp the purpose, problem, and prescription of marriage—from God's perspective. They need a gospel-centered heart understanding of creation-fall-redemption.

- *Creation—God's Ultimate Purpose for Marriage* (chap. 1). God's Marital Design: Shifting from self-centered marital goals to gospel-centered marital goals.
- *Fall—Our Core Problem in Marriage* (chap. 2). Our Marital Heart Disease: Confessing that problems in the home begin with problems in my heart.
- *Redemption—Christ's Central Prescription for Marital Healing* (chap. 3). Christ's Death for Sin and Our Death to Self: Surrendering to the reality that problems in my heart require Christ-dependence, not self-dependence.

[margin note:] Couples will tend to want to use communication & roles for their own gain. It is to meet their needs.

[margin note:] Bk of the self-focus, the solutions are meant to meet our needs, rather than the true goal of glorifying God.

Maturing as a Biblical Marriage Counselor
Solution Focused or Soul-u-tion Focused?

1. Travis and Britney had two diagnoses for their marriage problems: (a) We fight because we miscommunicate with each other. We need better communication skills. (b) We fight because we misunderstand each other. We need better teaching about roles and responsibilities in marriage.

    a. What are the strengths of each of these diagnoses?

    > (a) the strength of this is that communication is essential to a healthy marriage. The weakness is what that communication accomplishes. We can be effective communicators at getting our sinful needs met.
    > (b) Not have clear goals, roles & responsibilities in marriage can be an issue. However, we can use these roles & responsibilities to manipulate & demand.

    b. What are the weaknesses of each of these diagnoses? What is missing? What heart issues might they need to consider?

    > See above.

2. Travis uses his communication skills in a self-centered way to manipulate Britney—his training in communication skills has created a *more effective manipulator*. If you were counseling Travis, how could you help him see the way he is misusing biblical communication tools? How could you address his heart issues?

    > The bible never calls us to advocate for ourselves. We advocate for the other person, trusting that Christ will see to our final vindication. This glorifies God, rather than giving us what we think we need.

3. Britney uses her understanding of marital roles and longings in a self-sufficient way to self-righteously applaud herself and to judge Travis—her training about marital roles has created a *more self-sufficient sinner*. If you were counseling Britney, how could you help her see the way she is misusing biblical principles? How could you address her heart issues?

4. Had you ever thought about and contrasted *solution*-focused marriage counseling and *soul-u-tion*-focused marriage counseling, or are these new ways of thinking about marriage counseling? We are just beginning to describe the differences. So jot down your preliminary, working definition and description of each.

   a. *Solution*-focused marriage counseling

   b. *Soul-u-tion*-focused marriage counseling

Seeing the Gospel-Centered Marital Foundation in Ephesians

Ephesians 5:21–33, where Paul discusses marital roles and relationships, has to be the most often explored passage by biblical marriage counselors. That is true in my ministry. Yet Paul does not start Ephesians in chapter 5. So we should not start marriage counseling or our understanding of marriage in Ephesians 5 but rather in Ephesians 1:1 and following.

Glorifying God: Ephesians 1:1–23

When we start where Paul starts, our marital narrative changes. This is vital because the first calling of a biblical marriage counselor is to help couples define or redefine marital reality. Apart from Scripture, our marital reality contains a self-centered focus: *Marriage is about meeting my needs. Marriage is about making me happy.* In contrast, Paul's marital narrative teaches that marriage is all about glorifying God.

Paul begins with a hymn of praise to the Trinity (1:1–14). Everything in life, including marriage, is to be to the praise of the glory of the Trinity's grace. Paul continues by praying that we might grasp the Trinity's grace-love and avail ourselves of Christ's resurrection power.

These realities change our marital narrative from "It's all about me" to "It's all about him—Father, Son, and Holy Spirit." These truths change our marital focus from "I can make my marriage work on my own" to "We need Christ's resurrection power in our marriage so our marriage can glorify God."

Guilty before God: Ephesians 2:1–3

Paul next moves to our absolute need for God and his grace. We are totally depraved—dead in our trespasses and sins, self-centered to the core, and objects of just judgment.

In ourselves, we are helpless and hopeless. Sin is not just a sickness; it is a terminal disease that has already taken our spiritual life. These realities change our marital narrative from "Our marriage requires a better strategy for changing my *spouse*" to "Our marriage requires *my* humble repentance of *my* sinful self-sufficiency and self-centeredness."

Grace from God for Salvation and Sanctification: Ephesians 2:4–5:17

Thankfully, beginning in Ephesians 2:4 and continuing through 5:17, Paul transitions using the two greatest words in the English language: "But God." Though we were dead in sin, through our Father's grace we are resurrected to new life in Christ—grace for salvation. Paul does not stop there. From 2:10 through 5:17 he hammers home the point that the grace that saves is the grace that sanctifies. "For we are his workmanship, created in Christ Jesus to do good works, which God prepared in advance for us to do" (2:10). We are saved by grace apart from works, but we are saved by grace to do good works empowered by God for the glory of God.

Our old marital narrative claims, "Marriage is a self-improvement project done in my strength for my benefit." Our new biblical marital narrative insists, "Marital health begins with saving grace. Marital growth continues with God empowering us to put off the old self-focused ways and to put on the new death-to-self ways."

You were saved by grace to walk out by the Spirit in obedience for His glory.

Growth through God's Spirit: Ephesians 5:18–20 and 6:10–20

Because the fleshly inclination to make life work on our own is so strong, Paul continues the theme of growth through God's Spirit in Ephesians 5:18–20 and 6:10–20. Sometimes we fail to notice how Paul surrounds family life with spiritual empowerment. This is because we think Paul's teaching on the family ends with instructions for parents and children in Ephesians 6:4. However, in ancient Near Eastern culture the home included three couplets of relationships: husband and wife (5:21–33), parent and child (6:1–4), and master and servant (6:5–9). In Paul's day, teaching on these three relationships was known as the household code.

With this reality in mind, now consider what immediately precedes and immediately follows Paul's teaching on the home:

- *Be filled with the Spirit.* "Instead, be filled with the Spirit" (5:18).
- *Be empowered by the Lord.* "Finally, be strong in the Lord, and in his mighty power" (6:10).

Paul sandwiches family living between the reality that we must be filled with the Spirit and be strong in the Lord. I never lead a couple to explore Ephesians 5:21–33 without *first* reading these verses that surround Paul's marital principles. I tell couples:

> Contextually, it's appropriate to paraphrase these verses like this. "*Husband and wife,* if you are to fulfill the roles, responsibilities, and callings of a spouse, then first you must be filled with the Spirit. If you want your marriage to follow the God-honoring pattern of Ephesians 5:21–33, then first, *husband and wife,* you must be strong in the Lord and in his mighty power for your marriage. You must first put on the whole marital armor of God."

The old marital narrative says, "The solutions to our marital problems are within our own strength." The new marital narrative says, "The soul-u-tions to our marital problems are God-dependent; they require the filling of the Spirit and the power of the Lord."

Maturing as a Biblical Marriage Counselor
Seeing the Gospel-Centered Marital Foundation in Ephesians

1. Most of us as biblical marriage counselors naturally head to Ephesians 5:21–33 as our main go-to passage for marriage counseling. But in this chapter I suggest that we start with Ephesians 1:1–5:20 and 6:10–20.

   a. How could having that as a starting point help you as a marriage counselor build a biblical foundation for marriage?

   b. How could having that as a starting point reorient the couple to biblical marital narratives and biblical purposes for marriage?

2. In Ephesians 1:1–23, Paul highlights *glorifying God*. This can change our marital narrative from "It's all about me" to "It's all about him." And from "I can make my marriage work on my own" to "We need Christ's resurrection power in our marriage so our marriage can glorify God." How could you interact with couples using this passage to explore their understanding of the purpose of marriage and God's power to fulfill that purpose?

3. In Ephesians 2:1–3, Paul emphasizes our being *guilty before God*. This can change our marital narrative from "Our marriage requires a better strategy for changing my *spouse*" to "Our marriage requires *my* humble repentance of *my* sinful self-sufficiency and self-centeredness." How could you interact with couples using this passage to help them see their absolute need for God's grace in their life and in their marriage?

4. In Ephesians 2:4–5:17, Paul focuses on *grace from God for salvation and sanctification*. This can change our old marital narrative that says, "Marriage is a self-improvement project done in my strength for my benefit." It can create a new marital narrative that says, "Marital health begins with saving grace. Marital growth continues with God empowering us to put off the old self-focused ways and to put on the new death-to-self ways." How could you interact with couples using this passage to help them see their need for God's power in order for their marriage to change?

5. In Ephesians 5:18–20 and 6:10–20, Paul surrounds his marital teaching with the ideas of being filled with the Spirit and being strengthened by God's mighty power. How could you interact with couples about these passages to help them put off the old marital narrative that says, "The solutions to our marital problems are within our own strength" and put on the new marital narrative that says, "The soul-u-tions to our marital problems are God-dependent; they require the filling of the Spirit and the power of the Lord"?

The Ultimate Purpose of Marriage: Glorifying God

In Ephesians, Paul casts a biblical vision for marriage: *the grand purpose of every marriage is to glorify God.* Messed up, messy marriages have a great opportunity to bring God glory. When change occurs, a couple can become a praise testimony to the glory of God's grace at work in their marriage. The Bible reveals at least three ways that marriages glorify God.

Marital Purpose #1: Every Marriage Is Meant to Represent the Trinity

In the beginning, God created us male and female in his image. He blessed Adam and Eve, the husband and wife, and commanded them to be fruitful and multiply, to fill the earth, subdue it, and rule over it (Gen. 1:26–28). Adam and Eve, male and female, husband and wife, were created to reflect God. Within the Trinity there is unity, diversity, and equality. Within every marriage there is to be unity, diversity, and equality—distinct but equal.

God designed marriages to reflect the intimacy within the Trinity. John 1:1 echoes Genesis 1:1: "In the beginning was the Word, and the Word was with God, and the Word was God." That little word "with" means "in the presence of; face-to-face with." Father, Son, and Holy Spirit experience the intimacy of eternal communion.

Another little word—"was"—is also instructive. John could have used a past tense that indicates a snapshot: if we happened to travel back in time to the beginning, perhaps we might catch the Trinity in a moment of togetherness. Instead, John uses a past tense that indicates continuous action, which pictures an ongoing video: *whenever* we happened to travel back in time, Father, Son, and Holy Spirit would *always, forever, continuously* be in never-ending soul-to-soul communion. To reflect this intimacy, God created image bearers—male and female—who could unite and become one.

Marital Purpose #2: Every Marriage Is Meant to Reflect Christ and the Church

From Ephesians 5:21–33, every biblical marriage counselor knows that marriages are meant to reflect Christ and the church. A wife's respectful, loving relationship with her husband reflects the church's relationship to Christ. A husband's sacrificial, shepherding love for his wife reflects Christ's relationship to the church. When the onlooking world observes a Christian marriage, they are to step back in awe and give praise to God for the eternal loving relationship between Christ and his bride.

Marital Purpose #3: Every Marriage Is Meant for Couples to Nurture Each Other to Become More Like Christ

what are you doing that helps your spouse be like Jesos more, not for your benefit but theirs? How are you hindering this?

The husband-wife relationship is meant to be the most fertile ground for growth in grace. Husbands are to shepherd their wives so they increasingly reflect the beauty and purity of the Lord (Eph. 5:25–32). Wives are to live such godly lives that even without words their husbands are won over to Christ and become more like Christ (1 Pet. 3:1–6).

In Colossians 3:18–19, we find a shortened version of Paul's household code: "Wives, submit to your husbands, as is fitting in the Lord. Husbands, love your wives and do not be harsh with them." In the context immediately preceding those instructions, we see Paul encouraging us to minister to one another. Contextually, we could appropriately paraphrase Paul, "*Husbands and wives*, let the peace of Christ rule in your hearts, since as members of one body you were called to peace. *Husbands and wives*, let the word of Christ dwell in you richly as you sing psalms, hymns, and spiritual songs with gratitude in your hearts to God" (Col. 3:15–16, author's paraphrase).

When counseling couples, I like to say:

God is calling the two of you as husband and wife to be each other's *best biblical counselor*. You're to be each other's most vital one-another minister, most important encourager, most intimate spiritual friend. You're to speak and live gospel truth in love with one another so that you both grow up together in Christ.

Our marriages have the calling, opportunity, and privilege of being living pictures of the Trinity, of Christ and the church, and of maturing image bearers. The purpose of marriage is to reveal God's glory as we represent the Trinity, reflect Christ and the church, and enhance the maturity of our spouse. This should make a daily and an eternal difference in our marriages and in our marriage counseling.

Maturing as a Biblical Marriage Counselor
The Ultimate Purpose of Marriage

1. Marital Purpose #1: Every marriage is meant to represent the Trinity.

    a. If you are married, what difference could it have made in your last marital disagreement if you and your spouse were consciously aware of the truth that your marriage is meant to represent the Trinity's relationship of oneness?

---

b. As a marriage counselor, what difference could this truth make in your next marriage counseling session with a couple in conflict?

2. Marital Purpose #2: Every marriage is meant to reflect Christ and the church.

   a. If you are married, during your last public interaction, what difference could the truth of displaying to the world the love between Christ and his bride have made?

   b. As a marriage counselor, what difference could this truth make in your next marriage counseling session with a troubled couple?

3. Marital Purpose #3: Every marriage is meant for couples to nurture each other to become more like Christ.

   a. If you are married, when you ponder the purpose of your interactions with your spouse, what difference could it make if you focused on your calling of helping your spouse to become more like Christ?

   b. As a marriage counselor, what difference could this truth make in your next marriage counseling session with a struggling couple?

4. The purpose of marriage is to reveal God's glory as we represent the Trinity, reflect Christ and the church, and enhance the maturity of our spouse.

   a. If you are married, what daily and eternal differences could this make in your marriage?

   b. What difference could this make in your goals as a marriage counselor?

A Gospel-Centered Application of the Four Pillars of Oneness in Marriage

Every pastor and biblical counselor wants to help couples enjoy a God-glorifying, mutually meaningful marriage. In doing so, many of us have used the four pillars of marital oneness—leave, cleave, weave, and receive—from the creation narrative in Genesis 2:23–25.

Why, then, are so many Christian marriages still struggling? Perhaps because we have used these four pillars to focus on solutions instead of on gospel-centered soul-u-tions. I confess I did that for several years of marriage ministry. Here I want us to learn how to use these pillars to address *heart motivation* when seeking to build oneness in marriage.

Oneness in Marriage Pillar #1: Leaving

In Genesis 2:24 we read, "That is why a man leaves his father and mother . . ." The Hebrew word translated as "leave" means to sever, cut, or untie. Today we might say "cut the apron strings"—meaning to cut the umbilical cord of dependence upon parents. Throughout the first five books of the Old Testament, Moses uses this Hebrew word with the idea of forsaking, especially forsaking one allegiance for another.

Husbands and wives are to shift their *core* loyalty from parent to spouse. There will always be a parent-child loyalty and fidelity, even as an adult child to adult parents. However, the core loyalty, the principal commitment, now transfers to our spouse as our most important human devotion.

Why is leaving vital from a gospel-centered, Spirit-dependent perspective? Ponder how this idea might be misused without a gospel-centered reality. "Finally! I'm free from Mom and Dad!" The heart implication is still, "It's all about me! Leaving and shifting loyalty is all about my freedom."

Consider how to apply leaving from a gospel-centered point of view. "Our core loyalty to each other displays our core loyalty to Christ. ~~Our marriage relationship is ultimately all about being marital ambassadors who show the world how Christ and his bride are faithfully devoted to each other.~~"

The biblical principle of leaving can be applied to a self-centered heart or to a Christ-centered heart. The marital application will be entirely different depending on the heart motivation. Does that mean we cannot make practical applications? Not at all. But be sure to hear our central point—*address the heart first*. Apply truth to a heart growing in Christlikeness instead of applying truth to a hard, self-centered heart.

When I teach on leaving, I start with heart motivation, and then I share *three "in-law bylaws"* as one possible way to apply this principle.

In-Law Bylaw #1: Other-Centered. Seek to understand and appreciate your spouse's family of origin—their culture, way of doing things, likes and dislikes, etc.

In-Law Bylaw #2: Christ-Centered. Seek to create one new family culture to honor Christ—merge, blend, and integrate your two different families of origin into one new, united "you."

In-Law Bylaw #3: Marriage-Centered. Prioritize the husband-wife relationship over all other human relationships—honor your parents, love your children, encourage your church, and engage your community, but prioritize your marriage for God's glory.

There is no magic in these three applications. They are my current best attempt to contextualize these biblical principles—with a gospel-centered focus. You can collaborate with your counselees to apply the pillar of leaving to their marriage—in gospel-centered ways that uniquely glorify God.

Oneness in Marriage Pillar #2: Cleaving

Moses continues in Genesis 2:24, "and is united to his wife." The Hebrew word translated as "united" has the idea of attachment, permanence, keeping together, bonding, and tying a knot. We might picture it as superglue or Gorilla Glue. The word is used in the Old Testament for the attachment of muscle to bone and for the life-and-death grip of the hand to a sword in combat.

I recall participating in a wedding early in my ministry. The pastor who performed the majority of the ceremony was from India, as was the couple. During the ceremony, the minister looked at the groom with utmost seriousness and said, "What God has joined together, let no one separate." Then, making eye contact with the bride, he repeated, "What God has joined together, let no one separate." The silence in the sanctuary was deafening. Looking at the parents and then at the rest of the gathered celebrants, he repeated a third time, "What God has joined together, let no one separate." I was trembling at this point—and I was not the one getting married! The sacredness of that moment and the sanctity of the marital vows crushed down on me in a fresh way. Marriage is a permanent cleaving together.

Even this sacred truth of cleaving can be misapplied when our hearts are hard. If we could read the mind of the bride or groom, they might be thinking, "Finally! I can feel loved. Someone will be devoted only and always to *me*!" At one level, the *longing* for marital love is pure and proper. But we can poison that pure longing by turning it into the *demand* that *I* be loved so that *I* feel like a somebody.

What might cleaving sound like from a gospel-centered, Spirit-dependent perspective? "Lord, thank you that we can focus on loving each other. May our love be a reflection of your faithful covenant loyalty to us in Christ. When folks marvel at our commitment, may we point them back to your eternal commitment and our eternal security in Christ."

For the soft heart clinging to Christ, what are some practical implications of cleaving to one another? Consider these *four gospel communion and communication principles* from Ephesians 4:25–32.

1. *Speak truthful words with love* (4:25). "Father, as we cleave together, empower us toward the *mutual ministry* of speaking gospel truth to each other for your glory."

2. *Speak controlled words with patience* (4:26–28). "Father, we are not ignorant about Satan's schemes. He wants to use our anger to separate what you have joined together. In our anger, help us not to sin, but to seek sanctification *together* in Christ."

3. *Speak encouraging words with wisdom* (4:29–30). "Father, help us to *know each other so well* that our words uniquely and specifically bring life to each other."

4. *Speak gracious words with humility* (4:31–32). "Father, when sin seeks to separate, remind us of your forgiving grace; grant us strength to *give each other grace*."

Oneness in Marriage Pillar #3: Weaving

Adam spoke poetic words of weaving in Genesis 2:23: "This is now bone of my bones and flesh of my flesh; she shall be called 'woman,' for she was taken out of man." Moses spoke similar words in Genesis 2:24: "and they become one flesh." Moses is portraying the merging of two into one. This idea is not just physical, sexual union, though the act of marriage does portray that oneness. The Hebrew word translated as "flesh" (*basar*) is consistently used for the whole person—body, soul, and spirit. Moses is speaking not only of bodily oneness but also of soul oneness.

The Old Testament illustrates this concept of oneness using the image of strands of silk woven into a beautiful, resilient tapestry. In modern times we seek to illustrate this concept with the unity candle, where two separate flames merge to form one new flame. In weaving, two independent beings become interdependent and intertwined in one glorious tapestry.

Even this beautiful portrait can be marred by our sometimes ugly hearts. Without a gospel-centered perspective, our attitude toward weaving may simply be, "Finally, someone will love me and be one with me—complete me—and my self-image and self-esteem will blossom!" There is nothing wrong with marital completion, but that longing can be marred by a self-centered focus. Or we might think of weaving as, "Finally, fun sex without guilt!" As Scripture says, the marital bed is undefiled and meant to be joyous. However, if the primary or only goal of marriage is sexual pleasure *for me*, then I have missed the gospel beauty of marriage—even of marital sexuality.

To the gospel-centered, Spirit-dependent heart, the mindset behind weaving can be, "Thank you, Lord, for the marital joy of oneness in body, soul, and spirit. May I bring my spouse pleasure in every way, and may our mutual oneness reflect the Trinity's eternal dance of unity!"

To gospel-centered hearts, I'll sometimes share three tapestry principles.

1. *Realize that to unravel is to ruin.* Distance, discord, divisiveness, and divorce all tear apart body, soul, and spirit, because the two are now one.

2. *Discover who you are together in Christ.* God has fearfully and wonderfully made you as individuals. Now as one, seek to discern and celebrate your joint identity in Christ.

3. *Weave together one shared husband-wife grace narrative.* Your marriage is one page in Christ's grand redemptive narrative. What's the title of your grace narrative?

Oneness in Marriage Pillar #4: Receiving

Moses concludes his inspired creation narrative of the first marriage with the idea of receiving. "Adam and his wife were both naked, and they felt no shame" (Gen. 2:25). Naked and unashamed portrays intimacy in the sense of *into-me-see*. Another person sees into my soul and does not judge me but accepts, treasures, and values me. The idea is grace-knowing—awareness of my flaws, faults, imperfections, blemishes, weaknesses, and sins without rejection. And awareness of my uniqueness, beauty, strengths, gifts, and Christ-likeness without demanding that I have to be perfect to be accepted, wanted, and valued.

For Adam and Eve, originally there was no sin to cause any shame. Unlike them, we need a Romans 5:8 grace-knowing approach to our spouse: "But God demonstrates his own love for us in this: While we were still sinners, Christ died for us."

Without a gospel-centered focus, receiving can become a demand that my spouse wink at my sins, ignore my faults, and accept me without seeking to help me toward maturity in Christ. With a gospel-centered, Spirit-dependent mindset, because we are safe and secure in Christ, we invite our spouse to speak into our life—with challenge when needed, with encouragement when desired, or with affirmation when appropriate.

To a couple with soft hearts, I'll share *three intimacy instructions.*

1. *Risk openness.* To be seen, you must be vulnerable and transparent, real and raw. Because you are secure in Christ, you can risk exposure with your spouse—so you can grow together in grace.
2. *Respond graciously.* This involves applying Matthew 7:3–5 to your marital relationship—being willing to see and address the log in your own eye.
3. *Restore humbly.* When your spouse fails Christ or you, this means applying Galatians 6:1 (responding gently and humbly) with a desire not to protect your spouse's self-image but to promote the image of Christ in both of you.

As marriage counselors, will we use biblical marriage principles in a solution-focused, spouse-centered way? Or will we help couples use God's truth for God's glory in a soul-u-tion-focused, gospel-centered manner?

Maturing as a Biblical Marriage Counselor
A Gospel-Centered Application
of the Four Pillars of Oneness in Marriage

1. I confessed that in the past I had used the Genesis 2:23–25 principles of leaving, cleaving, weaving, and receiving in a solution-focused way instead of in a gospel-centered way—addressing the heart first. In which way have you used Genesis 2:23–25?

2. We started the sections on leaving, cleaving, weaving, and receiving with a discussion of the biblical, gospel-centered meaning of each pillar. If you are married, which of the four pillars seems most important to you in your marriage? If you are a counselor, which seems most important in your marriage counseling ministry?

3. With each of the four pillars, we compared and contrasted a self-centered mindset with a gospel-centered mindset. Think about couples you have counseled—how might they seek to apply these principles from a self-centered perspective? From a gospel-centered perspective?

4. At the end of each section on the four pillars of oneness in marriage, we shared some practical implications. These are simply my current best attempt to apply the biblical marital concepts in our modern context. What gospel-centered practical implications might you make for

    a. Leaving?

    b. Cleaving?

    c. Weaving?

    d. Receiving?

CHAPTER

TWO

Marriage My Way . . . or the Highway!

Introduction: Shame, Blame, Claim, and Maim

A nanosecond before their fall into sin, "the man and his wife were both naked, and they felt no shame" (Gen. 2:25). Distrusting God's good heart and disobeying God's wise command, they eat from the one forbidden tree. Immediately, Adam and Eve change from being naked and unashamed to realizing "they were naked; so they sewed fig leaves together and made coverings for themselves" (Gen. 3:7). At the very moment of their fall, Adam and Eve transform from leave, cleave, weave, and receive to shame, blame, claim, and maim.

In their shame, they hide from God. God pursues them and calls to Adam, "Where are you?" Adam answers, "I heard you in the garden, and I was afraid because I was naked; so I hid" (Gen. 3:9–10). *Shame.*

When God asks Adam who told him he was naked and whether he had eaten from the tree, "the man said, 'The woman you put here with me—she gave me some fruit from the tree, and I ate it'" (Gen. 3:12). Moments earlier Adam praised Eve as the one who was "taken out of man" and "bone of my bones and flesh of my flesh" (Gen. 2:23). Now she is simply the one God "put here with me." And she is the cause of it all—"*she* gave me some fruit." *Blame.*

Then, speaking to Eve, God says, "Your desire will be for your husband, and he will rule over you" (Gen. 3:16). Desire can be pure and beautiful. Here, however, God is speaking of the consequences of marital sin. God uses the same word when he speaks to Cain in Genesis 4: "Sin is crouching at your door; it desires to have you, but you must rule over it" (4:7). The concept of desire in Genesis 3:16 and 4:7 is the negative sense of demanding to have, manipulate, control, own, or clutch. *Claim.*

While Eve, in her fallen state, will manipulatively demand control, Adam in his fallen state will "rule over" her (Gen. 3:16). Context is king. "Rule over" is not a statement about loving, sacrificial, Christlike headship. It is a statement about the consequences of marital sin. Like sin in Genesis 4:7, Adam is crouching at the door like a roaring lion seeking to devour his wife—rule over and overpower. *Maim.*

How does sin impact the marital relationship? Husbands and wives move from leave, cleave, weave, and receive to shame, blame, claim, and maim. We shame—making each other feel worthless and dirty, weak and small. We blame—making the other person feel like everything is their fault. We claim—manipulatively demanding that my spouse meet my needs. We maim—retaliating against each other and hurting each other.

Maturing as a Biblical Marriage Counselor
Shame, Blame, Claim, and Maim

1. In marriage we *shame* each other—making each other feel worthless and dirty, weak and small.

   a. What are examples you have witnessed (in your counseling or in your own marriage) of couples sinfully shaming each other?

   b. As a marriage counselor, how can you expose this shaming process without adding more shame?

2. In marriage we *blame* each other—making the other person feel like everything is their fault.

   a. What are examples you have witnessed (in your counseling or in your own marriage) of couples sinfully blaming each other?

b. As a marriage counselor, how can you expose this blaming process without adding more blame?

3. In marriage we *claim* each other—manipulatively demanding that my spouse meet my needs.

    a. What are examples you have witnessed (in your counseling or in your own marriage) of couples sinfully claiming (manipulating) each other?

    b. As a marriage counselor, how can you expose this claiming process without demanding that the counselee make you look good by agreeing with your assessment?

4. In marriage we *maim* each other—retaliating against each other and hurting each other.

    a. What are examples you have witnessed (in your counseling or in your own marriage) of couples sinfully maiming (harming) each other?

    b. As a marriage counselor, how can you expose this maiming process in a gentle, humble, other-centered way?

Exposing the Marital Log in My Eye

As horrible and painful as all this is, there is a greater marriage counseling problem. Sit a troubled couple in front of you, tell them about shame, blame, claim, and maim, and this is what you will hear: "Yes! That's right. Darla does all of that all the time!" Or, "You tell him, Pastor. That's exactly what Jared does to me every single day, day after day!"

Sinful shaming, blaming, claiming, and maiming are substantial problems in troubled marriages. Sin's deceitfulness and blindness are substantial obstacles toward progress in marriage counseling. God calls us to see to it that no one "has a sinful, unbelieving heart that turns away from the living God" (Heb. 3:12). How do we do this as biblical marriage counselors? By encouraging one another daily so that no one is "hardened by sin's deceitfulness" (Heb. 3:13).

Sin blinds us to our faults, to the log in our own eye, to our sinful role in our marital struggles. Couples need the light of Scripture to expose their spiritual blindness.

This is a central marriage counseling issue: couples come to us so hurt by each other that they are blind to and deceived about their own marital faults. They focus on what the other person is doing wrong or not doing right. They mercilessly judge each other. Our calling in marital counseling is to help them to take the log out of their own eye.

Biblical marital counseling is not about pointing out your spouses issues. It is working on your own to resolve your side of the conflict.

> Why do you look at the speck of sawdust in your [spouse's] eye and pay no attention to the plank in your own eye? How can you say to your [spouse], "Let me take the speck out of your eye," when all the time there is a plank in your own eye? You hypocrite, first take the plank out of your own eye, and then you will see clearly to remove the speck from your [spouse's] eye. (Matt. 7:3–5)

This is a great question to ask in marriage counseling b/c it exposes the heart issues

When asked, "What's the reason for your marriage problems?" all spouses are sinfully hardwired to answer with blame. "My spouse is the cause of our marriage problems!" "It's him!" "It's her!"

We are all slow to apply Matthew 7:3–5—slow to see the large log in our eye and slow to focus on our own issues. Instead, we are quick to see the speck in our spouse's eye and quick to focus on them as the root cause of all our marital fights and quarrels. When I am more concerned about my spouse's issues than my own heart issues, my marriage will never become a Christlike, Christ-centered marriage.

Maturing as a Biblical Marriage Counselor
Exposing the Marital Log in My Eye

1. Who has been a Hebrews 3:12–13 brother or sister in your life? (You may list more than one.)

   a. How has this person been an encourager who lovingly, humbly, and graciously shines the light of Scripture into your soul so that your blindness to your sin is exposed?

   b. How has this person's ministry positively impacted your life for Christ?

2. In whose life have you been a Hebrews 3:12–13 brother or sister? How have you been an encourager to another Christian by lovingly, humbly, and graciously shining the light of Scripture into their soul so that their blindness to sin is exposed?

3. God calls a husband and wife to be each other's Hebrews 3:12–13 brother and sister.

    a. If you are married, how well are you and your spouse doing at encouraging each other to be more like Christ by lovingly, humbly, and graciously helping each other to become aware of blind spots to sin?

    b. If you are single, share about a married couple you have observed offering each other encouragement that reflects Hebrews 3:12–13.

4. A central marriage counseling issue is that spouses come to us so hurt by each other that they are blind to their own marital issues. Do you agree or disagree? Why or why not?

5. Reread Matthew 7:3–5.

    a. As a marriage counselor, what are examples you have experienced of a person being unaware of the log in their own eye while being totally aware of the speck in their spouse's eye?

    b. How have you sought to help a person become aware of the log in their own eye while at the same time not minimizing the log (or speck) in their spouse's eye?

What Really Causes Our Marital Fights and Quarrels?

In James 4 the pivotal relational *and* marital diagnostic question is posed: "What causes fights and quarrels among you?" (James 4:1). The fact that James asks this question indicates that in the midst of marital tensions we are poor judges of the root source of our relational conflicts. We need the light of Scripture to understand the heart issues lurking beneath our marital struggles. Consider this marriage counseling paraphrase of James 4:1–4.

> What causes your marital fights and quarrels? Don't they come from within *you*—from *your* self-centered demands and *your* sinful responses to *your* unmet marital desires that battle within *you*? *You* desire and demand *your* happiness, *your* agenda, *your* kingdom, but *you* do not get what *you* want from *your* spouse.
>
> In response, *you* covet—*you* manipulate: "I'll do whatever I can to get you to meet my needs." When that doesn't work, in anger and frustration *you* lash out at your spouse—*you* retaliate: "You hurt me; I'll hurt you!"
>
> But you still can't get what you want from your spouse. That's why you quarrel and fight. Your marital issues are ultimately rooted in a spiritual issue in *your* heart and in *your* relationship to God. You do not have because you do not ask God *humbly*. Instead, you keep subtly demanding *your* will be done, *your* kingdom come.
>
> Even when you do get around to asking God, you do not receive, because *you* ask with wrong, selfish motives—that you may spend what you get on *your own* pleasures. You become a taker, a consumer, a demander, instead of a sacrificial giver.
>
> You know what that makes you? *A spiritual adulterer!* That's right. You forsake God, your Spring of Living Water, and try to make your spouse come through for you as your messiah. You seek to make your spouse do for you what only God can do, what only the Savior can do—quench the deepest thirsts of your soul. But no spouse makes a good savior. So you end up turning to a broken cistern—your imperfect, finite spouse—that holds no thirst-quenching water.

God's Real and Raw Description of Our Marital Warfare

God pulls no punches when he talks about our relational boxing matches. He describes them as fights and quarrels. Revelation 12:7 uses the word "fight" to describe our feverish warfare with Satan. In James 3:13–17, the word "fight" depicts evil, bitter, selfish turf wars that are demonically inspired. This is a great reminder to couples that their spouse is not the enemy; Satan is. God calls husbands and wives to be intimate allies fighting against Satan.

The Greek word translated as "quarrels" in Revelation 12:7 refers to vicious verbal battles. In 2 Timothy 2:23–24, Paul uses it to picture argumentative debates. John 6:52 uses it to depict sharp disagreements. Paul selects the same word in 2 Corinthians 7:5 to portray harassing conflicts. And in Titus 3:9 the word highlights hurtful interactions. This sounds familiar to marriage counselors: verbal battles and debates filled with resentful, sharp, cutting words that hurt, harm, and harass.

God's Insight into Our Fights: The Problem in My Marriage Is *Me*

James answers his own question with a rhetorical question about the source of our fights. "Don't they come from your desires that battle within you?" (4:1). The problem in my marriage is *me*!

The battle begins in my heart: who is on the throne of my marriage—Christ or me?

Marriage is a battleground between two kingdoms: the kingdom of God and the kingdom of self. Marriage is always a war between the kingdom shaped by Christ, with an agenda focused on holiness and glorifying God, and the kingdom shaped by self, with an agenda focused on one's own happiness and satisfaction.

I Fight You When I Demand That You Fulfill Illegitimate, Misdirected Desires

James diagnoses two types of marital heart sins. First, he points to misdirected, illegitimate desires. This is the meaning of the Greek word for "desire" used in James 4:1—*hedonon*—from which we get our English word "hedonist." In our fallen state, we have an insatiable demand for self-gratification that wages war within our soul. We sinfully corrupt good desires into illegitimate demands.

Consider Margaret and Nate. In counseling with Margaret, it did not take long to detect that her legitimate desire for Nate to sacrificially love her had morphed into an illegitimate demand that Nate perfectly interpret her every mood so he could impeccably meet her every need. Nate could make a million changes—and he sure tried—but Margaret's root issue was not Nate's failure to love her. Her root issue was her demand that he be her flawless emotional genie.

In counseling with Margaret, my goal was *not* to kill her legitimate desire for cherishing, nourishing love. God put that longing into her soul (Eph. 5:23–33). My desire was to help Margaret recognize how she had transformed her desire into an illegitimate demand.

I Fight You When I Mishandle My Unmet Legitimate Desires

James, as a biblical soul physician, identifies a second root source of marital conflicts: "You want something but you don't get it" (James 4:2). The Greek word translated as "want" is a neutral term that can refer to either legitimate longings or sinful lusts. In context, James is talking about legitimate, God-designed desires—that go unmet. I fight you when I mishandle my unmet legitimate desires. These are not corrupt desires but a corrupt response to unmet desires.

Margaret legitimately desires Nate to love her with cherishing and nourishing love. When he fails to fulfill his biblical calling (Eph. 5:22–33), Margaret is going to hurt, to thirst. "Hope deferred makes the heart sick"—that is, depleted, empty, weak, faint (Prov. 13:12). In her thirst and emptiness, Margaret could humbly call out to God, her Spring of Living Water, for his compassion, healing hope, and strength to love sacrificially.

Margaret could recognize that marriage is not a container for her happiness. She could be consumed by kingdom thoughts: "Marriage is a receptacle for receiving God's grace and for sacrificially giving Christ's grace to my spouse. My broken spouse—like every spouse—is a God-given opportunity for me to be a grace-giver. My spouse's failure is an opportunity for me to be a grace-dispenser." Or, like a lot of us, Margaret could respond sinfully to the unmet desires and unquenched thirsts of her soul.

[margin note:] These is nothing wrong w/ legit. desires & we are told the heart grows sick from unmet legit. desires. However, we are to turn to God for fulfillment.

[margin note:] We often view our spouse as a need-meeter rather than for us to be a grace-dispenser

Our Sinful Responses to Unmet Marital Desires

Put yourself here. Picture it. Feel it.

I deeply desire something from my spouse—and it's a legit, biblical desire placed in my soul by God. But I'm not receiving it. My hope is deferred. My heart is depleted. How will my hurting, hungry heart respond to my spouse and my Savior?

Sinfully Responding to My Spouse with Manipulation: Claim

James emphasizes two potential sinful responses to our spouse when we can't get what we want: we kill and we covet (James 4:2). We will start with the second response—coveting. The Greek word can have a positive meaning, as in desiring or coveting a spiritual gift (1 Cor. 14:1). As it's used here in James, however, it has the negative meaning of jealously, zealously insisting upon, demanding, clinging to, and desperately needing something. When this occurs in our heart, even a good desire can become an idol. To use an image from Jeremiah 2:13, a good desire becomes a broken cistern that holds no water. We foolishly choose our broken spouse over God, the Spring of Living Water. We replace the Creator with the creature—our spouse.

Nate felt as if he never measured up to Margaret. He longed for her respecting love but could not sip a drip of it. In his heart he was saying, "I must have your respectful love in order to survive! I'm not receiving it. Rather than taking my emptiness to God, I'm going to demand that you be god for me."

This hints at another aspect of the word "covet." In covetous zeal, I exert myself *on my behalf*. I expend my energy *manipulating* you to meet my need. Nate, like a lot of us, acts more like a toddler than a mature Christian adult. "I want what I want and I want it now!" However, Nate has the savvy of an adult, so he imagines and creates an arsenal of manipulative ways to seek to obtain from Margaret what his soul desperately desires.

Sinfully Responding to My Spouse with Retaliation: Maim

James says we not only manipulate, we also retaliate—we kill. In 1 John 3:15, John links the word "kill" with murderous hatred, a seething rage. We might imagine Margaret and Nate each secretly thinking, "No matter what I do, I can't get you to come through for me. Fine! See if I'll come through for you. You've hurt me. Now it's your turn to feel the pain!"

I am not suggesting that most counselees have a clear awareness of this underlying agenda. Remember that sin blinds and deceives us. Only the Word of God used by the Spirit of God through the people of God can melt hardened hearts and give sight to blind eyes.

What has James taught us? Our marital expectations are not rooted in the gospel. They are rooted in self. My unstated and sometimes unrecognized marital expectation is that my spouse will make me happy, satisfy me, fulfill me, fill me, make me feel good about me, and complete me. Communication skills won't help—they only make for a more effective manipulator. Only heart repentance will help.

Sinfully Responding to My Savior with Idolatry

James now guides us on a vital mindset shift. Ultimately, *our sin in our home is due to sin in our heart*. Our sin against one another is eventually traceable to sin against God. Our social sin flows from our spiritual sin. "You do not have, because you do not ask God" (James 4:2). *Ask* is the key word. It means to humbly ask on loan, to ask submissively.

We do not ask God, because we think we can self-sufficiently manipulate others into meeting our needs. We do not ask God, because we go back to the first sin in the garden—we doubt God's good heart. We imagine God to be a thou-shalt-not god who is withholding something good that we need and desire (Gen. 3:1–3).

My biggest problem in my marriage is me—putting myself on the throne of my kingdom of self, trusting myself more than I trust God.

Sinfully Responding to My Savior with Carnality

According to James, when we finally get around to asking God, we ask amiss. "When you ask, you do not receive, because you ask with wrong motives, that you may spend what you get on your pleasures" (James 4:3). The Greek word *kakos*, translated as "wrong motives," means impure, corrupt, carnal motives. James is indicating that most of our marital prayers are hedonistic, carnal, and self-serving rather than other-centered and God-glorifying. Rather than living a life of ministry, we live marital life as a consumer. Our belly has become our god (Rom. 16:18; Phil. 3:19).

James is teaching that I do not need to be rescued from my spouse. I need to be rescued from *myself*! I need to be rescued from my self-centered, demanding, carnal heart.

Sinfully Responding to My Savior with Spiritual Adultery

Unless we are versed in the Old Testament portrayal of sin as spiritual adultery, the imagery James uses in 4:4 may seem out of context: "You adulterous people, don't you know that friendship with the world means enmity toward God? Therefore, anyone who chooses to be a friend of the world becomes an enemy of God."

When I demand that my spouse be god for me, I become a false worshiper. I love my spouse more than I love God. Or perhaps more accurately, I think I *need* my spouse more than I need God. Spiritual adultery is my frantic, frustrated effort to survive and thrive without needing God. Who seems better equipped to quench my thirst than my spouse? But spouses make horrible God substitutes. Even at their best, spouses are broken cisterns that can hold no water—false sources of the life that in reality only God can provide. Spouses pale in comparison to God, the Spring of Living Water (Jer. 2:13). The root source of my fight with my spouse is my flight from God and my fight with God.

God's Prescription for Marital Harmony: Relational Repentance

James, inspired by God, clearly understands the cause of our marital fights and quarrels. He also understands God's prescription for marital harmony. Marital conflict will be halted only by repentance of the self-sins: selfishness, self-sufficiency, and self-trust.

This is why James transitions from the concept of spiritual adultery to the scriptural truth that "God opposes the proud but gives grace to the humble" (James 4:6 ESV). When we see that our demanding heart is the core problem in our marriage, then we become desperate for Christ's grace. Then we begin to look at our marriage and our spouse with grace eyes. And we begin to realize that there is no marriage problem so deep that the grace of Jesus isn't deeper.

Our teaching on marital roles and communication falls not only on deaf ears but also on cold hearts, unless those hearts are thawed by Spirit-prompted repentance.

Come near to God and he will come near to you. Wash your hands, you sinners, and purify your hearts, you double-minded. Grieve, mourn and wail. Change your laughter to mourning and your joy to gloom. Humble yourselves before the Lord, and he will lift you up. (James 4:8–10)

This is relational repentance—coming near to God. It is the spiritually adulterous spouse returning to God our Husband. It is the prodigal son coming to his senses and returning to the father. Repentance is a change of relationship—relational return to God as our refreshing Spring of Living Water, as our forgiving Father, and as our gracious Husband.

Mind Renewal for Marital Renewal: Marriage as Soul School

Repentance is also a change of heart and mind. We repent of and put off the old way of thinking and living (Eph. 4:22), we are renewed in the spirit of our mind (4:23), and then we put on the new way of thinking and living (4:24).

In James 4, James instructs us in a mindset shift. He reminds us that *marriage is soul school.* In God's kingdom agenda, marriage is not about my *happiness*; marriage is about my *holiness.* God uses my unholy, imperfect, finite, failing spouse to sanctify me—to mature me increasingly into the image of Christ's sacrificial, other-centered, giving love. That's the mind renewal that biblical marriage counselors pursue with counselees—before we pursue behavioral change or teach about marital roles or instruct on communication skills.

In biblical marriage counseling, we have to first create the foundation b/f we can address the practical skills.

According to Matthew 6:33, we are all kingdom seekers. The question is, In my marriage am I seeking the kingdom of God or the kingdom of self? Is the secret agenda of my marriage to get my spouse to come through for me, to make me happy? Or is the spiritual agenda of my marriage to glorify God by loving my sinful spouse with Christ's *agape*, giving, other-centered, sacrificial grace-love?

When I get mad at my spouse for not coming through for me—that's kingdom of self stuff! I have reduced marriage to me—my needs, my wants, my preferences, my desires, my happiness—me. "You're in the way of what I want and what I think I need! That ticks me off!"

Marital conflict is caused by the preexisting conflict in my heart between surrendering to the kingdom of God and living for my kingdom of self. When two people cling to their own kingdoms, it's no wonder marriage is filled with endless conflict and emotional turf wars.

What did we expect at the altar? If we're honest, we married our spouse because we thought they were the whole package—they had what we needed so that they could fill us up. We were attracted to them because we sensed what they could do for us. That attraction dissipates as soon as we see our real spouse—our sinful, finite, imperfect, selfish spouse.[1]

Here is our secret marriage vow: "All I want is for my spouse to make me happy, to be my own personal messiah!" That is not God's purpose for marriage. Our marriage problem is rooted in our secret heart sin of ME and MY happiness!

We believe the lie that what we signed up for in marriage was personal happiness. So we say, "This isn't what I signed up for. You're not who I signed up for. You make me mad because you're not making me happy!" That is not biblical love.

Why would an all-wise and all-loving God put two immature, self-centered people together in marriage? Because *marriage is a principal tool of sanctification*. Marriage is a workroom for two people to become more like Christ. Marriage is soul school. God intends marriage to break us of our self-sufficiency and self-centeredness.

Marriage involves two conflicting marital agendas. While we are working on our *happiness* in marriage, God is working on our *holiness* in marriage. While we are working on our *comfort* in marriage, God is working on our *conformity* to Christ in marriage.

Rather than being reasons for our rage, our spouse's sinfulness and immaturity are opportunities for our maturity. The more we witness our spouse's weakness and wickedness, the greater our opportunity for our own personal holiness.

Jesus did not shed his blood to make my little kingdom of self work. Jesus shed his blood to crucify my kingdom and to invite me into his kingdom of grace-love for others. God calls us into a messy, imperfect, sinful marriage so we can grow in our love for our spouse in their darkest, most wicked, ugliest moments—and so we can move toward them with Christlike grace.

Redemption and Regeneration Required

If you've been tracking with this renewed way of thinking, and if you are married, then you have to be thinking, *This requires God's grace and strength!* The more honest we are about our own wickedness and weakness, the greater our awareness of our need for Christ's grace and the Father's resurrection power. We can't love like Christ in our own strength.

Redemption is what is required to move from shame, blame, claim, and maim to Christlike sacrificial love. We don't need recovery. We need regeneration. We need the good news of our good God sending his perfect Son to die for us to forgive our sins *and* to change our nature.

We cannot ignore the bad news of Genesis 3, Matthew 7, and James 4. However, we must never forget the good news of redemption. In the next chapter we'll shake off our gospel amnesia to remind each other of how Christ changes us as husbands and wives. We'll learn that changed spouses connect and commune together to fulfill their marital calling.

Maturing as a Biblical Marriage Counselor
What Really Causes Our Marital Fights and Quarrels?

1. How would you answer the foundational question, What causes marital fights and quarrels? How does your answer impact your focus in biblical marriage counseling?

2. James teaches two core truths about marital conflict: (a) I fight you when I demand that you fulfill my illegitimate, misdirected desires, and (b) I fight you when I mishandle my unmet legitimate desires.

   a. Share illustrations of each of these types of responses—from your own marriage or from your marriage counseling experiences.

   b. Role-play or write out a scenario involving each of these sinful marital responses. How do you provide biblical marriage counseling in each scenario?

3. James teaches three central ways we sin against God: idolatry, carnality, and spiritual adultery.

   a. Share illustrations of each of these types of responses—from your own marriage or from your marriage counseling experiences.

b. Role-play or write out a scenario involving each of these sinful marital responses. How do you provide biblical marriage counseling in each scenario?

4. Prayerfully ponder James 4:8–10 as it relates to marriage and marriage counseling. How could you apply this passage to your marriage? How could you help couples apply this passage to their marriage?

THREE

Marriage Christ's Way

Introduction: The Relevancy of Scripture—Eternally and Daily

When Jake and Miranda completed their paperwork before our first marriage counseling appointment, Jake was quite honest. In response to a question asking him to describe his relationship to Christ, he answered "nonexistent."

About forty-five minutes into our first session, after listening to Jake and Miranda's concerns about their marriage, I addressed Jake's response. I expressed appreciation for his honesty. Then I shared that while I would not be beating them over the head with the Bible, I would seek to derive my counsel from God's Word. I asked Jake, given his current relationship with Christ, how comfortable he would be with pastoral marriage counseling based on the Bible.

Jake responded, "I've heard good things about you and your counseling. That you have a lot of practical wisdom and you're caring and compassionate. I can see that's true already. So I'm good." Jake's voice trailed off, then picked up again as he finished with these words: "I just have a lot of questions about the Bible and Christ."

I was silently praying about whether I should immediately pick up on Jake's last sentence and move from counseling to evangelism. I determined initially to be more invitational than directive. "Again, thanks, Jake, for your honesty. At any point during our counseling, if you have questions about the Bible and Christ, I'm here for you. If you'd like to do a breakfast or lunch, just the two of us, and talk about those questions, just let me know . . ."

We then shifted back to their marital concerns. That first meeting lasted nearly two hours. During our time, Jake and Miranda's issues with each other became crystal clear. And it became apparent to me how one verse—Ephesians

5:33—encapsulated almost two hours of interaction. I shared that with Jake and Miranda.

> I like you guys! You're both so refreshingly honest. Here's what I've heard. Let me know if I'm on or off target. Jake, you're dying for Miranda to believe in you, to be your cheerleader. You're hungry for her encouragement. You want to know that Miranda's interested in what's important to you and that she admires you deeply. You long for her respect. And you're terrified that you've lost it or are going to lose it.

The entire time, Jake was nodding in agreement. So I continued, now focused on what I had heard from Miranda.

> Miranda, here's what I've sensed from you. You're dying for Jake's intimate interest in you. You want to know that you're his one and only and that Jake is madly in love with you—instead of mad at you. You're thirsty for his tender involvement that shows that he's captivated by you—like he used to be. You long for his cherishing love. And you're afraid that you've lost it or are going to lose it.

Now it was Miranda's turn to keep nodding in agreement, to keep saying, "Yes. Yep. Absolutely."

I then wrapped up our first meeting with these words of counsel *and* evangelism. Picking up my Bible, I shared:

> This is why I love and trust God's Word. It's so rich. So relevant. Let me share my paraphrase of Ephesians 5:33, a verse that captures everything I've heard the two of you saying for almost two hours: "Husband, love your wife. Wife, respect your husband." God's Word, written two thousand years ago, perfectly summarizes and clearly describes what you have been sharing with me and what you've been longing for from each other. And that's just one verse. God gets you. He understands your marriage. He cares about you and your marriage. The Bible has crucial wisdom for your life, your relationship, and your marriage.

Jake didn't get on his knees, say the sinner's prayer, and surrender his life to Christ as I concluded my sharing. However, by the end of our three months of counseling together, Jake did commit his life to Christ. As he said it:

> I came to believe God and his Word because *it knew me.* It was like the Bible ripped my soul open and looked inside me. It exposed how messed up I was—how selfish and sinful. I saw how I couldn't fix this mess—me and our marriage—on my own. The Bible not only has real answers about our marriage—it is spot on. Jesus is not only *the* answer. Jesus is my caring, wise Savior.

Jake is right. The Bible is spot on about everything—including marriage. In this chapter, we will explore how God's written Word (the Bible) and living Word (Christ) redeem marriage through

- Redeemed Marital Communion/Connection: Resurrected Oneness
- Redeemed Marital Calling/Character: Transformed Hearts and Renewed Relational Roles

These two redeemed marital realities are so unlike anything our fallen world and our fallen hearts would manufacture on their own. So before we begin our redemptive marital journey, it will help if we explore the divine irony of death to self through resurrection to life.

Maturing as a Biblical Marriage Counselor
The Relevancy of Scripture—Eternally and Daily

1. On a scale of 1 to 10, with 10 being the highest, how confident are you in the *relevance of Scripture* to provide practical wisdom for the couple sitting before you and for you as a marriage counselor?

   a. How could you keep growing in confidence in the Bible's relevance for marriage counseling?

   b. As a marriage counselor, what do you do that specifically demonstrates your confidence in the Bible's relevance for marriage counseling?

   c. How do you help couples grow in their confidence in the Bible's relevance for their marriage?

2. Without knowing it, Jake and Miranda aligned their diagnosis of their marital problems with Ephesians 5:33—love and respect.

   a. In your experience as a marriage counselor, in what ways have you seen *the husband's calling to love his wife like Christ loves the church* to be a central issue?

   b. In your experience as a marriage counselor, in what ways have you seen *the wife's calling to offer her husband respecting love* to be a central issue?

   c. If you are married, in what ways have you seen *the husband's calling to love his wife like Christ loves the church* to be a central issue in your own marriage?

   d. If you are married, in what ways have you seen *the wife's calling to offer her husband respecting love* to be a central issue in your own marriage?

Divine Irony: Death to Self through Resurrection to Life

Godly marriage involves a divine irony. Spouses must avail themselves of Christ's power to resurrect us from the dead—in order to die! Our resurrected marital life in Christ involves daily dying to self. Like Christ, we die to self and live for God's glory and the good of our spouse and others.

Both husband & wife are called to a task far beyond their abilities. Yet, by the spirit, both are to love each other in a way that is truly mind-boggling God calls the husband, whose wife has just shamed, blamed, claimed, and maimed him, to love her with Christ's sacrificial, death-to-self *agape* love. This is impossible in the flesh. It is insane from the world's perspective.

God calls the wife, whose husband has just shamed, blamed, claimed, and maimed her, to love him with the church's respect for Christ. This is impossible in the flesh. It is insane from the world's perspective.

The Scriptural Sanity of Death to Self

Death to self was inconceivable to the early hearers of Christ's gospel message—including his disciples. A suffering messiah? No! A reigning and ruling messiah? Absolutely!

Think about Peter's reaction when Jesus "began to explain to his disciples that he must go to Jerusalem and suffer many things at the hands of the elders, the chief priests and the teachers of the law, and that he must be killed and on the third day be raised to life" (Matt. 16:21). Immediately, "Peter took him aside and began to rebuke him. 'Never, Lord!' he said. 'This shall never happen to you!'" (16:22). Rebuking the Lord? What a contradiction. What an indictment of our aversion to death to self.

"Jesus turned and said to Peter, 'Get behind me, Satan! You are a stumbling block to me; you do not have in mind the concerns of God, but merely human concerns'" (16:23). Living a self-focused life of self-glory is Satan's vision, not God's. Here is God's vision for life and marriage: "Then Jesus said to his disciples, 'Whoever wants to be my disciple must deny themselves and take up their cross and follow me. For whoever wants to save their life will lose it, but whoever loses their life for me will find it'" (16:24–25). Loving the one who hurts us is totally sane from the Word's perspective.

Paul concurs. Consider the verses that serve as a header to Paul's family wisdom. "Follow God's example, therefore, as dearly loved children, and walk in the way of love, just as Christ loved us and gave himself up for us as a fragrant offering and sacrifice to God" (Eph. 5:1–2).

In marriage, Christ is not commanding us to do anything he has not already done. To make marriage work, we are to be imitators of God. What he did, we are to do. We are to live a life of love in marriage just as Christ loved us.

What is a primary goal of marriage counseling? To help the husband and wife together to live a life of love—to walk in love, to have a pattern of other-centered care and concern. That would be an interesting question to place on a Marital Personal Information Form (MPIF): "On a scale of 1 to 10, with 10 being the highest, rate how well you are consistently living a life of other-centered love toward your spouse."

Of course, we must define love if we are to accurately rate how well we are loving. Biblical love cannot be defined as an infatuated feeling of romantic interest because someone makes me feel good about me. Jesus defines and embodies biblical love: "just as Christ loved us and *gave himself up for us* as a fragrant *offering and sacrifice* to God" (Eph. 5:2). This is biblical love—sacrificially giving up ourselves, our rights, our wants for the benefit of another person. So another good MPIF question would be, "On a scale of 1 to 10, with 10 being the highest, rate how well you are consistently dying to self by losing your life through sacrificially giving up your rights and wants for the benefit of your spouse."

Maturing as a Biblical Marriage Counselor
The Scriptural Sanity of Death to Self

1. Godly marriage involves a divine irony. Spouses must avail themselves of Christ's power to resurrect us from the dead—in order to die! Our resurrected marital life in Christ involves daily dying to self. How could this biblical marital vision shape or reshape your marriage counseling ministry?

2. Christ said, "Whoever wants to be my disciple must deny themselves and take up their cross and follow me. For whoever wants to save their life will lose it, but whoever loses their life for me will find it" (Matt. 16:24–25). How could his vision reshape the way spouses relate to each other?

3. This section suggested the following exercise: "On a scale of 1 to 10, with 10 being the highest, rate how well you are consistently living a life of other-centered love toward your spouse."

   a. How would most of the couples you counsel answer this question? How could you help them grow in this area?

   b. If you are married, how would you answer this question? How could you grow in this area?

4. This section suggested a second exercise: "On a scale of 1 to 10, with 10 being the highest, rate how well you are consistently dying to self by losing your life through sacrificially giving up your rights and wants for the benefit of your spouse."

   a. How would most of the couples you counsel answer this question? How could you help them grow in this area?

b. If you are married, how would you answer this question? How could you grow in this area?

5. Christ's redemptive prescription for marital healing shifts our gaze to Christ's death for us and our death to self. It shifts our mindset to the reality that marital problems in our heart require resurrection power—Christ-dependence, not self-dependence. As a marriage counselor, how can you help couples make this shift?

The Resurrection-to-Life Power behind Death-to-Self Marriage

Any honest Christian is going to have one of two answers to such a convicting question: "If that's God's marital standard, then I'm much closer to a 1 than a 10!" Or, "That question isn't even on my radar. To even think about loving like that takes strength I don't have."

Death to self is not on our radar because many of us falsely see the gospel as our ticket to divine *earthly* blessings. We come to Christ for the gifts rather than coming to Christ in worshipful awe of the Giver—who gave his life sacrificially *so that* we might lose our life in serving him and others.

In order to die to self we need resurrection to life. This is why Paul couches Ephesians 5 in Ephesians 1. This is why Paul prays a prayer that should be every biblical marriage counselor's prayer and every spouse's prayer:

> Glorious Father, sacrificial Son, and Spirit of wisdom, enlighten the eyes of our hearts to know you better so that we can grasp and apply your incomparably great power for us who believe. In our marriage, help us to tap into your resurrection power that is like the working of your mighty strength, which you exerted in Christ when you raised him from the dead and seated him at your right hand in the heavenly realms. (Adapted from Eph. 1:17–20)

Biblical marriage counseling offers impossible counsel. (Don't tweet that sentence out of context!) Counseling a hurt and empty spouse to die to self is impossible apart from resurrection-to-life power. Christ's redemptive prescription for marital healing shifts our gaze to Christ's death for us and our death to self. It shifts our mindset to the reality that marital problems in our heart require Christ-dependence—resurrection power.

This is not a mechanical process. It is *relational*. Which is why Paul tells us to be imitators of God "as *dearly loved children*" (Eph. 5:1). Our spouse may leave us empty of love, but we are never empty of our Father's love. We love our finite, failing spouse in the strength of Christ's resurrection (Eph. 1:17–20), through the overflow of our Father's love (Eph. 5:1), and by the filling of the Spirit (Eph. 5:18) as we are made strong in the Lord's mighty power, which we put on as our marital armor of God (Eph. 6:10–18).

God did not design marriage to be two empty people sucking life from each other. God designed marriage to be two people being continually filled individually and together by the Trinity. Out of the overflow of that filling they sacrificially give life to each other so that they grow together in Christ-like service for others.

Redeemed Marital Communion/Connection: Resurrected Oneness

Sadly, couples typically come to us not as intimate allies and soul mates but as angry adversaries and hurting rivals. This is so counter to the communion, connection, and oneness that Paul speaks of in Ephesians 5:31–32. "'For this reason a man will leave his father and mother and be united to his wife, and the two will become one flesh.' This is a profound mystery—but I am talking about Christ and the church." Paul repeats the marital message from Genesis 2, adding that this union and oneness, this cleaving and weaving, is a *mega-mysterion*—a great mystery, a spiritual secret revealed only in Scripture. What is this sacred secret?

Reenacting the Eternal Love Story

Here's the sacred secret—our earthly marriage reenacts the eternal love story. As Ray Ortlund explains, the dramatic super-reality of the Son of God leaving heaven to pursue and woo his bride with deep and loyal love is the breathtaking reason why human marriage even exists. Marriage is not a human invention. Its origin is divine and its purpose is spiritual.

It is not that Christ and the church are the metaphors. Christ and the church are *the reality* and human marriage and the husband/wife relation are the metaphor. Our marriage is to signify the union between Christ and his church. Every Christian married couple is called to represent, embody, exemplify, and incarnate the dazzling beauty of the eternal sacred romance.[1]

The Stunning Beauty of Our Union with Christ

The gospel's sacred romance is foreign to many of us. While we may rightly know the gospel as justification, we often fail to grasp the stunning beauty of the gospel as union with Christ. A tour through the book of Ephesians provides a beautiful glimpse.

> In *love*, the Father *chose us in Christ* and *adopted us into his forever family*. He *lavished* his grace upon us to bring us *into unity with himself*. He *invited* and *included us* in Christ and *sealed us forever with his Spirit*, demonstrating his *passionate, loyal love*. He *longs for us to know and love him more intimately*. We are the fullness of the One who *fills everything*. *Christ is intimately and indissolubly united with us as his bride, and he loves us with profound, boundless, and steadfast love.* He is the head and we are his *body in the closest possible bond of unity, connection, and communion*. *Because of his great love for us*, God made us alive *with Christ*, raised *us with Christ*, and *seated us with Christ*. He has given us his *incomparably rich grace* expressing his *unfathomable kindness* to us. We are his *beloved poem*, his handcrafted masterpiece. Once far away, we are now *brought intimately near* to his heart. We are *his family, his children, his bride*. We are *joined together* and have *become a dwelling place* by his Spirit. We are heirs *together*. We can approach his *heavenly throne* with *freedom and confidence*. Christ *dwells in our hearts* through faith. The Father *wants to root us in his love* and wants us *to grasp more and more every day how wide, long, high, and deep Christ's love is for us*. The Father wants us *to experience his love that surpasses knowledge*. He wants us *to be filled with the fullness of God*. As our head, Christ *grows us up, knitting the body together in unity* as *his dearly loved children*. Christ *sacrificially loves us* by *giving himself up for us and making us holy*, presenting us to himself *as a stunning, spotless, radiant bride* that he *cherishes*. He left his Father's home *to be wedded to us*.

Union with Christ, Marital Oneness, and Marriage Counseling

In the beginning, God declared that it was *not good for the man to be alone*. God designed Adam for intensely intimate relationship of oneness with a strong helper-companion who would complement and complete him (Gen. 2:18–22). God intends marriage to bring us into more intense proximity with another human being than any other relationship. Two lives become one life fully shared in intimate and unbreakable attachment.

Although the marriage relationship was broken by the fall, Christ's death, burial, and resurrection restore our capacity for marital oneness. It is because of our union with Christ in the eternal romance that we marry in the earthly romance. God's love story—and our safe, secure place in it—is what motivates our marital love story. It is not only that marriage is to showcase the ultimate marriage. Marriage is *because of* this ultimate marriage. Marriage declares, *Because I am one with Christ, I can be one with you.*[2]

When God designed marriage in Genesis 2, he already had the relationship of Christ and his redeemed bride in mind. According to Paul, the essence of marriage involves a communion/connection of oneness in which I make a sacrificial commitment to love my spouse out of a profound understanding that we are now united as one just as Christ and the church are united. The gospel and marriage explain and picture each other.

This has multiple implications for couples and for counseling couples. We will consider two of these implications. First, spouses need help envisioning and enacting this coupling process. It is no longer "I" but "we." We establish our identity interdependently. Together we ask and answer questions such as, Who are we? What is our new joint story? What is the essence of our new combined DNA? How do we help each other to become more like Christ together? Often, these are the last thoughts on a hurting spouse's mind. We must prayerfully and patiently help them shift their mindset to life being all about reflecting Christ and the church *together*.

Second, the biblical marriage counselor needs to know how to get out of the way so the couple can couple. Yes, there are times when we might schedule individual meetings. Yes, there are times in joint sessions when we might focus on the husband or the wife. However, as you will read more than once in this book, marriage counseling is not individual counseling with an audience—with one spouse watching you counsel the other spouse. The art of marriage counseling involves *equipping the couple to be each other's biblical counselor.* It helps somewhat if a marriage counselor empathizes with a hurting husband or wife. It helps immensely if a hurting spouse empathizes with the spouse they have hurt.

Maturing as a Biblical Marriage Counselor
Redeemed Marital Communion/Connection

1. Couples typically come to us not as intimate allies and soul mates but as angry adversaries and hurting rivals.

    a. What premarital measures can churches take to lessen this typical reality?

b. What preventative measures can churches take to lessen this typical reality with couples who are already married?

2. Reread the tour through Ephesians, about the stunning beauty of our union with Christ.

   a. What aspects stand out to you—that you marvel at and rejoice over the most?

   b. Craft your own psalm of praise in response to your marvelous union with Christ.

3. Marriage declares, "Because I am one with Christ, I can be one with you."

   a. How could you help couples understand, grasp, and apply this reality?

   b. How might it impact couples to know that their union with Christ is the foundation for their oneness as husband and wife?

4. How can you help spouses to envision and enact the coupling reality that it is no longer "I" but "we"?

5　The biblical marriage counselor needs to know how to get out of the way so the couple can couple. What are the implications of this principle for your practice of marriage counseling?

Redeemed Marital Calling/Character:
Transformed Hearts and Renewed Relational Roles

When Jake and Miranda first sat down across from me, not only were concepts like redemption, resurrection, death to self, transformation, and renewal not on their minds, they were not even part of their vocabulary. Jake was not a redeemed, transformed person. Two primary issues were on their hearts:

I'm hurting. Fix my feelings.

My spouse is hurting me. Fix my spouse.

As I listened to their heart-cries, I empathized with both Jake and Miranda. I could feel their pain, their confusion. I listened to the story of their souls.

I also invited them, even unbelieving Jake, to listen to God's story of soul-u-tions. We read Ephesians 5:18 and 6:10–18 as bookends where Paul explains that to make marriage work couples need to be empowered by God. We read Ephesians 5:30–32, which says that, rather than fighting against each other, Jake and Miranda needed to become one with each other and with Christ in their fight to save their marriage.

Marriage as Mutual Ministry: Transformed Spouses Transforming Spouses

We also looked at Ephesians 5:25–28 and 1 Peter 3:1–2. These passages don't shout, "Fix my feelings! Fix my spouse!" Instead they plead, "Father, help us to help each other become more like Christ." Notice this mutual ministry message contained in each of these passages.

Husbands, love your wives, just as Christ loved the church and gave himself up for her to make her holy, cleansing her by the washing with water through the word, and to present her to himself as a radiant church, without stain or wrinkle or any other blemish, but holy and blameless. In this same way, husbands ought to love their wives as their own bodies. (Eph. 5:25–28)

Wives, in the same way submit yourselves to your own husbands so that, if any of them do not believe the word, they may be won over without words by the behavior of their wives, when they see the purity and reverence of your lives. (1 Pet. 3:1–2)

While we often talk about these passages in terms of marital roles, it would be beneficial to first highlight the calling behind these roles. God calls a husband to love his wife sacrificially *so that* she will become more holy—be sanctified. God calls a wife to love her husband with purity and reverence *so that*, in this case, he will become holy—be saved.

What does a gospel-centered marriage look like? We are to give each other grace-love that God uses to transform us increasingly into the character of Christ. As Tim Keller explains, "Marriage is a major vehicle for the gospel's remaking of your heart from the inside out and your life from the ground up."[3]

Marriage is for helping each other become our future-glory'selves. As biblical marriage counselors, we want to help a fighting couple say to each other, "I want to partner with you and God in the journey of Christlikeness."

As I noted earlier, our role as biblical marriage counselors is to equip spouses to be each other's best biblical counselor. Paul Tripp talks about "people in need of change helping people in need of change."[4] Great phrase. As it applies to marriage, I like to say "transformed spouses transforming spouses." That's very different from our exploration of James 4 back in chapter 2, where we saw that the motivation was essentially, "Fix my spouse for my benefit, because they are the problem!" That's a vicious cycle. Here the vision is, "Lord, transform each of us so we're empowered to be an instrument for mutual transformation in each other's life." That's a victorious cycle.

A Husband's Ministry Calling: An Empowering Shepherd Who Loves Sacrificially

Entire books have been devoted to the marital roles of husbands *or* wives. I'm devoting a third of a chapter to the roles of husbands *and* wives. Why so little? First, there is no reason to reinvent the wheel. Check the bibliography for excellent books on marital roles. Second, it is so vital to highlight the heart behind the role. Motivation matters. Transformation matters.

My counsel for marriage counselors: help couples get Christ-dependent communion and calling right. Lead them toward affirming, "We're united in our mission of the mutual ministry of spiritual transformation." When their hearts are captivated by this vision, then they will happily read and humbly apply books you recommend on marital roles.

Ministry Calling #1: Husband, Be an Initiator Who Starts the Chain of Love

God designed men as initiators. God placed Adam in the garden as a caretaker and road-maker (Gen. 2:15–17). Adam was to take care of the garden—to guard and protect it, keep it safe, watch over it. God called Adam to the fundamental task of working hard to care for creation. He was to be an undershepherd who cared for all God would place under his loving, servant headship. Adam was also to work the garden—to diligently, creatively do pioneering work and courageously create order by confronting chaos. God called Adam to responsibility and resiliency.

This calling is foundational to the rest of the husband's ministry callings. As initiator, the husband takes the lead in ministering to his wife. Rather than saying, "I'd serve my wife if she would just . . . ," the mature husband says, "I'll start the chain of love by fulfilling my calling."

Ministry Calling #2: Husband, Be a Sacrificial Shepherd Who Loves Passionately

God calls husbands to love their wives as Christ loved the church and gave himself up for her. The husband *takes the lead in dying.*

This is passionate love in the sense of the sacrificial paschal Lamb. This is biblical *agape*, which is giving, initiating love. It is Christlike love that proclaims, "We love because he first loved us" (1 John 4:19). It is the grace-love of Christ dying for the ungodly. Of God demonstrating his love in this: "While we were still sinners, Christ died for us" (Rom. 5:8).

Show me a husband who loves sacrificially, and I'll show you a growing marriage. Show me an unhealthy marriage, and I'll show you a husband who lives for himself instead of dying for his wife.

Ministry Calling #3: Husband, Be a Sanctifying Pastor Who Offers Impacting Love

The husband dies to himself for the purpose of offering new life to his wife—making her holy, being the major player in her sanctification process, being his wife's pastor.

In the ancient Near East, it was customary for the groom-to-be to prepare the home and for the bride-to-be to purify herself. Ephesians 5:26–27 turns this custom upside down. The husband lives to assist his wife to be radiant. The idea is movement toward splendor—glory, honor, high esteem. The husband is to envision and empower his wife toward her God-destined greatness, potential, inner beauty, and future glory. A mature husband builds up and promotes his wife's virtue, purity, and maturity. A mature husband meets his wife's longing for someone who is consumed with her well-being. He lives out the relationally dignifying purpose of putting his wife's growth first. He cares about her life and the direction she is heading—not only today but also her ultimate spiritual maturity and relationship to Christ.

Ministry Calling #4: Husband, Be the Head Who Offers Nourishing, Cherishing, and Honoring Love

As every man feeds and cares for his own body, so every husband as head is responsible to nourish and cherish his wife (see Eph. 5:29–30). "Nourish" pictures treating luxuriously, to be indulgent, extravagant. It is related to the word for daily bread. The husband seeks to provide for his wife's daily needs—body, soul, and spirit. "Cherish" means to gently protect, care for, warm, and provide for. Paul uses the same word in 1 Thessalonians 2:7 when he writes of a nursing mother giving of her own body to feed her infant.

In 1 Peter 3:7, Peter adds the calling to treat one's wife with respect and precious honor. Throughout the New Testament, "honor" speaks of great, precious, tender care given to people we highly value. It is even used of how we treat God! The sense in this verse is, "Assign to your wife the priority position of precious treatment. Reserve your greatest energy, excitement, and enjoyment for relating to her in ways that communicate the high value she has to you. Delight in and prize her."

Ministry Calling #5: Husband, Be a Servant Leader Who Offers Empowering Love

As an initiator and as the head, every husband has a leadership style. Before the fall, Adam was an empowering leader. After the fall, Adam and all males veer off in one sinful direction or another. Some of us misuse our power by overpowering others. We lord it over others through heavy-handed, domineering, abusive misuse of power (see Matt. 20:25–28; 1 Pet. 5:1–3). We push others down, attempting to master and enslave them. Paul specifically warns husbands against this in Colossians 3:19 when he exhorts the husband not to be harsh with his wife—not to be bitter or poisonous toward her.

Others of us misuse our power by being overpowered by others. Like Adam in the garden, we abdicate our role of protective leader. We are cowardly, intimidated by the thought that our wife might be better at something than we are, so we push her down rather than build her up.

Instead, God calls men to use their innate strength to serve and empower others. In doing so, men follow the model of Christ, who "did not come to be served, but to serve, and to give his life a ransom for many" (Matt. 20:28). Husbands become great by becoming servants who empower their wives (see Matt. 20:27). In 1 Peter 3:7, Peter exhorts the husband to be considerate of his wife as the weaker partner. The word "weaker" is not a pejorative, negative, demeaning term. Rather, it is a statement that women are not designed to be primarily focused on power, competition, potency, or power plays. So a godly husband will maintain an empathetic sensitivity to how his wife, a female, is designed by God. We can summarize it like this:

> Know your wife's God-designed feminine longings and thirsts, and nourish them by empowering her. She is not primarily about power, so be sensitive. Do not abuse your wife with your nature which is oriented around strength. Your wife is designed as a recipient of strength. If you withhold strength, she will be malnourished. If you abuse your strength, she will be harmed. Empower—put power into—your wife.

A Wife's Ministry Calling: An Encouraging Intimate Ally Who Loves Respectfully

God handcrafted male and female to complement, correspond to, and fit together—body and soul—like puzzle pieces. There are corresponding longings, desires, and thirsts that husbands and wives experience and fill in each other. What God designed the husband to long for, he created the wife with the capacity and wiring to fulfill, and vice versa.

Ministry Calling #1: Wife, Be a Suitable Helper Who Offers Responding/Corresponding Love

While God designed the male to be an initiator who is responsible to start the chain of love, he created the female as a responder who openly, vulnerably, and trustingly receives loving initiative. Of course, this does *not* mean that the husband is more valuable or less needy.

In fact, it was Adam—the male, the husband—whose neediness and aloneness prompted God to create a suitable helper (Gen. 2:18–22). The Hebrew word *ezer* ("helper") is used of Yahweh, who is our "shield and helper" (Deut. 33:29) and "the helper of the fatherless" (Ps. 10:14). In 1 Kings 20:16 the word describes an alliance of thirty-two kings—strong allies. Throughout the Old Testament *ezer* highlights rescuing out of compassion and aiding by surrounding.

The wife is a *suitable* helper—one who is intimately before, openly in front of, corresponding to, completing, matching; a fit, equal counterpart. The wife is suitable to meet the aloneness, separation, isolation, and sense of being incomplete that the husband experiences—suitable to fill a relational aloneness, suitable to responsively complete the initiating male soul.

Taken together, "suitable helper" portrays the essence of the feminine soul. She is comfortable with intimately responding to and relationally completing the masculine soul. God calls the wife to sustain and heal, comfort and encourage her husband's masculine soul by coming alongside to strongly help. She is her husband's formidable helper, his intimate ally.

Ministry Calling #2: Wife, Be Vulnerably Submissive as You Openly Receive Loving Headship

God calls all Christians, as brothers and sisters in Christ, to mutually "submit to one another out of reverence for Christ" (Eph. 5:21). He also calls all of us in humility to consider others better than ourselves, to look not only to our own interests but also to the interests of others, and to have the same other-centered, self-emptying attitude of Christ (Phil. 2:3–5). Biblical submission is a voluntary spirit, mindset, and attitude of Christlike humility, ranking oneself under another and putting the other first.

To mutual submission, Paul adds the specific submission of the wife to her husband (Eph. 5:22–24). As God calls a husband to loving, sacrificial headship where he takes the initiative in feeding and caring for his wife, so God calls a wife to a gracious disposition of openly responding to and receiving her husband's nourishing and cherishing ministry. Marriage is a waltz where the husband graciously initiates and the wife joyfully responds. Her response is done "to the Lord" (Eph. 5:22) as an act of vulnerable trusting worship of God.

The godly wife asks in her attitude, "How can I respond to my husband and represent to the world something of the joyful, respectful, helping, complementing submission of the church to Christ? How can I communicate to my husband that I am open to and want his giving, sacrificial love, wisdom, and strength? How can I communicate to my man that I will turn to no one else for the deepest satisfaction of my feminine soul?"

Ministry Calling #3: Wife, Be an Encourager Who Offers Respectful Love

As God calls a husband to offer unconditional love, so he calls a wife to offer unconditional respect (Eph. 5:33). This never means winking at sin. Instead, it communicates to the husband, "I believe in you, even when you don't believe in yourself. I respect and believe in your God-given capacity to be the man, the husband, God calls you to be. I so believe in you that I'm confident you are strong enough to hear difficult but loving feedback."

"En-courage" pictures putting courage into. God calls men to courageously confront chaos in a fallen world. It is hard, discouraging work. Life dis-courages—it drains of courage. A godly wife en-courages—she fills up her husband with courage. She has a clear vision of her husband's strengths and consistently affirms them. She recognizes her husband's victories and regularly applauds him. She esteems him, high-fives him, and fist-bumps him.

Peter speaks of the beauty of a wife's reverence (1 Pet. 3:3). The contentious woman of Proverbs 27:15–16; 19:13; and 21:19 is the distorted image of this. She stirs up strife; she wrangles and debates. Not a refuge-giver, she is a desert wasteland of death words, a dream crusher, doubter, naysayer, value-subtractor. Here in 1 Peter 3, we witness the godly image. In the face of a harsh, unbelieving husband, a godly wife wins him without words by the purity and reverence of her behavior. "Reverence" means to honor and respect—to lift up, build up, support, and be a value-adder. It speaks of believing in, stirring up, and blessing another with life words. It depicts watering what God plants and giving life to what the husband creates.

Ministry Calling #4: Wife, Be a Refuge-Giver Who Offers Loving, Gentle Strength

Peter continues painting his portrait of the godly wife. Her adornment is "the unfading beauty of a gentle and quiet spirit" (1 Pet. 3:4). The Greek word for "gentle" (*praus*) is the same word Christ uses of himself in Matthew 11:28–30, where he describes himself as a rest-giver. A Christlike wife is mild, not weak; humble, not aggressive; a bridge-builder, not a wall-builder. Her mantra is, "I will give you rest for I am restful in Christ. I will give you refuge, because I find my refuge in Jesus." The vexing woman of Proverbs 21:19 is the distorted image. She stirs up rage, trouble, turbulence, and commotion. She is not at peace, so she is unable to offer peace. She is the perfectionistic, negative, fault-finding, defeating, and deflating wife.

Not so the godly wife of 1 Peter 3:4, whose quiet spirit speaks of a soft responder. The quarrelsome woman of Proverbs 19:13 and 21:9 is loud, scolding, clamorous, and disquiet. She is a brawler. She is an umpire who enjoys calling her husband out at home! But in 1 Peter 3, "quiet" implies unperturbed, calm, and tranquil. The godly wife finds her shalom (wholeness, health, holiness, peace) in Jesus, so she is at peace with responding to and receiving her husband's loving initiative.

Maturing as a Biblical Marriage Counselor
Redeemed Marital Calling/Character

1. God calls a husband to be an empowering shepherd who loves sacrificially.

   a. As a marriage counselor, how could you walk alongside a husband and wife to help the husband grow as an initiator who starts the chain of love?

   b. As a marriage counselor, how could you walk alongside a husband and wife to help the husband grow as a sacrificial shepherd who loves passionately?

   c. As a marriage counselor, how could you walk alongside a husband and wife to help the husband grow as a sanctifying pastor who offers impacting love?

   d. As a marriage counselor, how could you walk alongside a husband and wife to help the husband grow as the head who offers nourishing, cherishing, and honoring love?

   e. As a marriage counselor, how could you walk alongside a husband and wife to help the husband grow as a servant leader who offers empowering love?

2. God calls a wife to be an encouraging intimate ally who loves respectfully.

   a. As a marriage counselor, how could you walk alongside a husband and wife to help the wife grow as a suitable helper who offers responding/corresponding love?

   b. As a marriage counselor, how could you walk alongside a husband and wife to help the wife grow vulnerably submissive as she openly receives loving headship?

   c. As a marriage counselor, how could you walk alongside a husband and wife to help the wife grow as an encourager who offers respectful love?

   d. As a marriage counselor, how could you walk alongside a husband and wife to help the wife grow as a refuge-giver who offers loving gentle strength?

PART 2

Practical Training for Biblical Marriage Counselors

How to Develop 22 Marriage Counseling Relational Competencies

FOUR

Mapping Biblical Marriage Counseling

Our Marriage Counseling GPS

Introduction: Theology Matters

As we launch our focus on the *methodology* of biblical marriage counseling, we should remind ourselves why we spent three chapters on the *theology* of marriage counseling. Every counseling approach is based on some theory, some worldview.

Over two decades ago, in my PhD program at Kent State University (KSU), three marriage counseling approaches were prominent: family systems, narrative therapy, and solution-focused therapy. As we learned each approach, every class spent up to half the time on the theory and worldview behind the model.

While professors at KSU would not have called their theory a theology, they covered theological terrain. Each model explored the same three areas we explored in chapters 1–3:

- *Understanding People*: A theory of couples—understanding how couples are to function and relate in healthy ways. Because we are exploring a *biblical* approach to marriage counseling, we call this Creation: understanding God's design for healthy marriage relationships.
- *Diagnosing Problems*: A theory of why couples struggle—diagnosing what is wrong inside each spouse and/or between spouses. Because we are exploring a *biblical* approach to marriage counseling, we call this Fall: understanding how our heart sin leads to relational sinning.

- *Prescribing Solutions*: A theory of how to help couples—prescribing how to move from unhealthy to mutually healthy relationships. Because we are exploring a *biblical* approach to marriage counseling, we call this Redemption: understanding how Christ changes us and how we relate.

Theology matters in our ten chapters on methodology. In this chapter, we outline how a biblical creation-fall-redemption theology of marriage shapes three areas of marriage counseling:

- *Our Focus*: Encouraging couples to couple through gospel connection.
- *Our Role*: Envisioning ourselves as collaborators (co-laborers) through gospel coaching.
- *Our Approach*: Equipping couples to care for each other through gospel conversations.

We can consider these our GPS: Gospel Positioning Scripture. The gospel matters eternally and it matters daily. The gospel matters in marriage and in marriage counseling.

Maturing as a Biblical Marriage Counselor
Theology Matters

1. Think back to the Creation theology of chapter 1. What are the top two or three implications for marriage counseling from chapter 1?

2. Think back to the Fall theology of chapter 2. What are the top two or three implications for marriage counseling from chapter 2?

3. Think back to the Redemption theology of chapter 3. What are the top two or three implications for marriage counseling from chapter 3?

Our Focus: Encouraging Couples to Couple through Gospel Connection

As we saw in chapter 1, God calls couples to couple. "'This is now bone of my bones and flesh of my flesh; she shall be called "woman," for she was taken out of man.' That is why a man leaves his father and mother and is united to his wife, and they become one flesh. Adam and his wife were both naked, and they felt no shame" (Gen. 2:23–25).

If we are not careful, as marriage counselors we can displace the husband and wife as the primary instruments for comfort, encouragement, restoration, and wisdom. Yes, as counselors we must connect deeply with both spouses. However, the hurting husband and wife, having left their parents as their primary connection, should not primarily attach to their marriage counselor.

Attaching to the counselor is a temptation for them because they are so hungry for connection. It can also be a temptation for us as their counselor. If we are not maturing in Christ, we will *need* them to attach to us. It fills us up, makes us feel necessary and useful. Instead of being their marriage counselor, we become their marriage messiah. But there is only one Messiah— and it is *not* us.

In chapter 6, you will learn several marriage counseling competencies to connect with the couple *so that* they connect with each other. I am raising the issue now as a foundational mindset shift for us as marriage counselors. Our mindset should not be "How can I rescue their marriage?" Instead, our mindset needs to be "How can I encourage this couple to connect to each other, to Christ, and to the body of Christ so their marriage glorifies Christ?"

If the theology of marriage from Genesis 2–3, Matthew 7, Ephesians 1–6, Colossians 3, James 4, and 1 Peter 3 that we explored together in the first three chapters means anything, it is that the counselor is not the most important person in their marriage—Christ is and they are. So before, during, and after every marriage counseling session, we should be asking marriage counselor questions like:

- How can I help this couple find their gospel comfort in Christ so they can comfort each other (2 Cor. 1:3–8)?
- How can I help this couple find their gospel encouragement in Christ so they can encourage each other (2 Cor. 1:8–11; Phil. 2:1–5)?
- How can I help this couple find their gospel restoration in Christ so they can forgive each other, reconcile with each other, and have their marriage restored in Christ (2 Cor. 5:17–21; Eph. 4:30–5:2)?

- How can I help this couple to discover and apply gospel wisdom from Christ and his Word so they can discern together what is best and pure and glorifying to Christ (Phil. 1:9–11)?
- How can I help this couple unite together in Christ so they can experience gospel leaving, cleaving, weaving, and receiving (Gen. 2:23–25)?
- How can I stir up this couple to tap into the gospel resources residing in them so their marriage can bear the fruit of the Spirit's power, love, and wisdom (2 Tim. 1:6–7)?

Maturing as a Biblical Marriage Counselor
Our Focus

1. You read that if we are not careful, as marriage counselors we can displace the husband and wife as the primary instrument for comfort, encouragement, restoration, and wisdom.

   a. Have you ever seen this happen in marriage counseling—that you either observed, received, or offered? If so, what was the impact?

   b. How can marriage counselors avoid this pitfall of displacing the couple?

2. You read, "Instead of being their marriage counselor, we become their marriage messiah."

   a. Have you ever seen this happen in marriage counseling—that you either observed, received, or offered? If so, what was the impact?

   b. How can marriage counselors avoid this sin of displacing Christ?

3. Which of the marriage counselor mindset questions seems most important to your ministry as a marriage counselor? Why? How could you apply these mindsets to your ministry?

   a. How can I help this couple find their gospel comfort in Christ so they can comfort each other?

   b. How can I help this couple find their gospel encouragement in Christ so they can encourage each other?

   c. How can I help this couple find their gospel restoration in Christ so they can forgive each other, reconcile with each other, and have their marriage restored in Christ?

   d. How can I help this couple to discover and apply gospel wisdom from Christ and his Word so they can discern together what is best and pure and glorifying to Christ?

   e. How can I help this couple cleave together to Christ so they can experience gospel leaving, cleaving, weaving, and receiving?

   f. How can I stir up this couple to tap into the gospel resources residing in them so their marriage can bear the fruit of the Spirit's power, love, and wisdom?

Our Role: Envisioning Ourselves as Collaborators through Gospel Coaching

Since we are not marriage messiahs, what are we? What images capture our calling as biblical marriage counselors who seek to encourage couples to couple?

A Gospel Coach

Coaches do not play the game for their players. They empower their players to play powerfully. So it is with marriage ministers—through Christ's power we empower couples to love with the uniqueness God designed into them. We draw out, stir up, provoke, encourage, and fan into flame their gifts.

A Gospel Choreographer or Conductor

Marriage counselors are like the choreographer of a dance scene in a Broadway musical. We are like the conductor of a philharmonic orchestra. We sense a couple's unique marital dance and assist them to flow (to leave, cleave, weave, and receive). We listen to the harmony of their unique marital music to help them blend and co-create a beautiful new symphony.

A Gospel Cheerleader

Marriage counselors offer hope and provide encouragement. We look with spiritual eyes to spot resources and successes and point these out to couples. With faith eyes we envision together what God is up to and how couples can cling to Christ to join what he is doing in and through their marriage.

A Gospel Care-Fronter (Confronting in Care)

We are not naïve. We do not ignore problems, weaknesses, and sins. We confront out of concern—we are care-fronters. We humbly speak gospel truth in love (Gal. 6:1; Eph. 4:15). We gently expose sin (2 Tim. 2:24–26). We help couples to face their heart sins, repent, find forgiveness (James 4:1–8), and experience the power of grace to change (Titus 2:11–14).

A Gospel Church Representative

Regardless of the setting—church or parachurch—as biblical counselors we envision ourselves as shepherds representing the body of Christ. This means we never see counseling simply as something done alone in an office. We do not want churches *with* biblical counseling. We desire churches *of* biblical counseling—where one-another ministry saturates everything. This means we always see the one hour a week of marital counseling as a subset of the larger, ongoing ministry of the church. We connect the couple with the body of Christ: worship, preaching, small groups, advocates, personal Bible study, spiritual disciplines, and more.

A Gospel Craftsman

A true craftsman, whether an expert carpenter or a renowned artist, moves beyond rudimentary skills. True craftsmen spontaneously use the gifts of God implanted in them by his Spirit. You will take Kellemen stuff and make it your own. Taking some here. Leaving some there. Weaving in your own biblical studies and counseling experiences here. Blending in the biblical teaching of others there. Be yourself—your healthy, maturing, Christlike self.

A Gospel Construction Foreman

We are not the architect—God is. He is the Designer who has given us the blueprint for marriage. But we can be like the construction foreman. We use the blueprint God has given us, and we work with the crew (the couple) to empower them to get the job done. We help the couple to organize themselves as one united organism.

A Gospel Co-creator

Frequently couples enter counseling living the shame, blame, claim, and maim narrative we looked at in Genesis 3. With Christ and the couple we co-create and co-author a new marital narrative of grace, forgiveness, acceptance, and responsibility.

A Gospel Cop

This is a startling image. However, it is a necessary one because sometimes couples come to us in such disarray that they need to be protected from each other. Someone strong needs to step in to "protect and serve." Within a session, this means saying, "While I want the two of you to be honest, that tone and those words are destructive. I can't allow that during our meetings." Between sessions it may mean anything from calling the appropriate authorities to carrying out church discipline to recommending a temporary separation for the safety of a spouse.

A Gospel Collaborator (Co-laborer)

If the image of a cop was startling, then the image of a co-laborer is meant to be summarizing. We co-labor with Christ, the couple, and the body of Christ to produce something beautiful. We co-labor with them so that they find Christ's power to sustain, heal, reconcile, and guide one another—which leads us to our final focus for this chapter.

Maturing as a Biblical Marriage Counselor
Our Role

Review the ten images of a biblical marriage counselor:

Gospel Coach	Gospel Craftsman
Gospel Choreographer/Conductor	Gospel Construction Foreman
Gospel Cheerleader	Gospel Co-creator
Gospel Care-Fronter (Confronting in Care)	Gospel Cop
Gospel Church Representative	Gospel Collaborator (Co-laborer)

1. Which two or three of these images stand out to you as most important for you to develop as a biblical marriage counselor? Why? How could you grow in those two or three areas?

2. Which two or three of these images are already strengths for you? How did Christ grow them in you to this point? How could you keep growing in those two or three areas?

3. What additional images would you add to this list? Describe each image.

Our Approach: Equipping Couples to Care for Each Other through Gospel Conversations

Picture Trish and DeWayne. They committed to love each other for better, for worse, and right now they are in the for worse period. Trish is irate because she is not sure she can trust DeWayne. She says, "He lost his job and lied to me about it for weeks!" DeWayne feels condemned—even before he lost his job. He says, "There's nothing I could ever do that would measure up to Trish's perfectionistic standards!" They are deeply hurt by each other. And they are deeply hurting each other.

As we noted in the book's introduction, individual counseling is messy enough. But marriage counseling is exponentially messier. So we need a GPS—Gospel Positioning Scripture—wisdom to know where to start and where to move. Biblical marriage counselors need the prayer Paul prayed in Philippians 1:9–11.

> And this is my prayer: that your love may abound more and more in knowledge and depth of insight, so that you may be able to discern what is best and may be pure and blameless for the day of Christ, filled with the fruit of righteousness that comes through Jesus Christ—to the glory and praise of God.

We want to share Christ's love with DeWayne and Trish with biblical counseling wisdom that best encourages their love to be pure and their relationship to be filled with Christ's righteousness so their marriage glorifies God.

But where do we start? Well, any counselor is going to say, "We start by listening to more of their story." Agreed. Let's say we have done that. Any biblical counselor would then say, "We focus on their heart issues, not just on surface behavioral matters." Agreed. But whose heart issues first? And which heart issues—the heart of their hurt and their suffering? Or the heart of their hurting each other and their sinning? What is our biblical guide?

Two Guideposts for Biblical Marriage Counseling

In *Gospel-Centered Marriage Counseling*, we will follow a GPS derived from God's Word and the history of Christian soul care. It provides two guideposts and four compass points for biblical marriage counseling.

Our biblical approach to marriage counseling will address both marital suffering and marital sin, both hurting hearts and hard hearts, both comforting and confronting. In the words of Frank Lake, "Pastoral care is defective unless it can deal *thoroughly* with the evils we have suffered as well as with the sins we have committed."[1]

Guidepost #1: Biblical Marriage Counseling for Suffering

Clearly, both DeWayne and Trish are suffering. What does the Bible offer them in their marital pain? Among the many New Testament words for spiritual care, *parakaleo* ("to comfort, encourage, or console") predominates, appearing 109 times. In 2 Corinthians 1:3–11, Paul pictures God as the Father of compassion and the God of all comfort (a form of the word *parakaleo*). Paul then teaches that the best comforters are those who go to God for comfort because he is the one "who comforts us in all our troubles, *so that* we can comfort those in any trouble with the comfort we ourselves receive from God" (2 Cor. 1:4).

The word *parakaleo* emphasizes personal presence—one called alongside to help. It also highlights the idea of empathy and suffering with another person or couple—weeping with those who weep (Rom. 12:15). The English word "comfort," when broken down, pictures well the biblical idea: co-fortitude— shared sorrow is endurable sorrow.

In *parakaletic* marriage counseling, we seek to turn Trish and DeWayne's desolation into consolation through hope in God. The word "encouragement," when broken down, pictures the idea well: en-courage—to put courage into. Encouragers come alongside to help struggling, suffering spouses through personal presence coupled with scriptural wisdom that directs the couple's gaze and focus to God's eternal perspective.

When Christ ascended, he sent the Holy Spirit to be our *Parakletos*—our Comforter and Advocate called alongside to encourage and help us in times of suffering, trouble, grief, injustice, and hardship. The Spirit performs his ministry by being in us and by revealing truth to us (John 14:16–17). As the Spirit of Truth, his ministry is the exact opposite of Satan's, who is the father of lies (John 8:44). Satan is called the accuser (Rev. 12:10), and his core strategy is to speak lying words of condemnation to us. The Spirit is called Encourager and Advocate, and his ministry is to speak gospel truth in love about our justification and reconciliation in Christ.

Think about what Paul is saying to *you*. You don't need a PhD in marital therapy to become a competent parakaletic marriage counselor. You have the resource planted within you—the *Parakletos*, the Holy Spirit—so that you can comfort and encourage Trish and DeWayne to hope in God and to believe that God is good even when their marital life is bad.

Guidepost #2: Biblical Marriage Counseling for Sin

In Romans 15:14, Paul says that the Christians in Rome are competent to counsel, instruct, and disciple. Here he uses a form of the Greek word *noutheteo*, which occurs eleven times in the New Testament. Jay Adams, the founder of the National Association of Nouthetic Counselors (now the Association of Certified Biblical Counselors), describes nouthetic counseling as confronting for change out of concern.[2]

Noutheteo emphasizes inner heart change leading to relational change. The foundational meaning of the word comes from the root *noeo*, meaning to direct one's mind, to perceive, and from *nous*, which refers to the heart, the mind, the seat of spiritual, rational, and moral insight and action. The mind is the place of practical reason leading to moral action. The emphasis is not merely on the intellect but also on motivation and affections. *Noutheteo* means to impart understanding, to set right, to lay on the heart. Nouthetic impartation of truth can take on many forms, such as encouraging, urging, spurring on, teaching, reminding, admonishing, reconciling, guiding, and advising.

Paul uses *noutheteo* in Colossians 1:20–29 to describe one aspect of his multifaceted pastoral ministry. God commissioned him to present Christ's gospel of grace to people (1:20–25), infusing people with the hope of who they are in Christ (1:26–27), with the goal of presenting them mature in Christ (1:28), through personal, passionate, persistent involvement in their lives (1:28–29) by Christ's resurrection power (1:29).

Paul is saying in Romans 15:14 that believers like you are competent to disciple couples like DeWayne and Trish toward communion with Christ and conformity to Christ through the personal ministry of the Word—biblical marriage counseling. Through loving nouthetic ministry, they can internalize the truth that God is gracious even when their marital relationship is sinful and that his grace that saves is also his grace that sanctifies and changes their marriage.

Four Compass Points for Biblical Marriage Counseling

While marriage counseling can be complex and messy, we will keep our GPS as simple as possible. Just as a map has the four compass points of north, south, east, and west, so our biblical marriage counseling model has the four compass points of sustaining, healing, reconciling, and guiding. Figure 4.1

Figure 4.1

Comprehensive and Compassionate Biblical Marriage Counseling

Parakaletic Biblical Marriage Counseling for Suffering Spouses

- **Sustaining**: Like Christ, we care about each other's hurts.
- **Healing**: Through Christ, it's possible for us to hope in God together.

Nouthetic Biblical Marriage Counseling for Sinning Spouses

- **Reconciling**: It's horrible to sin against Christ and each other, but through Christ it's wonderful to be forgiven and to forgive.
- **Guiding**: It's supernatural to love each other like Christ, through Christ, for Christ.

---

illustrates this for us.[3] For each of our compass points, we will first explore what it looks like in individual counseling. Then we will make the transition to what it looks like in marital counseling.

Biblical Compass Point #1: Sustaining—"Like Christ, we care about each other's hurts."

Sustaining involves joining with others in their suffering—comforting them as we weep with them. We grieve together, empathizing with them and compassionately identifying with them in their pain. Sustaining gives the other person permission to grieve. It communicates the biblical truth that it's normal to hurt when our fallen world falls on us. Sustaining enters the other person's troubling earthly story of suffering and despair.

I use a rather macabre image to capture the essence of sustaining ministry: *climbing in the casket*. I've developed this picture from 2 Corinthians 1, where Paul says he does not want his brothers and sisters in Christ to be ignorant about the hardships he has suffered. Paul writes, "We were under great pressure, far beyond our ability to endure, so that we despaired of life itself. Indeed, we felt we had received the sentence of death" (2 Cor. 1:8–9). When Paul despaired of life and felt the sentence of death, he wanted the Corinthians to "climb in his casket"—to identify with what felt like a death sentence.

It's important that we learn to offer DeWayne and Trish our sustaining comfort. However, remember a vital principle that we will repeat often: *marriage counseling is not individual counseling with an audience*. If DeWayne watches me comfort Trish, and then Trish watches me sustain DeWayne, that's good—but it's not best (remember Phil. 1:9–11). What is best is when they begin to communicate to each other, *"Like Christ, we care about each other's hurts."* Ponder how extraordinary that is. DeWayne and Trish are at each other's throats, causing each other's hurt. They are focused almost exclusively on their own pain. But in Christ, they can move to deep heart change where they start caring deeply about their spouse's pain—pain they have often caused.

In chapters 6 and 7, we will learn biblical marriage counseling competencies that can help Trish and DeWayne climb in each other's casket, give each other permission to grieve, and weep with each other. They will become each other's best parakaletic biblical counselor by sustaining each other in Christ through restoring each other's trust in the Father of compassion. We do this by asking ourselves the sustaining question we identified earlier: How can I help this couple find their gospel comfort in Christ so they can comfort each other?

Biblical Compass Point #2: Healing—"Through Christ, it's possible for us to hope in God together."

In biblical counseling through healing, we journey with sufferers to Christ, encouraging them to live today in light of Christ and his eternal hope. When bad things happen to God's people, Satan attempts to crop Christ out of the picture. He tempts couples like Trish and DeWayne to conclude, "Our marriage is bad. God is sovereign. So God must be bad too!" God calls us to *crop Christ into their picture*. We have the privilege of journeying with DeWayne and Trish so they listen together to God's eternal story of healing hope in Christ alone. We move with them to the place where they can say with conviction, "Life is bad, but God is good. He's good *all* the time—the cross of Christ forever proves this!"

To balance the sustaining image of climbing in the casket, I capture the essence of healing ministry with *celebrating the empty tomb*. Earlier we read 2 Corinthians 1:8–9. I purposefully stopped before the end of verse 9. Paul continues, "But this happened that we might not rely on ourselves but on God, who raises the dead." Paul does not remain in the casket, because Jesus did not remain in the tomb! Because of the resurrection, it is always possible to hope.

Consider again the subtle yet vital mindset shift we must make in marital counseling compared to individual counseling. DeWayne and Trish meet with me one hour a week, which of course means they are apart from me the other 167 hours in the week. It is not enough for me to be the one who points each of them individually to Christ's healing hope.

This is why in chapters 8 and 9 we will learn biblical marriage counseling competencies that will help Trish and DeWayne say, *"Through Christ, it's possible for us to hope in God together."* They must become each other's biblical en-couragers—putting Christ's courage into their dis-couraged hearts and dis-couraged marriage. What an amazing change this is. DeWayne and Trish have been crushing each other's hearts. Now, we have the joyful privilege of equipping them to be soul physicians for each other—doing open heart surgery on each other and infusing each other with hope in God! We do this by asking ourselves the healing question we identified earlier: How can I help this couple find their gospel encouragement in Christ so they can encourage each other?

Biblical Compass Point #3: Reconciling—"It's horrible to sin against Christ and each other, but through Christ it's wonderful to be forgiven and to forgive."

People come to us not only hurting but also hurtful. They not only need biblical comfort and encouragement through parakaletic sustaining and healing; they also need biblical discipline and discipleship through nouthetic reconciling and guiding.

In reconciling, God calls us to expose sin humbly yet firmly—speaking gospel truth in love (Eph. 4:15). Like the early Christians, we are aware of the deceitfulness of sin, so we commit to being sure that no one has a sinful, unbelieving heart that turns away from the living God (Heb. 3:7–19). Like the prophet Nathan did with King David, we have the ability to paint pictures that say, "See your sin in all its horrors!" Like the Puritans, we are able, when necessary, to "load the conscience with guilt" so that hard hearts are softened by God's Spirit of truth.

Biblical reconciling never stops with the exposure of heart sin. God also calls us to be skillful at magnifying grace—to communicate that where sin abounds, grace mega-abounds (Rom. 5:20). We not only communicate that it's horrible to sin but also convey that it's wonderful to be forgiven. In biblical reconciling, we communicate that God is gracious to us even when we are sinful. We don't just load the conscience with guilt; like the Puritans, we lighten the conscience with grace.

The image I use to communicate reconciling is the picture of every Christian as a *dispenser of grace*. Grace is God's medicine of choice for our sin. Grace is God's prescription for our disgrace.

What does this look like in *marital* counseling? In chapters 10 and 11, we will learn biblical marriage counseling competencies that will help couples like Trish and DeWayne confess their sin to Christ and to each other, receive Christ's forgiveness, and forgive each other. In addition to Trish and DeWayne realizing that it's horrible to sin, they communicate to each other that *it's horrible to sin against Christ and each other*. They each begin to take the marital plank out of their own eye (Matt. 7:1–5) and begin to accept responsibility for their own sinful responses (James 4:1–4). Because they each have been recipients of Christ's great grace, they also begin communicating to each other that *through Christ, it's wonderful to be forgiven and to forgive*.

Nothing is more wonderful than watching Christ's amazing grace melt the hard hearts of couples like DeWayne and Trish. We do this by asking ourselves the reconciling question we identified earlier: How can I help this couple find their gospel restoration in Christ so they can forgive each other, reconcile with each other, and have their marriage restored in Christ?

Biblical Compass Point #4: Guiding—"It's supernatural to love each other like Christ, through Christ, for Christ."

In biblical guiding, we help people discern how God empowers them to put off the old sinful ways and put on the new ways of the new person in Christ. We help them practice the biblical spiritual disciplines that connect them with Christ's resurrection power (Phil. 3:10). We assist them in thinking through the implications of their identity in Christ and what Christ has already done for them (the gospel indicatives), and the implications of commands to obey Christ out of gratitude for grace (the gospel imperatives). We practice what first-century Christians practiced in spurring one another on to love and good deeds (Heb. 10:19–25).

In marriage counseling, we help couples live out the truth that *it's supernatural to love each other like Christ, through Christ, for Christ*. Their marital love reflects Christ's love, their love is empowered by Christ, and their love has glorifying Christ as its ultimate goal. The grace that saves them is also the grace that empowers them to grow. Their growth in grace involves responding to and availing themselves of Christ's resurrection power—the same power that raised Christ from the grave is in them (Eph. 1:15–23; Phil. 3:10).

The picture I use for guiding is *fanning into flame the gift of God*. Our role is not to place power within our counselees. Our role is to stir up and fan into flame the gift of God *already* in them, just as Paul stirred up the gift of God in Timothy (2 Tim. 1:6–7).

In chapters 12 and 13, we will learn biblical marriage counseling competencies that will help Trish and DeWayne be each other's spiritual director. In marriage counseling, we disciple Trish and DeWayne to disciple each other. They envision together their individual and joint identity in Christ. They empower each other to tap into Christ's resurrection power. They equip each other to put on the full marital armor of God so that instead of fighting each other, together they fight against Satan—in Christ's strength. Through the Spirit's power they live out Ephesians 5 by loving each other like Christ. We do this by asking the guiding question we identified earlier: How can I help this couple to discover and apply gospel wisdom from Christ and his Word so they can discern together what is best and pure and glorifying to Christ?

Maturing as a Biblical Marriage Counselor
Our Approach

1. Regarding the *two guideposts*: We all tend to be a tad more inclined toward focusing on either comforting the suffering or confronting the sinning. Which are you more inclined toward? How could you further develop your skillfulness in the other?

2. Regarding the *four compass points*: We all tend to be a tad more inclined toward one of these four: sustaining, healing, reconciling, or guiding. Which are you more inclined toward? How could you further develop your competencies in the other three?

3. This section (and this book) makes the repeated point that marriage counseling is not individual counseling with an audience. This means our calling as biblical marriage counselors is not just to sustain, heal, reconcile, and guide each spouse. Instead, we are to *equip them* to sustain, heal, reconcile, and guide *each other*. You will develop these skills in subsequent chapters, so respond to the following questions based on your current understanding and competency.

a. "Like Christ, we care about each other's hurts." How important do you think it is to help spouses live this out? How hard do you think this will be? What skills do you think you need to develop?

b. "Through Christ, it's possible for us to hope in God together." How important do you think it is to help spouses live this out? How hard do you think this will be? What skills do you think you need to develop?

c. "It's horrible to sin against Christ and each other, but through Christ it's wonderful to be forgiven and to forgive." How important do you think it is to help spouses live this out? How hard do you think this will be? What skills do you think you need to develop?

d. "It's supernatural to love each other like Christ, through Christ, for Christ." How important do you think it is to help spouses live this out? How hard do you think this will be? What skills do you think you need to develop?

Marriage Counseling as "Spaghetti Relationships"

Reviewing our GPS, you might think marriage counseling is a nice, neat, easy, linear process where you quickly move directly from sustaining, to healing, to reconciling, to guiding. No. Not at all.

I often call counseling "spaghetti relationships." It is mixed up and messy. Yes, sustaining, healing, reconciling, and guiding provide a comprehensive map or GPS. However, the marriage counseling journey is filled with detours, mountains, valleys, road closures, obstacles, and even accidents. So don't imagine a straight line and don't see sustaining, healing, reconciling, and guiding as a straitjacket. View marriage counseling as a creative and artistic endeavor led by the Spirit as you and the couple dance together.

FIVE

Infusing HOPE
in the Midst of Hurt

Resurrection-Focused Marriage Counseling

Introduction: How Do We Spell Marital HOPE?

As I write, I am in the midst of numerous appointments with my oral surgeon. Actually, it is my *second* oral surgeon. The first oral surgeon I visited planned to perform some pretty major surgery on my jaw in his office. Trusting him, I was okay with that until his medical assistant looked at my chart, looked at me, and said, "He's going to do *that* surgery in our *office*?" If that wasn't enough to raise my blood pressure, about five minutes later the office manager (with thirty-five years of experience) looked at my chart, looked at me, and said, "Doctor's going to do *that* surgery in the *office*?"

I decided to obtain a second opinion from another oral surgeon. After he looked at my X-rays and examined my jaw, his diagnosis was similar to the first surgeon's; however, his treatment plan was quite different. "Bob, there's been some damage to your jawbone underneath tooth 32," he said as he showed me the X-ray. Continuing, he shared, "I don't want to speak against your first oral surgeon, but my fear is that if we went in right now and took out that impacted wisdom tooth, you'd end up with a broken jaw that had to be wired shut." He then immediately reassured, "We're not going to let that happen. Here's what I'm prescribing. First, we'll do an outpatient surgery that will help your jawbone start to heal. You'll be totally out under anesthesia. Then, for six months we're going to monitor the progress of your bone growth. I've done this scores of times. In six months your bone should grow back significantly. This will give your jaw plenty of strength for us to then do a second, more major surgery where we'll remove that impacted tooth without doing any damage to your jawbone. Again, you'll be under anesthesia in the outpatient surgery center."

Both surgeons diagnosed the problem similarly—and it was pretty serious as teeth and jaw issues go. One minimized the seriousness of it and gave me little confidence in a successful outcome. The other surgeon never minimized my problem; however, he maximized my confidence in his ability to move from description to prescription, from problem to solution.

That is what this chapter is about—*infusing hope in the midst of hurt.* My second surgeon was up-front about the seriousness of my condition—he did not pretend. However, he also did not panic. He had a plan and he had experience implementing that plan.

Biblical marriage counselors are soul physicians who serve under the Great Soul Physician. When we meet with a hurting couple, we do not pretend that their problems are nonexistent. We take their hurts and their problems seriously—so seriously, in fact, that we prescribe major heart surgery. But we also do not panic. God has *the* plan for marriage and marital healing—we examined it in chapters 1–3. Additionally, the Bible and church history provide a road map for biblical counseling—we examined it in chapter 4.

Here in chapter 5, we provide one vital *preliminary* addition. Because couples frequently come to us having lost all hope, before we do anything else we launch the marriage counseling process by infusing hope in the midst of hurt. We put into action resurrection-focused marriage counseling. Here is how we spell marital HOPE:

H Having Hope as a Marriage Counselor: Practicing Resurrection-Focused Counseling

O Offering Hope to Hurting Couples: Trusting God to Do Abundantly More Than We Can Imagine

P Promoting God's Perspective: Joining the Eternal Story

E Enlightening Couples: Believing and Growing Together in Christ

Maturing as a Biblical Marriage Counselor
How Do We Spell Marital HOPE?

1. In your life, what is it like when someone offers you "quick hope"—rose-colored glasses that do not take into account your real struggles?

2. In your life, what is it like when someone empathizes with your hurt but seems to get stuck there with you—all hurt and pain with no hope and growth?

3. In marriage counseling, how do you attempt to balance empathizing with the couple's very real struggles while also offering couples hope in the midst of their hurts?

4. What passages do you turn to that provide a biblical balance of identifying with hurt while also addressing the sure hope we have in Christ?

Having Hope as a Marriage Counselor: Practicing Resurrection-Focused Counseling

In marriage counseling, somebody better have hope, because the typical couple comes to us not with resurrection hope but with the fear that their marriage is dead. As they share with us their problem-saturated stories of despair, they are in desperate need of hope—the hope that God can resurrect dead marriages.

Our role is to join with them in their pain and hurt *but not in their despair*. To use the language of chapter 4, our role is to climb in the casket with them but not to close the casket lid on all three of us.

Mingling Hurt and Hope

In chapter 7, I call this approach "empathetic encouragement"—entering a couple's marital story of pain while helping them enter God's eternal story of hope. The Scriptures constantly mingle hurt and hope. In Romans 8, before Paul speaks of God working all things together for good (Rom. 8:28–39), he speaks of suffering and groanings that cannot be put into words (Rom. 8:17–27).

Jesus relentlessly mingles hurt and hope. In John 16:33, he sandwiches hope around hurt: "I have told you these things, so that in me you may have peace [hope]. In this world you will have trouble [hurt]. But take heart! I have overcome the world [hope]."

Paul consistently mingles hurt and hope. "We were under great pressure, far beyond our ability to endure, so that we despaired even of life itself. Indeed, we felt we had received the sentence of death [hurt]. But this happened that we might not rely on ourselves but on God, who raises the dead [hope]" (2 Cor. 1:8–9). God raises dead people—like the couple sitting in front of us. God raises dead things—like dead marriages.

In our initial interactions with hurting couples, it is not either/or—either we enter their story of hurt or we enter God's story of hope. Instead, it is both/and—we enter their story of hurt *and* we journey with them into God's story of hope. The movement between hurt and hope is a delicate dance—which is why we devote an entire section in chapter 7 to empathetic encouragement. Here in chapter 5, our focus is on the need to infuse hope early on in marriage counseling.

The Struggle for Hope

How we perceive and define situations is critical. Do we so define problems that we make them unsolvable? Modern Christianity has lost hope. We have succumbed to a pessimistic, negative mindset. This is so unlike New Testament Christianity.

- "And we rejoice in the hope of the glory of God" (Rom. 5:2 ESV).
- "But thanks be to God! He gives us the victory through our Lord Jesus Christ" (1 Cor. 15:57).
- "You, dear children, are from God and have overcome them, because the one who is in you is greater than the one who is in the world" (1 John 4:4).
- "For everyone born of God overcomes the world. This is the victory that has overcome the world, even our faith" (1 John 5:4).

Recently I have been pondering why we are blind to our resources in Christ.

- We are not praying for enlightenment to know God's power and love (Eph. 1:15–23; 3:14–21).
- Satan blinds us to God's good work in us (2 Cor. 4:1–18).
- We fail to stir up, provoke, encourage, and fan into flame the gift of God within each other (2 Tim. 1:6–7; Heb. 10:24–25).
- We look at life with eyeballs only rather than with spiritual eyes (2 Cor. 10:4–7).

- We forget that Paul's marriage and family principles in Ephesians 5–6 are sandwiched between the Spirit's filling and God's spiritual armor (Eph. 5:18–21; 6:10–18).

When three couples in a row enter our office with seemingly impossible and intractable problems (like the couples I mentioned in the introduction to this book), it is easy for us as the counselor to begin to lose hope. The first battle in marriage counseling is the counselor's battle for hope.

Bathing Our Minds in Gospel Hope

Our hope is not in the situation, not in the couple, not in our training, skillfulness, winsomeness, or experience. Our hope is in the God who resurrects dead things, including dead marriages. Biblical marriage counselors must constantly remind themselves of the Bible's redemptive metanarrative. Everything in Scripture is moving toward resurrection hope. Everything in Scripture is saturated with the good news of the God who declares, "I am generously good and gracious." Everything in Scripture moves toward Paul's inspired declaration in Romans 8:31–32, "What, then, shall we say in response to these things? If God is for us, who can be against us? He who did not spare his own Son, but gave him up for us all—how will he not also, along with him, graciously give us all things?"

We can practice resurrection-focused marriage counseling if we keep bathing our minds in gospel truths like:

- Since God is the great Rewarder (Heb. 11:6), he will provide grace to help for all those couples who diligently seek him in their time of marital need (Heb. 4:16; 11:6).
- Where sin abounds, grace superabounds (Rom. 5:20); therefore, God provides us with all the resources we need to experience Christ-honoring marriages (2 Pet. 1:3–4).
- Since God hates divorce (Mal. 2:16), he offers us his spiritual resources (Eph. 1:15–23) and resurrection power (Phil. 3:10) to defeat Satan, the great divorcer (Eph. 6:10–18).
- Because marriage has the eternal purpose of reflecting Christ's marriage to the church (Eph. 5:21–33), God will stop at nothing to protect his reputation and display his glory through saving our marriages (Eph. 3:1–21).

If we believe that God provides everything couples need for life and godliness, then we will see their marital problems as God's opportunity to reveal more of his love, grace, and power. As we receive the initial contact via email, phone call, text message, or in person, these are the sort of resurrection-focused thoughts that could be dancing through our minds:

- What amazing and surprising work is God up to in this marriage?
- Who do they want to become together in Christ, and what biblical process would guide them there?
- What unique resources do they possess that we can fan into flame?
- The very fact that they called tells me that they've not given up all hope. I wonder how they've cooperated with God to maintain hope in the midst of their troubles.

Maturing as a Biblical Marriage Counselor
Having Hope as a Marriage Counselor

1. The Bible is hope-centric. We listed just a few of the myriad biblical passages on hope—Romans 5:2; 1 Corinthians 15:57; 1 John 4:4 and 5:4. What are *your* go-to passages on hope?

2. "The first battle in marriage counseling is the counselor's battle for hope." When a couple comes to you deceived by Satan, defeated by their situation, and hopeless, how do you as their counselor battle for hope—in *your* soul, in *your* mindset?

3. "How we perceive and define situations is critical. Do we so define problems that we make them unsolvable?"

   a. How do you help a couple to develop a biblical, hope-filled perception of their problems?

   b. How do you undeceive a couple regarding Satan's lie that their situation and relationship are hopeless?

4. On page 95, you read biblical principles and passages for bathing your mind in gospel hope.

    a. Which of those passages and principles stand out the most to you? Why? How do you apply them in your life and in your counseling?

    b. What additional passages and principles would you use in order to bathe your mind in gospel hope?

5. On pages 95–96 I listed several resurrection-focused thoughts that could be dancing through our minds when we receive the initial contact from a troubled couple. How could those types of mindsets impact your hope-focused marital counseling?

Offering Hope to Hurting Couples: Trusting God to Do Abundantly More Than We Can Imagine

Armed with hope in God, as counselors we can now offer hope to hurting couples. Resurrection-focused marital counseling never denies suffering and sin. Just the opposite. Hope-based counselors keep their eyes wide open to suffering and sin while looking with spiritual eyes to the God who sustains and heals couples in their marital suffering and reconciles and guides couples to overcome their marital sinning.

Though we empathize with hurting couples, we do not join with them in their *shrunken perspective*. All too often couples wait so long to seek help that by the time they enter counseling their eyes are shut. They present to us shrunken marital narratives:

- *Concerning self*: "I don't have the resources, even in Christ, to deal with these problems."
- *Concerning their spouse*: "She's all to blame." "He doesn't want to work on this."

- *Concerning their marital partnership*: "We don't have what it takes to make this marriage work." "Our mess is beyond cleaning up; we may as well give up."
- *Concerning God*: "Where are your great and precious promises when we really need them?" "Where are you when we really need you?"

Our primary initial role involves *infusing resurrection hope*. We need to undeceive couples. They buy Satan's lie that their marriage is hopeless and they are helpless. They begin to give in to despair, and then despair creeps into shaming and blaming each other. Rather than joining together to hate Satan, the great divorcer, they begin to hate and emotionally divorce each other.

We offer couples a narrative with the subtitle *Building Loving Marriages That Last through All the Storms of Life*. We join with them so that they can divorce their old marriage and begin a new one with the same spouse.

To infuse hope, we must have respect for the couple. We must believe that because they are image bearers they have a God-created design and desire to leave, cleave, weave, and receive. Sometimes we cannot see that desire. It seems deeply buried, even carefully hidden. However, based on our theology, we can unconditionally respect their potential in Christ to avail themselves of God's resources to sustain, heal, reconcile, and guide each other.

Infusing Hope during the First Contact

Our word "crisis" has its etymological roots in the Greek verb *krinein*, which means "to judge, to choose." A marital crisis is a moment when spouses (and counselors) must choose among various perspectives and opportunities that present themselves. Couples can perceive a marital crisis as a time to cut and run. Or they can perceive a crisis as the time to run to the Father and turn more deeply to Christ. In our initial contact *we point couples to Christ in the midst of their crisis*.

We want to convey the resurrection reality that through Christ couples can revitalize their marriage. It does not happen overnight. It is not easy. But through God, couples can renew and deepen their loyal love for each other.

Imagine a hurting couple contacting you. You listen, empathize, pray, and arrange a first meeting. Your first contact is almost over and your first meeting may not be for a week. How do you leave them? What concrete acts of hope can they participate in?

Infusing Hope through Trialogues

To answer these questions, I need to introduce the concept of *trialogues*. One of the great advantages of the personal ministry of the Word (biblical counseling) is the ability to engage in back-and-forth conversations about how biblical principles and scriptural passages relate to life. I call these trialogues. In a monologue, I speak to the counselee or couple, teaching them truth. In a dialogue, we talk to each other. But in a trialogue, there are three conversation partners: me, the counselee or couple, and God through his Word. Trialogues are another way of picturing gospel conversations—we converse about the difference the good news of Scripture makes in the particulars of a marital relationship. I encourage the use of two types of trialogues.

- *Spiritual Conversation Trialogues*: We engage the couple in thinking about the application of relevant scriptural principles.
- *Scriptural Exploration Trialogues*: We engage the couple in discussing specific application of pertinent biblical passages.

Consider two examples.

Just a week ago a call came through to my church office number. Almost immediately the tears were so heavy I could barely understand what this troubled wife was saying. As I listened and empathized, I asked if I could pray for her, her husband, and their marriage. We arranged a first marriage counseling meeting, and then I asked her if she and her husband would do their marriage a favor.

> Many couples report that the act of asking for help starts a positive chain reaction. It's a biblical principle. When we are weak, then in Christ we are strong. God gives grace to the humble. God hears the cry of the needy. So, over the next few days, would the two of you be on the lookout for and jot down any positive changes in your relationship that God is helping you to make?

This is a trialogue that focused on pondering and applying scriptural principles: spiritual conversation.

About a month earlier, another husband and wife had asked to speak with me after church. As they haltingly and tearfully shared their marital hurts, I listened and we prayed together. We agreed to meet that coming Wednesday evening. They had mentioned searching Scripture about their marriage. I affirmed that and engaged them in a trialogue focused on exploring and applying a specific biblical passage: scriptural exploration.

> Between now and Wednesday, jot down the passages you've been exploring. And jot down where you see God's love, concern, comfort, and compassion for each of you and for your marriage. Also jot down the promises God gives you in his Word that you can begin claiming and applying . . .

Figure 5.1

Marriage Counseling Goals and Focus Form

1. What are the top two or three areas in **your** heart, actions, attitude, and way of relating to your spouse that **you** want help changing so that you can be more Christlike and your marriage can be more Christ-honoring?

2. What are the top two or three strengths that you see **in your spouse** that you want to affirm?

3. What are the top two or three aspects **of your marriage** that you want help changing so that your marriage can be more Christ-honoring?

4. Let's create an Ephesians 3:14–21 vision for your marriage (please read Ephesians 3:14–21).

    a. Think ahead three months. As God does exceedingly, abundantly above all that you could ask or imagine in your heart and in your marriage, what **two or three amazing changes are you envisioning, praying for, and hoping for**?

    b. What **needs to happen** in **your heart** and in **your relationship** so that through Christ's strength these amazing changes start occurring?

5. What else do you want us to know, think about, or focus on in our times together?

Infusing Hope through Initial Paperwork

While a detailed Personal Information Form (PIF) is very helpful, I have found that hurting couples often do not have the mental or emotional energy to share such exhaustive information *before* the first meeting. Plus, in some church cultures, the idea of completing a lengthy form before getting to talk to a pastor feels too clinical. So I typically reserve the longer PIF for *after* our first meeting. Before our first meeting, I ask each spouse to complete a one-page, five-question sheet (Marriage Counseling Goals and Focus Form) and return it to me before we meet. Figure 5.1 includes the five questions I ask (on the actual form, each question leaves space for a one-paragraph response).

I have never had a couple refuse to complete this form. Just this form gives us enough to interact about for weeks of resurrection-focused marriage counseling. Notice a few aspects of the Marriage Counseling Goals and Focus Form:

- It starts by getting each spouse to look at the plank in their own eye (question 1): "the top two or three areas in *your* heart." Couples come to us focused on the other person's faults. Question 1 gets each spouse to focus on their own issues. Over 90 percent of spouses can identify their own issues when asked. For the 10 percent who cannot—that communicates a great deal to us as counselors.
- It starts with an assumption of change and growth: "that you want help changing."
- It starts with a Christ-centered focus: "so that you can be more Christlike and your marriage can be more Christ-honoring."
- It asks for strengths to affirm in one's spouse (question 2). Even in the messiest marriages, husbands and wives have always been able to identify some strengths in their spouse.
- It does not ignore problems (question 3). It asks for the top two or three marriage problems that the couple wants us to address.
- It casts a future vision by pointing the couple to Ephesians 3:14–21 and getting them to think about what God can do in their marriage above all that they ask or imagine (question 4a). This is the most important hope-inducing question on the form, and I've never had a couple be unable to answer it.
- It connects Christ's strength and their heart change as the biblical foundation for marital hope (question 4b).

Maturing as a Biblical Marriage Counselor
Offering Hope to Hurting Couples

1. On pages 97–98, I share shrunken marital narratives that couples have about themselves, their spouse, their marital partnership, and God. What shrunken marital narratives have you heard from couples in those areas?

2. A marital crisis is a choice point—between running away from their marriage or running to Christ. What can you do to point couples to Christ in the midst of their marital crisis?

3. On page 99, you read two examples of trialogues that infuse hope during first contact. Write out two examples of trialogues you could use to infuse hope during the initial contact.

4. Reread the five questions on the Marriage Counseling Goals and Focus Form.

   a. Which of the questions seems most important to you in infusing hope?

   b. What question(s) would you add? Why?

5. Ponder a relational struggle or crisis in your life.

   a. Think ahead three months. As God does exceedingly, abundantly above all that you could ask or imagine in your heart and in your relationship, what two or three amazing changes are you envisioning, praying for, and hoping for?

   b. What needs to happen in your heart and in your relationship so that through Christ's strength these amazing changes start to occur?

Promoting God's Perspective: Joining the Eternal Story

Now the couple sits in front of you for the first time. Be prepared. All your pre-session, hope-focused intervention will not magically or biblically wipe away their hurt. Nor will it eradicate all their despair. Proverbs 13:12 tells us that "Hope deferred makes the heart sick." Such heart sickness is not healed by one pre-session growth project.

Additionally, even when hope takes hold, hurt does not evaporate. Consider Paul. "We are hard pressed on every side, but not crushed; perplexed, but not in despair; persecuted, but not abandoned; struck down, but not destroyed" (2 Cor. 4:8–9). Hope directs people to find Christ even when they do not find relief. Hope helps people cling to Christ whether or not their circumstances and feelings change.

Picture the image of "pivot feet." With one foot we are journeying with the couple in their earthly marital story of despair. With the other foot, we are inviting the couple to journey with us to God's eternal story of expectant hope.

The Bible teaches that hope is a key ingredient in the diet of healthy Christians, especially during times of suffering (Rom. 5:1–11; 8:14–39; Heb. 10:19–12:29). In the crisis of despair:

- We help people realize that their problems are not bigger than God and his resources.
- We focus on Christ's power at work in their weakness.
- We identify the couple's hopes and dreams and the biblical route for getting there.
- We search for unique God-given resources, gifts, and strengths to build upon and nurture.

At the very beginning of our first session we can create the atmosphere of expectant hope. I will often start by reviewing together the Marriage Counseling Goals and Focus Form (fig. 5.1). With questions 1 and 3, we are stepping into the couple's earthly story. With questions 2 and 4, we are entering God's eternal story. I make sure we reserve ample time for question 4 in particular.

> 4. Let's create an Ephesians 3:14–21 vision for your marriage (please read Ephesians 3:14–21).
>
>   a. Think ahead three months. As God does exceedingly, abundantly above all that you could ask or imagine in your heart and in your marriage, what two or three amazing changes are you envisioning, praying for, and hoping for?
>
>   b. What needs to happen in your heart and in your relationship so that through Christ's strength these amazing changes start occurring?

Throughout the first several meetings, there are additional hope-focused trialogues we can engage in.

- Both of you have experienced some deep hurts. I'm truly sorry for that. I'm also wondering how you've tapped into Christ's strength to maintain your commitment to each other.

- Though these issues seem almost insurmountable to you, you know that through Christ you can do all things. Christ can change you no matter how entrenched the patterns seem. What is going through your mind as I share that?
- These are hard issues. They've grown over time. However, with your commitment and through Christ's resources, we can see lasting changes. Would it be okay if the three of us each prayed right now, asking God to fill us with his hope, love, faith, and power?

The most important person in the hope-giving process is Christ. However, Christ also gives us gifted people within his body the church (Eph. 4:10–12). So it is totally legitimate to help the couple find hope through your involvement in their marital life.

- You've discussed several things you've tried, and I sense some exasperation in your voices. I want you to realize that in coming here you've added a third pair of eyes. You've added another voice, another perspective to the mix. So already you've taken a positive step that has changed the way you handle these issues. What do you think of that?
- You've experienced some very difficult things. I want you to know that as long as I'm your counselor, one of my roles will be to police how you treat each other. While you're here, I want you to be honest, but *lovingly* honest—speaking the truth in love. If I sense that either of you is speaking destructively, I'll call you on that. Do you both agree to this? Does it provide some safety for you?

Affirming the couple's God-given strengths is also hope-giving.

- As you talk about some of your struggles, I'm wondering if we also could explore some of the times God has given you victories.
- Through Christ, how have you learned to overcome [insert obstacle or struggle]?

By the time your first few meetings have concluded, your prayer is simple: "Lord, may you have used me to help them glimpse a vision of a better life together in Christ."

Maturing as a Biblical Marriage Counselor
Promoting God's Perspective

1. We emphasized that even when hope takes hold, hurt does not evaporate, that hope directs people to find Christ even when they don't find relief, and that hope helps people to cling to Christ whether or not their circumstances and feelings change.

   a. How could you relate these truths to situations and relationships in your life?

   b. How could these truths impact how you interact with and counsel couples?

2. On pages 103–4, you read several hope-focused early session trialogues. Write two or three hope-focused trialogues of your own.

3. We always point couples to Christ and the body of Christ. Since we are part of the body of Christ, I noted that "it is totally legitimate to help the couple find hope in your involvement in their marital life." This makes some counselors feel uncomfortable—as if I'm bragging or making it all about me as the counselor. How comfortable or uncomfortable are you in indicating that your involvement is a positive, God-given gift to the couple?

4. On page 104, you read sample trialogues for affirming the couple's God-given strengths. Write two or three of your own affirmations of a couple's Christ-dependent strengths.

How do we infuse hope after sessions, between sessions, and in subsequent sessions? Chapters 12 and 13 talk more about counselor homework and counselee homework—or growth projects. For now, we will focus specifically on resurrection-focused growth projects for between sessions.

The Counselor's Hope-Focused Communication

In chapter 7 we will discuss the value of communicating with couples between sessions. Figure 5.2 provides a sample hope-focused letter or email that you could send after an early session.

The Couple's Hope-Focused Communication

There are endless varieties of homework or growth projects that a couple can engage in between sessions. What follows are three sample pre-prepared assignments with a hope-focused mindset. The idea is to have the couple first work on these individually, then discuss them together before your next meeting, and finally the three of you interact about them in your session.

The first sampler is titled "Discussing Your Outlook on Your Marriage" (fig. 5.3). This would be a one-page form with space for a paragraph of writing after each question.

The second sampler is titled "Sharing about Our Marital Expectations" (fig. 5.4). This would also be a one-page form with space for a paragraph of writing after each question. You would only select one such growth project for a given week.

A longing fulfilled is like life-giving medicine (Prov. 13:12). The third sampler addresses marital longings (fig. 5.5). This would be a one-page form with space for a paragraph of writing after each question.

Figure 5.2

The Counselor's Hope-Focused Communication

Becky and Jim,

Wow! Quite a meeting for the three of us, huh? I know it was a very emotional time for both of you. I'm convinced it was another faith step along your path to a marriage that God will be strengthening week by week.

Given the level of tension and struggles, I was amazed to notice how well you complement (complete) each other. Jim, you were right there for Becky with your words and hugs when she needed you the most. And Becky, you hung on Jim's every word. You were able to sense what it has been like for him to go through this.

I'm wondering where God taught the two of you to connect so well, especially in the midst of hard times. How have the events of the past three months further sharpened your connection? How have they challenged your connection?

There's something else I'm curious about. I never heard a word of blame or shame. There was no finger-pointing. No fault-finding. Just honest, open sharing. How can you tap into Christ's resurrection power to keep this good sharing going?

God never ceases to surprise me. For the two of you, he's taking what has been so incredibly painful and making something beautiful out of it. Rather than allowing what Becky's boss did to cause the two of you to drift apart, you're using it to pull closer together. What role is your faith in Christ playing in your healthy response to this?

I'm wondering what might have happened between the two of you if you did not share such a strong faith . . . I'm wondering, too, about the prayers you have prayed through this ordeal, both separately and together . . .

Of course, it's not all roses—and every rose has its share of thorns. Be honest—how much do you each think you were on your best behavior for this meeting? How comfortable are the two of you sharing whatever is on your hearts? How safe do you feel being open and vulnerable about your hurts and concerns?

It's been three days since we met. Have you been able to start on your homework/growth project from Ephesians? How's it going? How can I be praying for you both and for your marriage over the next three days before we meet again?

In Christ's grace,
Pastor Bob

Figure 5.3

Discussing Your Outlook on Your Marriage

Before our next meeting, each of you complete your own sheet and then discuss your responses. Please bring your completed sheet to our next meeting.

1. What are two or three major issues you believe *you* need to work on in order for your marriage to improve?
2. How do you think your spouse would answer question 1 about you?
3. What are two or three major issues that you would like *your spouse* to work on in order for your marriage to improve?
4. What biblical passages and principles do you think most relate to the issues you and your spouse need to work on for your marriage to be more Christlike?
5. What will be the first signs that things are moving in the right, biblical direction in your marriage?
6. Share about some times when you have had real victory in your marriage.
   a. What is different about those times in terms of your relationship to Christ and each other?
   b. How do you see you, your spouse, and God keeping these victorious times going?
7. No doubt there will be ups and downs. During the down times, how could the two of you cling together to Christ?

Figure 5.4

Sharing about Our Marital Expectations

Before our next meeting, each of you complete your own sheet and then discuss your responses. Please bring your completed sheets to our next meeting.

1. When we got married:
   a. *My* expectations of my spouse were that he/she would . . .
   b. My spouse's expectations of *me* were that I would . . .

2. For the *wife*: On a scale of 1 to 10 (10 being the highest rating), share how well you sense your husband is doing in each of these areas:

   Unconditional Love (Nourishing)
   Leadership/Shepherding (Initiative)
   Gentleness (Cherishing)
   Understanding
   Communication
   Companionship/Friendship
   Sexual Fulfillment
   Family Commitment
   Financial Support

3. For the *husband*: On a scale of 1 to 10 (10 being the highest rating), share how well you sense your wife is doing in each of these areas:

   Respect
   Responsiveness to Shepherding
   Encouragement
   Understanding
   Communication
   Companionship/Friendship
   Sexual Fulfillment
   Nurture and Care
   Support

4. What other categories would you add to this list? How is your spouse doing in those categories?

Figure 5.5

Our Marital Desires and Longings

1. What do you think your spouse desires and longs for from you?
2. What do you desire and long for from your spouse?
3. What does the Bible say a husband longs for and desires from his wife?
4. What does the Bible say a wife longs for and desires from her husband?
5. What makes it difficult for you to focus on meeting your spouse's longings?
6. Through Christ, how can you meet your spouse's desires and longings?

   a. List specific actions you could take to meet your spouse's desires and longings.
   b. Ask your spouse to list specific ways you could meet his/her desires and longings.

Maturing as a Biblical Marriage Counselor
Enlightening Couples

1. In figure 5.2, you read a sample hope-focused letter or email.

   a. What are your thoughts about communication with couples between sessions?

   b. What impact do you think that letter might have on Becky and Jim?

2. In figure 5.3 you saw the tool "Discussing Your Outlook on Your Marriage." Write five to seven questions you would want a couple to discuss after their first or second meeting with you.

3. In figure 5.4 you saw the tool "Sharing about Our Marital Expectations." Questions 2 and 3 of that form list callings or responsibilities for the wife and husband, respectively. What would your list of the top five to ten biblical callings of the husband be? Of the wife?

4. In figure 5.5 you saw the tool "Our Marital Desires and Longings."

    a. If you are married, ask your spouse if the two of you could complete and discuss this form. After you do, jot down what that process was like for the two of you.

    b. To what Bible passages would you go to answer questions 3 and 4 about what Scripture says a husband longs for from his wife and what a wife longs for from her husband? What do those passages indicate about marital longings?

CHAPTER

SIX

Comforting Each Other with Christ's Comfort

Sustaining in Marriage Counseling, Part 1

Introduction: Climbing into Each Other's Marital Casket

Picture Trish and DeWayne again. When you connected with them in your first marriage counseling meeting, every word about their marriage dripped with hopelessness. Most of the words they spoke about each other oozed venom. Because their vision was obscured by hurt, neither could see the log in their own eye. Blinded by rage, they each saw the speck in their spouse's eye as a huge plank.

It has not been easy, and it has taken time and patience, but imagine you have been able to help both Trish and DeWayne begin to replace despair with glimmers of hope. You have helped them to call a temporary truce so they are not screaming in each other's face.

But they are not yet on each other's side and they do not have each other's back. Both Trish and DeWayne are still much more aware of their own hurt than of their spouse's pain.

They have each suffered real hurt, profound pain, and deep wounds at the hands of their spouse. No suffering hurts more. No words cut deeper than words spoken by the person who once vowed to love you for better, for worse. That person is now making your life worse than you ever imagined it could become. The person who swore to love you in sickness and in health is making you sick to your stomach.

Being human and being like most couples, DeWayne and Trish are not only deeply disappointed in each other; they are also struggling with doubts about God. Their faith that God is good even when life is bad is being tested—severely.

Now what? If this were individual counseling with Trish, then our counseling goal might be to enter her disappointment and doubt, compassionately identifying with her pain (Heb. 4:14–16). We would sustain her so she could draw a line in the sand and stop retreating from God. Shared sorrow is endurable sorrow—which helps Trish run to God in her pain (2 Cor. 1:3–7). We would sustain her by comforting her—co-fortitude, strengthening Trish as she experiences the compassion of Christ's body weeping with her as she weeps (Rom. 12:15).

If this were individual counseling, then we would direct Trish to lament to God. He is the Divine Counselor; we are only the human counselor. While our comfort and compassion help, God is the Father of compassion and the God of all comfort (2 Cor. 1:3).

All of these interventions are good, godly, and helpful. But this is *not* individual counseling. It is marital counseling. If Trish receives empathy primarily from us and rarely from DeWayne, then we might make matters worse. "DeWayne, why can't you be caring and compassionate like Pastor Bob?"

As you saw in chapter 4, it is not enough for the pastor-counselor to sustain each spouse during marriage counseling. It is more important that we help Trish and DeWayne sustain, comfort, and empathize with each other—climb into each other's casket. It is relatively easy to empathize with DeWayne or Trish. It is much more difficult to help hurting DeWayne to focus on empathizing with Trish's hurts.

That is the task we set our hearts to in the next two chapters. How does the gospel guide us to journey with couples so they move from self-centered anger and bitter disappointment toward other-centered love and grace-based compassion?

This is where marriage counseling differs from individual counseling. We direct Trish and DeWayne back to God and to *each other* (2 Cor. 1:4). As they receive God's comfort, they find God's grace to care about and comfort each other, sustaining each other—and their marriage.

Through sustaining marital counseling, our prayer is that Trish and De-Wayne begin to say, "Like Christ, we care about each other's hurts." They entered counseling focused almost exclusively on their personal hurts. We want the gospel—the Suffering Savior—to so impact them that they not only sense each other's pain but embrace each other in their mutual pain.

Do not let the depth of this shift too easily float by. Picture Trish and De-Wayne. Picture a couple you have counseled or you know who can't seem to stop hurting each other. Or picture a time in your own marriage or a close relationship where you were so deeply wounded that you felt it was almost impossible to care about the person who had hurt you.

Now picture any of these couples being so changed by the gospel that there is movement from vengeful hurting to compassionate caring. No longer is the thought, "They hurt me; I'm going to hurt them back." Instead, each thought is so taken captive by grace that the renewed mindset is, "They hurt me. Christ comforts me. They're hurting too. I want to comfort them with Christ's comfort." This is gospel-centered change.

Our gospel-centered calling is to help Trish and DeWayne move from being focused only or predominantly on their own hurt to focusing on each other's hurt and the Father's comfort. In chapters 6 and 7, we learn how to encourage such change through CARE:

C Coupling with the Couple: Empathizing with the Marriage (chap. 6)

A Assisting the Couple to Become Intimate Allies: Bridging the Couple (chap. 6)

R Renewing the Couple's Trust in the God of All Comfort: Clinging to Their Father of Holy Love (chap. 7)

E Engaging the Couple through Empathetic Encouragement: Connecting Couples in Their Hurts and Hopes (chap. 7)

Maturing as a Biblical Marriage Counselor
Climbing into Each Other's Marital Casket

1. Read 2 Corinthians 1:3–7.

   a. Describe a time when the Father of compassion and the God of all comfort comforted you.

   b. Describe a time when, out of the overflow of God's comfort in your life, you comforted another person with Christ's comfort.

2. Warren Wiersbe wisely notes:

   Only true Christian ministry can put grace in the heart so that lives are changed and problems are really solved. The best thing we can do for people is not to solve their problems for them, but so relate them to God's grace that they will be enabled to solve their problems and not repeat them.[1]

   a. Who has ministered to you like this—treating you maturely by empowering you to turn to Christ to solve problems, rather than by trying to solve your problems for you?

---

b. How did their ministry help you to grow in mature dependence on Christ?

3. Based on our focus in this chapter, we might tweak Wiersbe's quote:

    Gospel-centered marriage counseling understands that it is God's grace that changes us, teaching and
    empowering us to say no to sinful marriage relationships and yes to Christlike marriage relationships.
    The best thing a marriage counselor can do for a hurting couple is not simply to empathize with each
    spouse individually but to encourage each spouse to find comfort in Christ and then equip them to
    comfort each other with the comfort they've received from Christ.

    a. What is the potential impact of a marriage counselor focusing exclusively on
        empathizing with each hurting spouse?

    b. What is the potential impact of a marriage counselor seeking to help each spouse find
        comfort in Christ and to give Christ's comfort to each other?

Coupling with the Couple: Empathizing with the Marriage

Hurting spouses want their counselor to take their side. Biblical marriage
counselors, while empathizing deeply with each spouse, take Christ's side.
Our first calling is to help marriages glorify God. Our second calling is to be
on the side of the marriage. We are not on the wife's side. We are not on the
husband's side. We are on the marriage's side.

Our sustaining goal is to help the couple to couple with each other—
bridging. But before we can bridge the couple together, we need to *couple with
the couple*. We need to empathize with their joint marital disappointment by
joining and experiencing their marital dance.

Every couple has a unique dance. The images and metaphors we could
use for this are seemingly endless: their unique song, voice, routine, act,
story, drama, narrative, picture, style, or chapter title. This is as it should
be, since God calls couples to weave a joint tapestry (Gen. 2:23–25). When
couples leave, cleave, weave, and receive, they develop a recognizable pattern
of interaction—a dance.

Joining the Marital Dance

We connect with the couple, flowing as they flow, understanding and experiencing their relationship as they do. We resonate at the couple's frequency by tuning into them. How?

We listen empathetically to hear their joint story from their perspective. We do this by focusing on their style of relating, which is revealed through the dynamics of their interactions. We join the marital dance by watching the couple dance *in front of us*. This builds on our core principle that marriage counseling is not individual counseling with one spouse as the audience while we talk endlessly with the other spouse. Trish doesn't spend the bulk of her time listening to me talk to DeWayne. Instead, I spend the bulk of my time listening to Trish and DeWayne talk with each other and watching Trish and DeWayne dance with each other.

When couples are in deep distress, counselors fear having them talk to each other. We think, "It'll get too messy. It's too dangerous." But it's a whole lot messier and more dangerous when hurting couples are interacting outside the watchful eye of their pastor-counselor. So get the couple talking in front of you in the safety of the counseling office—even if the result is messy, ugly, and chaotic. God's Spirit does his most amazing work creating beauty out of ashes, crafting order out of chaos.

Becoming Their Dance Instructor: Picturing the Marital Dance

Several years ago my wife, Shirley, and I took ballroom dancing lessons. That will test a marriage! I learned more about counseling from the dance instructor than I did about dancing. He demonstrated the steps motion by motion, then we would have to dance in front of him. He'd observe. Suggest. Coach. Then, when we still didn't quite get it, he or his co-instructor would step in and dance with one of us.

That's similar to what marriage counselors can do. Consider this basic four-step alliterated dance instruction process:

- *Engage*: Get the couple talking to each other in your presence.
- *Encapsulate*: Watch for patterns, themes, and threads in how they relate.
- *Enlighten*: Formulate and share a creative depiction of their marital dance.
- *Empathize*: Express empathy for their individual pain, but more importantly, express empathy for their joint, united marital pain.

Engage

Trish and DeWayne come in, once again upset with each other and blaming each other. This time it is about how they each think the other person has been an insensitive instigator.

"Pastor Bob, she did it again," DeWayne begins. "She instigated all of this by having no concern about me and no awareness of how her words are like a knife in my back!"

"Tell Trish that," I say to DeWayne.

"Huh? What do you mean, Pastor Bob?"

"Instead of telling me, turn your chair so you can look Trish in the eyes. Collect your thoughts. As calmly as you can [he still won't be very calm] share with Trish your perspective on what happened. Then, Trish, I want you to . . ."

They will want to keep looking at you and talking to you. Keep directing them to talk it out with each other.

Encapsulate

As DeWayne and Trish talk, listen for patterns. Pray—ask God to help you encapsulate their marital dance in one major image or summary story. Seek to capture an image that speaks their language—coming from what you know about Trish, DeWayne, their history, and their marriage.

They finish talking—likely without a lot of helpful resolution at first. I say, "So, is this typical of how your conversations go at home?"

"Oh yeah! Only at home it's worse. We're on our best behavior because we're in the *pastor's* office!"

"Fair enough. Could I paint you a summary picture of what I just saw?"

Enlighten

Now share a creative depiction of their unique marital dance. Picture their relationship for them. As you do, express what you observe in a matter-of-fact summary. General ways you can introduce your summary picture include:

- You seem to be engaged in . . .
- It looks to me like . . .
- Here's a snapshot of what I just witnessed . . .

For Trish and DeWayne, it might sound something like this.

> We've talked about how your son and my son were both wrestlers. As I listened to the two of you, it reminded me of when I coached wrestling and what used to happen toward the end of the wrestling season at the end of a very long, exhausting practice. At the beginning of the year, my son and his drilling partner were good teammates for each other. But by this point they knew

each other's moves so well that they anticipated every move. So no one could accomplish anything and both of them would get *really* frustrated. On top of that, they were exhausted. Long season. Hard practice. And neither of them wanted to let the other one even try a new move. So neither of them improved. They went from being drilling partners who helped each other to wrestling opponents who frustrated each other constantly. Instead of teammates, they became opponents, enemies.

That's you guys. You can finish each other's sentences, but not in a helpful way. And you're so exhausted from all the infighting that you don't seem to care much about the fact that you're hurting your spouse. Frustrated and exhausted, you're like, "Can you for once just let me drill my move!" And both of you seem to want to be the alpha wrestler. You both have to end up on top, you both have to win. You've gone from being drilling partners and teammates to opponents and enemies . . .

How does this description fit for you?

While they may tweak your summary, if you have been tracking well with them, they are likely to own at least part of it. If they don't, then ask:

How would you describe the two of you together? Not how would you describe yourself or your spouse, but what picture would you give of the way the two of you relate?

Empathize

Once you've worked through an initial summary of their marital dance, first empathize with each of them individually. Next, empathize with their marriage.

EMPATHIZE WITH EACH SPOUSE

In empathizing with them individually, highlight the unique pain or disappointment each seems to experience. "Trish, as I listened to you and DeWayne talk, I could see times when you cringed, and I cringed with you. Your wrestling drill partner was so forceful that I could see your fear and defensiveness. That has to be really hard, really scary . . ." Then you and Trish interact . . .

Follow that up with, "DeWayne, that doesn't mean this is one-sided or that you alone are the problem. As I watched the two of you, I could sense your frustration. It especially happened when Trish would interrupt you and correct you, almost taking over the conversation . . . That has to be really discouraging . . ." Then you and DeWayne interact . . .

AFFIRMING AND OFFENDING

Individual empathy in marriage counseling is tricky. It's so tricky that years ago I gave it a label: *affirming and offending.* As we empathize with Trish, we are affirming her—her perspective, her pain. But in doing so, we risk the possibility of offending DeWayne. When I tell Trish, "That has to be really hard, really scary," then DeWayne is likely feeling that I have chosen Trish's side. How do we handle this possibility?

- At the start of counseling, caution the couple that affirming and offending may occur.
- Remain aware of the possibility and track the reactions (verbal and nonverbal cues) of each spouse.
- Attempt to remain unbiased, neutral, and balanced when offering feedback (affirming and offending each at various times).
- Take the calculated risk of offending one to affirm and empathize with the other.
- Talk openly with the spouse who feels offended.

Our prayer is that each spouse will ultimately affirm the other. Trish will empathize with the pain she is causing DeWayne. DeWayne will be offended by his own sin—by the pain he is causing Trish.

Empathize with the Marriage

For many people, empathizing with the marriage is a new concept. It requires that we see the couple the way God sees them—*as one*. Trish and DeWayne are one (Eph. 5:31). Their marriage is the merging of two souls into one. The one marital couple, the one marital unit, has a life of its own, a soul of its own.

Ask God to help you to *hurt for the marriage*. To hurt for Trish/DeWayne. I'll even mingle the letters of their names together on a whiteboard in my office: DTERWIASYHNE. Then I'll remind them, "That's you guys. One." What might it sound like to empathize with Trish and DeWayne's marriage?

> When you guys first came in, I asked you to tell me your marital story—including your dating story. What attracted you to each other. What you liked, loved, and admired about each other. I remember the joy you brought each other.
>
> Now my heart breaks when I see the current state of your marriage as two alpha wrestlers, each demanding that the other one loses . . . It breaks my heart for Christ. It breaks my heart for your marriage. It breaks my heart for each of you together . . . It's breaking your wedding vow. What God has joined together let no one tear apart. [I lace my fingers tightly then rip them apart.]
>
> Your one soul is now being ripped in two.

Now, stop talking. Be quiet. Let them reflect. Then interact. Ask them if they have wept for Christ's broken heart over the state of their marriage. Ask what it might be like if they wept for their marriage. Ask if they have wept for their spouse.

The goal of empathizing with their marriage is to expand the breadth and reach of their empathy. We want to expand their souls beyond the little world of "me" to the larger story of "you/us" and to the largest story of God.

We are all hardwired to focus on our own pain. That's not all bad—if we take our pain candidly to God in lament. But sin hardwires us to focus *only* on our own pain. Sin hardwires us to ignore the hurt and harm we are causing others. Sin uses our pain to create amnesia about God's purpose for our marriage.

Our goal is to resurrect Trish and DeWayne's memory of the biblical reason for their marriage—*to glorify God by reflecting Christ and the church as the two of them become one.* We want to enliven their memory of the reason they married *this* person—because they loved, liked, cared about, and would die for *this* person. We seek to raise their gaze beyond their own pain. Our goal is to couple them together in feeling joint pain over the current state of their once beautiful, Christ-reflecting, God-honoring marriage.

Maturing as a Biblical Marriage Counselor
Coupling with the Couple

1. Philippians 2:1–5 calls us to a Christlike focus on others. We are to give more consideration to others than to ourselves. We not only look to our own interests but also to the interests of others. This is especially hard when the other is a person who is hurting us. Philippians 2:1 explains that we can do this by tapping into: (a) the encouragement and comfort we have from the *Son,* (b) the fellowship we have with the *Spirit,* and (c) the tenderness and compassion we receive from the *Father.* Think about a painful relationship in your life. How could the Son's encouragement/comfort, the Spirit's fellowship, and the Father's tenderness/compassion empower you to care like Christ for this other (hurtful) person?

2. "Marriage counseling is not individual counseling with one spouse as the audience while we talk endlessly with the other spouse." What impact would it have on your marriage counseling if you focused more on the couple talking to each other than on you talking individually to each spouse?

3. Of the four aspects of becoming the couple's dance instructor (engage, encapsulate, enlighten, empathize), which one do you think you need to develop the most? Why? How might you go about growing in that area?

4. *Affirming and Offending*: Whether in formal marriage counseling or in informal interactions with any married couple, have you experienced the affirm/offend dynamic, where empathizing with one spouse leads the other spouse to feel you have taken sides? How could the awareness of this possibility shape your future interactions? What could you do moving forward to address this affirm/offend process?

5. *Empathizing with the Marriage*: How new is this concept to you? What impact might it have on your marriage counseling if you focused not only on empathizing with the individual spouse but also on empathizing with the pain of their broken marriage?

Assisting the Couple to Become Intimate Allies: Bridging the Couple

By joining with Trish and DeWayne, we become their therapeutic glue. We function as their conduit. We join with them so we can assist them to join with each other. They have drifted apart—living on separate islands. We help them build a bridge back to each other.

It is not simply our care that heals them. It is ultimately their mutual care for each other that helps them to experience Christ's healing care. They become "Jesus with skin on" for each other as we arm them to become intimate allies.

As marriage counselors, we assist, equip, and prepare them to become intimate allies by co-creating a renewed biblical narrative of:

- Other-centered empathy
- Their true enemy
- Each spouse's personal responsibility
- Mutual sustaining ministry

Co-creating a Renewed Biblical Narrative of Other-Centered Empathy

Trish and DeWayne have seen us empathize with their marriage and with each of them individually. We have asked them to imagine what it would be like to do that for each other. That is unlikely to happen during the session in which you initially empathize with the marriage. They each likely need time to think. Three homework assignments can prime the pump.

Homework Assignment #1: Pen a Lament Psalm about Your Own Pain

Marital suffering is real and raw, and lament is biblical. Asking Trish and DeWayne each to write their own Psalm 13 or Psalm 88—psalms of lament paraphrased for their situation and soul—can be very healing. Then schedule individual meetings with Trish and DeWayne to talk through their personal lament and to walk with them on their healing journey with Christ. Encourage them to begin praying for the ability to comfort their spouse with the comfort they have received from Christ.

Homework Assignment #2: Pen a Lament Psalm about Your Spouse's Pain

This is harder. It takes other-centered compassion. It often takes several rewrites. The lament for a spouse can quickly become a lament for self or a lambasting of the spouse. You may need to meet with them individually to help them write and rewrite their lament for their spouse.

"Where do you think DeWayne's hurts are?"

"What has Trish said to you, even if in moments of anger and disappointment, that helps you to put her hurt into words—even if she is lamenting you having let her down?"

"From the overflow of the Father's compassion for you and Christ's comforting you, express in writing the compassion you feel for your wife's loneliness/for your husband's emptiness."

Then meet together again. Have them read and share their mutual laments for each other. Encourage them to pray for each other's healing.

Homework Assignment #3: Co-create a Lament Psalm for Your Marriage

Now they work together. You have set the stage by your lament for their marriage—by the picture you have painted for them. For Trish and DeWayne, it was the picture of two wrestling teammates and drilling partners becoming enemies who drill each other into the ground.

Prompt them to shape their lament psalm as movement from *paradise to desert*. They write a paragraph or so about their past marriage paradise.

"Our relationship used to be so sweet and good and mutually satisfying and God-glorifying."

"When we dated, we loved how we _____ so well together . . ."

If their marriage was rarely good, which happens sometimes, then prompt them to write about what a biblical "paradise marriage" could be like. This is a great opportunity for them to read marriage and relationship passages together.

Then they craft a paragraph about what has been lost, what is missing, what is different now. Encourage them *not* to write attacks about each other. They are jointly to lament the loss of what used to be or what could have been in a healthy biblical marriage.

"What is *our* joint loss, *our* marital pain, *our* marital lament?"

"What title would we give that chapter of our story?"

Co-creating a Renewed Biblical Narrative of Their True Enemy

Trish and DeWayne have come to us seeing each other as their ultimate enemy. We take them back to Ephesians 6:10–18 to remind them that Satan is the true enemy of their marriage.

We say to the hate-filled couple:

> You want to hate? Hate the evil one trying to destroy your marriage. Satan is the enemy the two of you must join to defeat. God is calling you to join forces against the great divorcer, Satan himself. Don't divorce each other. Be intimate allies fighting together to defeat the great divorcer!

For Trish and DeWayne, we can fit this directly into their marital dance imagery.

> You want to wrestle against an enemy? Wrestle against Satan! Be drilling partners who practice spiritual disciplines together and who dress each other in the armor of God so you can fight the evil one [Eph. 6:12–17].

When God created Adam and Eve, he made them to be lovers in a love affair and heroes in a grand adventure. All married couples follow that model when they connect and create as intimate allies. Our role is to help couples to *cooperatively create*—to work together to grow love and ministry in their relationship. When spouses are separating and destroying, God calls us to help them create a new family narrative, one where they envision themselves fashioning, growing, nurturing, and empowering each other to love like Christ loves.

Co-creating a Renewed Biblical Narrative of Each Spouse's Personal Responsibility

Perhaps the chief roadblock to constructing the marital bridge is the principle we highlighted in chapter 2—the plank in one's eye (Matt. 7:3–5). Psalm 36:2 describes many hurting or hating couples: "In their own eyes they flatter themselves too much to detect or hate their sin."

I see with crystal clarity the log in my spouse's eye—because I constantly feel it stabbing and clubbing me. But my hurt and hardness blind me so that I cannot detect the log in my own eye—the one I keep beating my spouse with. Gently but consistently return to Matthew 7:3–5 and to James 4:1–4. What causes the fights and quarrels among us? Scripture says it's *me*. My sinful, demanding, self-centered, self-sufficient heart is the core reason for my deepest struggles.

Co-creating a Renewed Biblical Narrative of Mutual Sustaining Ministry

Another roadblock to marital bridge-building is the counselee's insistence that "I've heard all of this before. All I hear is how much they're hurting!" Most couples enter counseling having heard incessantly about their spouse's real or perceived hurts. They will tell you that they are sick and tired of hearing how they have failed their spouse and hurt their spouse. The last thing they want is more of the same. So what do we do?

Equip each spouse to find comfort and healing in Christ. Keep sending each spouse back to Christ. The more they receive Christ's comfort in their hurts, the more the overflow of Christ's comfort can wash over their spouse. If DeWayne can never or rarely comfort Trish, then he is not taking the plank out of his eye *and* he is not receiving his Father's comfort.

Empathize with the couple. Communicate to Trish and DeWayne:

I hear you. I realize that hearing about your spouse's hurts is old territory. You've heard them so much that now they only feel like complaints—like attacks on you and all your faults. But remember, there's a difference now. You have a third party here who we keep turning to—God! And you have a fourth party here—me. I'm not simply your referee. I want to be a coach who helps you to know what to do with what your spouse shares . . .

Explain typical marital patterns. You might say something like this to Trish and DeWayne:

Here's what I've noticed in a lot of hurting marriages. At first we try to communicate our hurt in a helpful way. Later, when that doesn't seem to get through to our spouse, we tend to share our hurt in a hurtful way—attacking and putting down our spouse. What started as an attempt to draw closer now becomes another reason to grow further apart. I'd like to get us back to the place of sharing our hurts in a way that helps you to understand each other, care about each other, and learn how you can experience the joy of comforting each other with Christ's comfort. Are you willing to give this a try?

Coach the Couple in Christlike Communication

Walk with the couple through passages like Ephesians 4:25–5:2. These are not simply communication skills. These are heart attitudes that result in other-centered listening and death-to-self speaking. Talk through being angry but not sinning. Talk through putting off falsehood and speaking truthfully—including the falsehood of coloring our descriptions with our self-focused perspective. Talk through refusing to let any poisonous words come out of our mouth, instead speaking only words that are nourishing because they are grace words that meet the specific need of our spouse in that specific moment. Talk through getting rid of bitterness, brawling, and slander—especially toward our soul mate. Talk through forgiving each other as Christ forgives us. Talk through loving like Christ loves us.

Then, structure the sharing.

> Trish, as you share, here's what I'd like you to do. Avoid blaming and attacking. Simply share with DeWayne two things. First, what you most long for from him. Second, what you feel like when you don't receive that. Help DeWayne to experience what your soul experiences . . .

Next, structure the listening and responding.

> DeWayne, here's your calling. Please don't interrupt. Listen quietly and attentively until I ask Trish to give you a chance to respond. While you're listening, I want you to think about two things. First, how you can summarize what Trish really longs for from you. Second, how you can put into your own words the hurt that Trish feels. And when you respond, don't defend or explain. This is not an attack. Your role is to try to really understand Trish so that you can comfort her with Christ's comfort. By the way, soon you'll have your chance to share your longings and hurts while Trish listens . . .

Couples bridge the gap they have allowed Satan to create between them by committing to climbing in the casket with each other, listening compassionately to each other's troubling story, empathizing with each other, offering Christ's comfort to each other, helping each other to cry out to God for help, asking forgiveness of each other, and granting grace to each other.

Maturing as a Biblical Marriage Counselor
Assisting the Couple to Become Intimate Allies

1. Ponder a time of suffering in your life. Prayerfully pen a psalm of lament—paraphrase your own Psalm 13 or Psalm 88—taking your pain to the God who cares and comforts.

2. In addition to Ephesians 6:10–18, what are some other passages you could use to show a couple that Satan is their true enemy? Craft several trialogues you could use to explore one of those passages with a couple.

3. "In their own eyes they flatter themselves too much to detect or hate their sin" (Ps. 36:2). What a convicting verse!

    a. During times of conflict in your relationships, what has God used to help you to begin to see the log in your eye?

    b. How could you use Psalm 36:2; Matthew 7:3–5; and James 4:1–4 to help spouses detect the log in their eye?

4. In addition to Ephesians 4:25–5:2, what other passages could you use to lead a couple in exploring Christlike communication? Craft several trialogues you could use to explore one of those passages with a couple.

5. Which of the four counselor competencies of bridge-building do you think is most important? Which are you currently best at? Which do you need to develop further and how
might you do that?

- Co-creating a Renewed Biblical Narrative of Other-Centered Empathy

- Co-creating a Renewed Biblical Narrative of Their True Enemy

- Co-creating a Renewed Biblical Narrative of Each Spouse's Personal Responsibility

- Co-creating a Renewed Biblical Narrative of Mutual Sustaining Ministry

CHAPTER

SEVEN

Clinging Together to Jesus in the Storm

Sustaining in Marriage Counseling, Part 2

Introduction: "I Surrender"

When they first started meeting with me, Emma and Logan each had the numbers of divorce attorneys saved in their cell phones. It was clear as I listened to their marital story that they were ready to raise the white flag of surrender.

So I used that imagery. "Emma, Logan . . . I sense your feelings of hopelessness. Each of you is ready to surrender—to give up, give in, and get out." Pausing, I made eye contact with each of them. "I want you to surrender."

They were shocked. And as you read my words, perhaps you are too.

Since I had their attention, I continued.

Christ has set a choice before you today. You could raise the white flag of surrender and give up on your marriage. Or you could surrender to God and give up on your own efforts to make your marriage work in your own strength. Based on the fact that you called me—your pastor—instead of your lawyer, I'm thinking you're ready to tap out and surrender to God and tap into Christ's power. What do you two think?

As Logan and Emma responded, I could hear shame in their voices as they expressed how helpless they felt to fix their marital mess. Rather than joining their shame, I chose to expose their wisdom. "I get it. None of us likes to feel powerless and incompetent. But you guys are actually at the best place possible—the biblical place. Let me show you what I mean . . ."

So I walked them through Ephesians, just like I walked you through Ephesians earlier in this book. I opened my Bible and turned to Ephesians 5:22–33.

A lot of biblical marriage counselors might start with you right here in Ephesians 5. I know you guys. You know this passage. And I know you feel this passage is an impossible standard given the current state of your marriage. Here's the good news—Paul doesn't start Ephesians with chapter 5. He starts with the glory of God's grace and the power of Christ's resurrection in chapter 1. Then he moves on to our helplessness in ourselves and our rescue in Christ alone in chapter 2. He continues in chapter 3 with the heavenly Father who can do exceedingly, abundantly above all that we could ask or imagine. Then Paul moves to chapter 4 and the body of Christ—the church—and our new life in Christ. It's pretty clear, isn't it, that Paul doesn't think we can pull off this marriage stuff on our own?

But there's still more. Let's look at the verses before and after Ephesians 5:22–33. Emma, could you read Ephesians 5:18–21? It starts out "Be filled with the Spirit." And Logan, would you then read 6:10–18? It starts out "Be strong in the Lord and in his mighty power." As you read, remember that these verses surround Paul's teaching about marriage and family life . . .

Emma and Logan, I'm glad you feel weak and incompetent—in yourselves—to change your marriage. I'm right there with you, because I'm powerless and incompetent to counsel you—in my own competency. How about the three of us join Paul and admit that we and every other human being are powerless apart from our all-powerful God? How about we surrender? What if we started our marriage counseling together by praying that God would fill us with his Spirit so he can change us? What if we started our marriage counseling together by praying that we would be strong in the Lord and in his mighty power?

Maturing as a Biblical Marriage Counselor
"I Surrender"

1. In this book's introduction, we discussed the value of counselors recognizing their incompetency in self. In this chapter's introduction, we highlighted the value of the couple recognizing their incompetency to change themselves and their marriage without Christ. How could you help couples to move to this recognition and to the point of saying, "I surrender"?

2. Read Ephesians 5:18–21 and 6:10–18. What difference could it make during your first marriage counseling session if everyone in the room prayerfully acknowledged that marriage and marriage counseling are dependent on the filling of the Spirit and the strength of the Lord?

3. Craft sample trialogues (scriptural explorations or spiritual conversations) you could use to help couples grasp the relevance of Ephesians 1:1–5:21 and 6:10–18 to their marriage and the marriage counseling process.

Ephesians 1

Ephesians 2

Ephesians 3

Ephesians 4

Ephesians 5

Ephesians 6

Renewing the Couple's Trust in the God of All Comfort: Clinging to Their Father of Holy Love

Exploring Ephesians with Logan and Emma was a helpful start. The theological concept of surrendering to God and turning to him for comfort was not hard for them to grasp. However, translating that theology from head to heart, from idea to marital life, was another story. What makes it so hard for hurting hearts to trust God's heart?

The Heart Disease That Blocks Heart Surrender

Think about this logically. When I voluntarily surrender to someone, I entrust myself to them *because* I trust them. Marriage counselors need to consider that simple logic. Am I asking Emma and Logan to entrust themselves to a

God they perceive to be untrustworthy? *Our biblical counsel will fall on deaf ears if our counselee has unbiblical beliefs about God.*

Think about this theologically. In Jeremiah 2, the Lord says of Israel, "I remember the devotion of your youth, how as a bride you loved me and followed me through the wilderness" (2:1). Only a few verses later we see Israel say, "I love foreign gods, and I must go after them" (2:25). So the Lord questions them in 2:31, "Have I been a desert to Israel or a land of great darkness?"

What in the world happened? Why would Israel move from a bride who so trusted God that she would follow him into the desert, to a spiritual adulterer who sees God as a dark desert?

God wonders that too. "What fault did your ancestors find in me, that they strayed so far from me?" (2:5). "Fault" is a mental imagery word. God is asking, "What faulty view of me, what lightweight subversion of me took hold of your mind and led your heart to distrust my heart?"

The Lord provides his diagnostic answer in Jeremiah 2:19: "Consider then and realize how evil and bitter it is for you when you forsake the LORD your God and have no awe of me." "Awe" is another mental imagery word. We forsake entrusting our hearts to God when our minds lose the sense of the awesomeness of God.

On the other hand, we entrust ourselves to God when we perceive him to be trustworthy. As Peter reminds us, we cast our cares on Christ *because* we believe that he cares for us (1 Pet. 5:7). Paul reminds us that it is "in view of God's mercy" that we surrender ourselves to God as living sacrifices (Rom. 12:1–2). The author of Hebrews teaches that we turn to Christ for grace to help in our time of need *when* we perceive him as our sympathetic High Priest (Heb. 4:14–16).

How we view God is the most important thing about us. We are naïve to expect couples to turn to God for comfort unless they believe he is the Father of compassion and the God of all comfort. This is why biblical marriage counselors must help couples restore a biblical image of God that counters the distorted lies of Satan.

The Biblical Portrait of God That Animates Heart Surrender

What image of God do couples need to cling to in their marital suffering? Isaiah provides our answer. "Comfort, comfort my people, says your God" (Isa. 40:1). For thirty-nine chapters, Isaiah has spoken about Israel's hard service and heartbreaking suffering. Now God's people are to be *perfectly comforted*—in Hebrew the repetition of the word "comfort" communicates ultimate comfort. But for God's suffering people to receive comfort, what do they need? They need to see God biblically.

The first word of Isaiah 40:10 is instructive: "See." It means "Behold!" or "Pay attention!" It is the Hebrew equivalent of a flashing neon sign. It is like a curator at an art museum saying, "This picture is the artist's masterpiece that best captures their life's work, their soul!"

To be comforted, we need to be still and behold the biblical image of God—our Father of Holy Love.

> See, the Sovereign LORD comes with power,
> and he rules with a mighty arm.
> See, his reward is with him,
> and his recompense accompanies him.
> He tends his flock like a shepherd:
> He gathers the lambs in his arms
> and carries them close to his heart;
> he gently leads those that have young. (Isa. 40:10–11)

Our comforting Father in heaven is *holy*. He is our sovereign God who, in the midst of our suffering, comes with power and rules with a mighty arm. He rewards us for clinging to him in our suffering, and he recompenses and deals with those who cause our suffering. He is our mighty King who works all things together for good. God is holy—infinite, above us, transcendent, sovereign, and in control.

Our comforting Father in heaven is *loving*. He is our affectionate Shepherd who, in the midst of our suffering, gathers us in his arms. He carries our hurting heart close to his tender heart. He gently leads us when we are most vulnerable. He is our Father of compassion who is able to sympathize and empathize with us when marital life is bad. God is love—near us, immanent, affectionate, and caring.

Our comforting Father in heaven is holy *and* loving. God is our Shepherd King of affectionate sovereignty who cares and controls. The biblical portrait of God is as our Father of Holy Love.

Satan's Sub-version of God

Previously we introduced the idea that Satan attempts to crop Christ out of our picture. Actually, Satan is all too happy to crop sub-biblical images of God into our picture. All of these sub-versions seek to crop out either God's holiness (sovereign control) or God's love (affectionate care).

To Logan, Satan might whisper:

You're suffering; it must mean God isn't really actively controlling things. Maybe he's like the watchmaker who wound up the watch and then went off duty. Or maybe he's grandfatherly, nice and kind, but he's not going to do anything about your messy marriage and mean wife. Maybe God's kinda like your dear ol' dad. Remember how henpecked and controlled Daddy Dearest was by your stepmother? Just like you are by Emma. It sure doesn't look like he's working all things together for good, does it? Look at the evidence and you'll see that you can't trust God to come through for you!

To Emma, Satan might hiss:

You're suffering; it must mean God doesn't care—he's not nearly as loving as he claims to be. Oh, he's big. He's infinite, in fact. But he's too big to concern himself with your puny problems. If he really loved you, he would never let your hubby get away with treating you the way he does. In fact, your hubby is just like your God—big and bossy, not kind and caring! Look at the evidence and you'll see you can't trust God to care for you!

Expanding a Couple's Biblical Image of God

One of our first tasks as marriage counselors is to *listen theologically to each spouse's functional image of God*. How do they seem to perceive God? How do they describe him? Which part of Satan's typical caricature of God are they believing—God as an uncaring despot or God as a caring but weak grandpa? Are they missing the mark on God's affection or God's sovereignty? Are they off the mark on God as Shepherd or God as King? Are they interpreting life through circumstances or through the cross?

- Emma and Logan, when you pray about this, how are you picturing God, seeing God?
- Who is God to you as you go through all of this? I'm not looking for your academic answer. In your heart, how are you seeing God in all of this?
- Where do you think God is as you go through all of this? Aloof? Involved? Distant? Near? Weeping with you? Judging you?

We then help people put off those old lies and put on the truth. We help them apply Isaiah 40 and God's holy love to their specific marital suffering. "So, Emma and Logan, let's explore Isaiah 40. Let's start by getting the context behind the words 'Comfort, comfort my people.'"

After discussing the context and the repetition of the word "comfort," we then read and jointly apply Isaiah 40:10–11.

- Emma and Logan, both verses are infinitely true of our God and how he relates to each of you. Does either verse resonate more for one of you? Does either verse seem to contain descriptions of God that you personally most need to believe and cling to?

- What would it look like to apply these verses together to your life and marriage?
- How do these verses counter Satan's lies about who God is as you go through this?
- Let's imagine these two verses as thick, strong, huge ropes intertwined again and again. How could the two of you *together* cling to God and these images as your rope of hope?

Or we help them apply 2 Corinthians 1 and God's compassion and comfort to their marriage.

- Emma and Logan, maybe I've been premature in urging you to turn to God in your suffering. Perhaps first we should talk about *who* God is *to you*. Let's look together at 2 Corinthians 1:3–7.
- Paul urges us to comfort each other based on the comfort we receive from God. But first he encourages us to see God as our Father of compassion and our God of all comfort who comforts us in every marital trouble.
- Let's talk about that word "Father." In your experience, what does that word even mean to you? What does it mean to you that God is your heavenly Father? And God is not just any Father but the Father of compassion. How does that biblical image of God square with how you've been perceiving and experiencing God?
- Paul also describes God as the God of *all* comfort. How could that image of God attract you to run to God in your suffering?

Maturing as a Biblical Marriage Counselor
Renewing the Couple's Trust in the God of All Comfort

1. "Our biblical counsel will fall on deaf ears if our counselee has unbiblical beliefs about God." (See Jer. 2; Rom.12:1–2; 1 Pet. 5:7.)
   a. What is your biblical assessment of that statement? What passages would you use to support your assessment?

   b. If the statement is true, what are the implications for your biblical marriage counseling?

---

2. "How we view God is the most important thing about us."

    a. What is your biblical assessment of that statement? What passages would you use to support your assessment?

    b. How does a faulty, sub-biblical image of God impact our lives? Our marriages?

3. We summarized a biblical image of God as our Father of Holy Love.

    a. What is your biblical assessment of that summary? What passages would you use to support your assessment?

    b. In your own life, have there been times you struggled to maintain both those aspects of God's character in your mind—his holiness and his love?

4. Reread Isaiah 40:10–11. Think about a recent or current time of suffering in your life.

    a. How could the biblical portrait of God in this passage bring you comfort?

    b. Based on Isaiah 40:10–11, craft a prayer for comfort from your Father of Holy Love.

Engaging the Couple through Empathetic Encouragement

In every marriage counseling session, counselors come to numerous choice points where we must decide "What do I focus on *at this moment*?" One of the many values of the sustaining, healing, reconciling, and guiding model of marriage counseling is the assurance it gives us that we are following a *comprehensive* approach. So we do not have to cover everything all at once. As in Ephesians 4:29; 1 Thessalonians 2:11–12; and 1 Thessalonians 5:14, we approach each person, each couple, by seeking to offer them what they most need at that moment.

Some of the options in marriage counseling include:

- *Focusing on Hurt (Sustaining Empathy)*: "Yes, your spouse has deeply hurt you, wounded you, abused you."
- *Focusing on Hope (Healing Encouragement)*: "You can endure all things and do all things through Christ who strengthens you."
- *Focusing on Sin and Forgiveness (Reconciling Exposure)*: "Your pain is not the ultimate issue. Your sin and God's grace are."
- *Focusing on Wise, Mature Relating (Guiding Equipping)*: "Your highest calling is Christlike love, whether or not your spouse reciprocates."

As we saw in chapter 5, in the early stages of engaging with a couple, they often need empathetic encouragement that focuses on hurt *and* hope. This relational competency involves recognizing both their deep pain (empathy) and their tremendous courage in not giving up (encouragement). We acknowledge their feelings (empathy) while acknowledging their resilience (encouragement).

- Emma and Logan, this must be so difficult to handle [empathy]. Tell me how the two of you together are managing to defeat these negative feelings through Christ [encouragement].
- With everything you've gone through in your marriage [empathy], how has Christ been strengthening the two of you so you're keeping your heads above water [encouragement]?
- I can tell that you both feel very hurt by the one you love the most [empathy]. Yet I also sense your deep commitment to each other. Logan and Emma, tell me how Christ is empowering the two of you to maintain your commitment in the midst of your pain [encouragement].

When we empathize with Emma and Logan, they know we care and that we take their pain seriously. When we expose glimpses of victory that they had become blind to, they gain new confidence and assurance. "Wow! We've not only survived these hard times; at times we've even thrived. Through Christ, we *can* change and grow in our marriage relationship."

Connecting the Couple in Their Hurts and Hopes

Our empathetic encouragement is to model for them how they can relate to each other. So perhaps we share something like this:

- Logan, you've heard me identify with some of Emma's hurt. And you've seen me affirm Emma's perseverance. I'd love to have you share with Emma right now about both of those areas.
- Where are some places you've seen Emma's pain? I know this is hard because you've been responsible for some of that pain. And I know it's difficult because Emma's been responsible for some of your pain. But I know you care about and feel for Emma.
- Logan, in addition to sharing the pain, I'd like you to share the gain—encourage Emma by letting her know some specific examples where you're amazed by her persistence, her courage, her stick-to-itiveness, her hope in God.
- Don't worry. When you're done, I'm going to ask Emma to share something similar with you . . .

Connecting the Couple's Hurts to Christ's Hope

We not only want the couple to speak into each other's lives, we want to help the couple see how Scripture speaks into their marital suffering with hope and help from above. While we will explore God's hope much more in chapters 8 and 9, this is another case where we mingle hurt and hope because Scripture mingles hurt and hope.

We have already introduced Logan and Emma to Ephesians as the backdrop and foundation for their marriage and our marriage counseling. Now we can trialogue with them, interjecting God's power into their problems. Perhaps you explore Ephesians 1.

- Paul starts Ephesians with a hymn of praise to the great grace of the Father, Son, and Holy Spirit in 1:3–14. Right now, you just want to survive. I get that. And I know it's difficult at times to figure out how the Father, Son, and Holy Spirit relate to our daily fights. Could we look at these twelve verses together and explore how they could give you comfort in your hurt, hope in your confusion, and purpose in your marriage?

Or you explore Ephesians 6:10–18.

- Let's paraphrase Ephesians 6:10–18, putting it into its marital context. Logan and Emma, in your marriage, be strong in the Lord and in his mighty power. As husband and wife, put on the full marital armor of God, so you can take your stand together against the devil's schemes. For your marital struggle is not against each other, but against the rulers, against the authorities, against the powers of this dark world and against the spiritual forces of evil in the heavenly realms. Satan is your enemy; your spouse is not your enemy. So, Emma and Logan, put on the full marital armor of God, so that when the day of evil comes, you may be able to stand your ground together, and after you have done everything, to stand. Stand firm then as husband and wife, with the belt of truth buckled around your waist, with the breastplate of righteousness in place, and with your feet fitted with the readiness that comes from the gospel of peace. Take up the shield of faith, with which you can extinguish all the flaming arrows of the evil one. Take the helmet of salvation and the sword of the Spirit, which is the word of God. And pray for your spouse and your marriage in the Spirit on all occasions with all kinds of prayers and requests.
- Emma and Logan, let's embed your most recent fight right into Ephesians 6:10–18. Picture yourself in the middle of that fight. Now picture this passage invading your hearts and minds right at that moment. What specific ways could the truths of this passage have impacted you at that very second?

Envisioning God's Work in the Midst of Their Marital Mess

This heading captures the essence of empathetic encouragement: *in the midst of their marital mess, see God at work—hurt and hope.* To use imagery from the Gospels, in the midst of their marital storm, look for Jesus walking on the water and hear Peter saying, "Help!" A struggling marriage can become a gift—a wake-up call, a reality check, a cry for help. Healthy couples learn well the truth that "We need Jesus!" The key word is "we"—couples not only need to hurt together but also to work together toward hoping together.

Too many couples want to wait until their spouse is perfect and their relationship is tranquil before they will agree to work as a team. Our goal is to help them start working together now—in the middle of the storm. Together they cry out to Jesus, "Help us hope again!"

Perceive Their Unique Way of Connecting, Cooperating, and Co-creating

With troubled couples, there may not be obvious, overt signs of clinging together to Christ so they can work together in Christ. So pray for spiritual eyes. Be curious.

Ask yourself questions. Who are these people? How do they relate? What are their special gifts? How do they dance? What are their unique strengths? How would this couple work together compared to any other couple? What is special and different about their relationship?

Activate Insight by Combining Their Hurt and Hope Story

As you prayerfully ponder a couple's uniqueness, you will likely begin to see how the very areas that frustrate them about each other can become complementary ways of working together. So share what you see in a captivating and motivating way.

- Emma and Logan, as you two interacted, even though it got a bit messy, a picture kept running through my mind. In *Star Trek*, Spock was the rational, logical one; Kirk was the passionate, emotional one. Alone, they were incomplete. Together, what a team! They complemented each other. I notice the same thing with the two of you. While I know those differences can be frustrating, even maddening, I'm wondering if you've noticed how God designed the two of you like puzzle pieces fitting together just right. Emma, you seem to tap into hope rationally, with specific verses. Logan, you seem to tap into hope relationally, with specific prayers. What if you guys combined all of that?

Provoke Joint Action

On the basis of their newfound insight, provoke joint action. Help the couple continue to see their connection and then to do more of the same.

- None of us is naïve. Logan and Emma, just because we've had a good start today, that doesn't mean everything will be perfect. Now you have a choice. You can focus on the negatives and on the ways you two are so different: "Why does he have to be so emotional—led by his heart?" "Why does she have to be so rational—all in her head?" Or you can look for positive areas of growth where you're helping each other *in your differences* to find hope when you're hurting. This next week I'd like each of you to write down times when you connect like Spock and Kirk. I know, those differences can be maddening, but we're trying to see how they can also be beautiful and helpful. So keep track of those times when you use the different ways God has wired you to help each other find God's comfort and hope. Maybe it will sound something like this: "I'm so glad Emma keeps me grounded in the truth of Scripture." "I'm so glad Logan stirs up my passion for closeness to Christ."

Expect the Best (and Deal with the Rest)

When the couple returns, expect the best.

- We'll definitely discuss struggles you may have had this week. But first, tell me what's different or better since our last meeting. Logan and Emma, how did God use your differences to help you find hope in your hurts?
- What was God empowering you to do this past week, even in the midst of the storm, that the two of you want to continue doing?
- Through Christ's strength, what did the two of you accomplish together in your relationship that you would like to continue to nurture?

When they report successes, keep the ball rolling.

- That's great! How did Christ empower you both to accomplish that?
- What does this say about your ability to unite your differences in Christ?
- I'm struck by your teamwork . . .

When they report no change, then respond with:

- That could be discouraging. How has Christ strengthened you so that you've been able to continue to cope with this as a couple?
- I'm sorry to hear that it feels like the same old, same old. With Christ, how have you managed to stay on top of things as a couple through all of this?
- No? Not even a little? Was there one time when you were able to experience a bit more victory together than previously?
- Are there actions, attitudes, or words that you would do differently if you had the week to do over again?
- What do you think kept you from drawing on God's power to do this together?

Maturing as a Biblical Marriage Counselor
Engaging the Couple through Empathetic Encouragement

1. This section focused on the somewhat unusual combination of acknowledging pain, hurt, and suffering (empathy) and expressing affirmation for someone's ability to endure that suffering (encouragement).

   a. Which do you tend more toward: expressions of empathy in pain or expressions of encouragement and affirmation for victory and growth and gain?

   b. Is this relational competency a new concept for you—combining both empathy and encouragement in one response? If not, how did you learn to do this? If so, how could you develop this competency?

2. One of the skills of empathetic encouragement is turning to Scripture to connect the couple's hurts to Christ's hope. Again, this can be somewhat unusual for us, as we often do one or the other—look for passages that express comfort in hurt or turn to passages that identify our hope in Christ. Is this relational competency a new concept for you? If not, how did you learn to do this? If so, how could you develop this competency?

3. Another skill of empathetic encouragement involves envisioning God's work in the midst of a couple's marital mess.

   a. This takes compassionate ears willing to listen well to the couple's earthly story. It also takes spiritual eyes able to see God's hand at work. How would you rate yourself on your ability to do both: listen with compassionate ears and look with spiritual eyes?

   b. This section noted Peter sinking in the water and crying out to Jesus for help as one example of God's work in the midst of life's storms. To what other biblical passages would you take couples to see how God works in the midst of their marital messes?

EIGHT

Interpreting Life from a Faith Perspective

Healing in Marriage Counseling, Part 1

Introduction: Hoping in God Together

When couples enter counseling, they typically are looking at one another and their marriage with eyeballs only—from a shrunken, self-focused, temporal perspective. No one has to tell them life is bad or their marriage is on the rocks. They feel separated and distanced from the one person they had hoped to cleave to and weave with. They feel hopeless and helpless. This is why we often begin marital counseling with infusing hope (chap. 5).

As we infuse hope, we are careful to listen compassionately to the couple's earthly story of marital hurt. This is the story we enter into with them in the sustaining process as we climb in their casket of marital loss, hurt, pain, and suffering (chaps. 6–7).

If we have witnessed God's sustaining and comforting work in their marital earthly story, then they are now in the casket *together*. They not only feel their own pain but they are empathizing with each other's pain. Having received comfort from Christ, they then comfort each other. Their shared sorrow is now endurable sorrow. Together they have invited Christ into their casket. Through Christ's comfort, they are communicating to each other, "Like Christ, we care about *each other's* hurts." Getting to this point of mutual empathy is a significant work of Christ.

Yet there is more work Christ empowers us to do in every couple's troubling story. In the marital healing process, Christ's eternal story begins to invade their earthly story, creating a *faith story* (chaps. 8 and 9). For the apostle

Paul, this occurred when he moved from despairing of life to trusting in the One who is the resurrection and the life. He writes, "Indeed, we felt we had received the sentence of death. But this happened that we might not rely on ourselves but on God, who raises the dead" (2 Cor. 1:9). Notice what Paul says next: "On him we have set our hope" (1:10). The earthly casket story is a good place to be if our casket experience causes us to *give up hope in ourselves and resurrects our hope in God.*

In sustaining, we seek to help couples offer each other grace *relationships*—empathy and Christ's present comfort. In healing, we seek to help couples co-create grace *narratives*—encouragement and Christ's eternal perspective. In sustaining, we tune into their emotions, pain, hurt, and suffering so they can be *comforted* together in Christ. In healing, we focus on their thinking, beliefs, mindsets, and perspectives so they can *hope* together in God.

Paul highlights this grace narrative, larger story, eternal perspective in 2 Corinthians 10:3–7. The contentious Corinthians were "judging by appearances" (10:7). "Appearances" means externals, from the surface. It literally means "face"—eyeballs only, where we are blind to Christ's grace perspective and we interpret life from an earthly, temporal viewpoint.

Paul, however, wants us to look at life with spiritual eyes, with an eternal perspective, with faith and cross-focused vision. The weapons Paul fights with are spiritual weapons that have divine power to demolish strongholds, arguments, and every pretension that sets itself up against the knowledge of God so that we can take every thought captive to Christ (10:4–5). Strongholds, arguments, pretensions, and thoughts all highlight fundamental, foundational beliefs and images that govern how we interpret life. They are hardened, fortified worldviews that shape how we perceive reality—how we view God, others, and ourselves.

Picture it like this. Tension erupts between my wife, Shirley, and me. The situation creates a choice point. Do I interpret what is happening and do I view Shirley through fleshly strongholds that are me-focused, condemning, judging, and self-centered? From this worldly mindset, my mental image of life screams, "Bob is the center of the universe! Bob is on the throne! I can only count on Bob. It's all about Bob!"

Or do I interpret what is happening and do I view Shirley through spiritual strongholds that are Christ-focused, forgiving, grace-giving, other-centered, and Christ-centered? This mental image of life cries out, "Christ is the center of the universe and of my marriage! Christ is on the throne of my heart and our marriage! I trust God's good heart. Everything, including our marriage, is all about Christ!"

Climbing in the casket together as a couple is an amazing start, but if a couple stays there and fights with earthly power and a smaller-story, self-centered, eyeballs-only perspective, they may as well close the casket lid on themselves. They need to see life through a gospel lens. They need our help in the healing process so they can say to each other, "Through Christ, it's possible for us to *hope in God together*." Biblical marriage counselors help couples hope in the goodness of God who raises the dead—including dead marriages—by developing a FAITH perspective:

F Fighting Satan's Lying and Condemning Earthly Narrative (chap. 8)

A Applying Christ's Truth and Grace Eternal Narrative (chap. 8)

I Inviting Couples to Crop the Life of Christ into Their Marital Life (chap. 9)

T Trialoguing about Christ's Truth and Grace Eternal Narrative (chap. 9)

H Healing Individually and Together in Christ (chap. 9)

Maturing as a Biblical Marriage Counselor
Hoping in God Together

1. As a counselor, your focus in *sustaining* is on building a grace *relationship* with the couple where you empathize with their hurt and help them climb in the casket with each other. This requires a depth of emotional connection on your part. Your focus in *healing* is on grace *narratives* where you help the couple identify the lies of Satan that they are believing and help them together see their marriage through the lens of Christ's resurrection hope.

   a. Which are you more inclined toward and naturally good at—grace relationships or grace narratives? Why? How?

   b. If you are not as strong at marital sustaining, which of the competencies in chapters 6 and 7 do you think you most need to keep working to develop?

   c. If you are not as strong at marital healing, what do you think the result might be if you empathize with couples in pain but do not help them to gain Christ's eternal perspective on their relationship?

2. Picture a recent disagreement or relational tension with someone, either in your marriage or in another close relationship.

   a. How would you view that situation, your role, your heart, the other person, and what should happen next if you view it from a fleshly stronghold that is self-focused, condemning, judging, and self-centered? Your heart is screaming, "I am the center of the universe! I'm on the throne! I can only count on me! It's all about me!" How would those mindsets and strongholds impact your response?

   b. How would you view that situation, your role, your heart, the other person, and what should happen next if you view it from a spiritual stronghold that is Christ-focused, forgiving, grace-giving, other-centered, and Christ-centered? Your heart is crying out, "Christ is the center of the universe and of this relationship! Christ is on the throne of my heart and this relationship! I trust God's good heart. Everything, including this relationship, is all about Christ!" How would those mindsets and godly strongholds impact your response?

Fighting Satan's Lying and Condemning Earthly Narrative

In chapter 7, we exposed Satan's lies so couples would receive comfort from their holy and loving Father. In chapter 8, we expose Satan's lies so couples can refuse to interpret God through the lens of their marital circumstances (the earthly story of despair) and instead choose to view God through the lens of the cross of Christ (the eternal story of hope).

To understand the pathway toward despair, recall two basic premises. First, *when our marriage stinks, our perspective shrinks*. We get squinty-eyed; we look at life through darkened, negative, hopeless lenses. Second, Satan is happy to join in at this point, seeking to *crop Christ out of our picture*. This is an equation for despair:

A horrible, rotten, terrible, no-good situation

+ A shrunken perspective

+ A shrunken Christ

= Despair

Identifying the Theme of Satan's Scheme: Condemnation

To offer biblical hope in the midst of marital despair, we need to help couples identify the theme of Satan's scheme. The apostle Paul sets the example for our biblical marriage counseling context in his instructions to the Corinthian church. First, he exhorts the Corinthians to confront a man who was having sexual relations with his own stepmother (1 Cor. 5:1–5). Then, when this man shows fruits of repentance, Paul encourages the church to forgive him, comfort him, and reaffirm their love for him. If they won't restore him, the man would become overwhelmed by excessive sorrow, guilt, and condemnation—an inability to grasp grace and receive the Father's forgiveness (2 Cor. 2:5–11).

In this intensely relational context, Paul explains that we must forgive—so that Satan does not outwit us, for we are not unaware of his scheme to overwhelm us by magnifying guilt while blinding us to grace (2 Cor. 2:8–11). *Satan's scheme always centers on condemnation.* First, he tempts us to condemn God by doubting God's good heart—Satan is the accuser of God (Gen. 3:1–5). Second, he tempts us to condemn ourselves and our spouse—Satan is the accuser of God's people (Rev. 12:10). Satan titles his narrative "Doubt God, Trust Yourself."

Identifying Satan's Condemning Narrative of God: "Doubt God's Good Heart"

Doubting God is the theme of the fallen story that Satan tells—over and over and over again. In chapter 7, we introduced the idea of Satan questioning our Father's holy love. That scheme began in the garden when Satan questioned God's good, generous, and gracious heart by trying to paint God as a "thou-shalt-not" god. Our generous Father had told Adam and Eve, "You are free to eat from any tree in the garden; but you must not eat from the tree of the knowledge of good and evil, for when you eat of it you will certainly die" (Gen. 2:16–17). Wonderful freedom with only one protective prohibition! But Satan twisted our Father's words. "Did God really say, 'You must not eat from any tree in the garden'?" (Gen. 3:1). Perceive the contrast.

- You are *free to* eat from *any* tree.
- You *must not* eat from *any* tree.

Satan questions God's generous, gracious love.

Next, Satan questions God's perfect holiness. God had said, "For when you eat of it you will certainly die" (Gen. 2:17). The serpent says, "You will not certainly die" (Gen. 3:4). According to Satan, God does not do what he says. He does not keep his word. He is not righteous. You can flaunt his will with impunity.

Then Satan questions God's very character. "For God knows that when you eat from it your eyes will be opened, and you will be like God, knowing good and evil" (Gen. 3:5). The serpent hisses out his fiendish fabrications: "God is a hoarder, not a rewarder. He is holding back his best from you. God is jealous of you. Your God is unloving, unholy, and jealously insecure. You cannot trust him! He does not have a good heart."

This is the filter Satan wants couples to place over every painful marital event, like he did with Emma and Logan in chapter 7 and with Adam and Eve in the garden. He insinuates, "You say God is sovereign. He allowed this horrible situation to happen in your marriage, so he must not be caring. Or maybe he's caring but he's just not in control; he can't protect you. Either way, when your marital life is bad, it means God must not be good—since you can't trust him, trust yourself! Since he won't protect you, protect yourself!"

Satan dupes couples into believing that suffering is God's way of getting back at them instead of realizing that suffering is God's way of getting them back to himself. This is why couples like Logan and Emma come to us not only with their backs to each other but also with their backs to God. This may not come across in seething anger. More often it is a subtle disappointment in and secret distrust of God.

Identifying Satan's Condemning Marital Narrative: "Hate Yourself, Crush Your Spouse, Trust Yourself"

Remember the marital results of the fall: shame, blame, claim, and maim. It is a confusing mixture of lies and condemnation designed to keep us continually off-balance. Satan starts with shame. "Hate yourself! You're at fault. You're faulty. Filthy. God doesn't want to have a thing to do with a fool like you. Give up. You don't have the resources to fix this marital mess!"

Already tempted to doubt God's gracious heart, now we see our own evil heart. No wonder we are filled with fear and shame. Instead of looking up to God for mercy to help in our time of need, our eyes look down because our condemned soul fears making eye contact with God. Like Job's wife (Job 2:9), we feel like cursing God and letting our marriage die—giving up on God and giving up on ourselves and our marriage.

Then Satan shifts tactics to blame and maim. "Crush your spouse. It's not *really* your fault. It's *all* your spouse's fault! Look at all the ways—make a list and check it twice—your selfish, no-good, lying spouse has let you down, sinned against you. It's payback time! They've hurt you; now it's their turn to feel the pain!" Satan messes with our minds by tempting us to mingle self-hatred with spouse-hatred.

He is still not done. Now he tempts us to claim—to manipulate and control. "Since you can't trust God and you can't trust your spouse, trust yourself. Demand what you deserve! You want what you want and you want it now— and you know how to manipulate your spouse into giving it to you. You can make this work—in your way, in your time, on your terms, through your own wisdom. Doubt God. Trust yourself!"

Taking Every Thought Captive: Collaboratively Exposing Satan's Couple-Specific Smaller Story

The power of the personal ministry of the Word is our ability to counter Satan's condemning narrative by applying universal biblical truths specifically to the couple sitting in front of us. As we sit with them, we ask ourselves, "What hopeless narrative is driving this couple to despair?"

Prayerfully Assess Their Earthly Story: Diagnostic Questions

To answer this question, as they share their earthly story, we prayerfully ask ourselves diagnostic questions like:

- What is the theme of their marital earthly story—from the husband's perspective? From the wife's perspective? What patterns do I keep hearing—patterns of hopelessness, despair, doubt, self-trust, unforgiveness?
- What negative images and condemning word pictures are pervading their minds as they describe their marital struggle?
- What specific lies is Satan telling them about God, themselves, their spouse, and their marriage?
- Where is God's eternal story missing from their story? Where is God absent? Where is Christ's grace absent? Where is resurrection hope missing?
- What filter are they using to interpret their marital situation? Self-hatred? Manipulation? Revenge? Hopelessness? Anger?
- If I were to give a title to their marital smaller story, what title would I choose?

Collaboratively Undeceive the Couple

It is not enough for us as the counselor to identify these earthly story themes. We need to do more than just tell them the themes we are hearing. We need to trialogue with them so they begin to identify and own the ways they are perceiving and interpreting their marital story.

Introduce the Idea of Level 1 and Level 2 Suffering

I seek to make this as simple as possible. I go to a whiteboard, trace on my Surface Pro, or draw on a napkin:

- *Level 1 Marital Suffering—Our Situation*: What is happening *to* me/us (our circumstances).
- *Level 2 Marital Suffering—Our Soul*: What is happening *in* me/us (our interpretation/lens).

Then, looking together at what I just sketched, I share something like:

- Logan and Emma, let's review your level 1 marital suffering—what's happening *to* each of you and *to* your marriage. I've heard you describe ____, ____, and ____. We've all wept over the pain of that. That's difficult stuff. Let's discuss an even deeper level—what's happening *in* your soul—your level 2 marital suffering. Satan wants to take your pain and hurt and turn it into hopelessness and helplessness. As we look together at your marriage, we need to realize that every person sees their pain through tinted lenses. [I'll often take off my glasses and look through them at this point.] Those lenses can be God-shaped and God-filtered lenses. But Satan wants us to interpret life *without* God. Remember how we talked about Satan trying to crop Christ out of the picture? So it's really vital that we start thinking about what is happening in you—in your soul.

  » How are you *seeing* your situation—in Christ-focused ways or in non-God ways?
  » How are you *perceiving* God—through biblical lenses or through Satan's lies?
  » How are you *viewing* each other—with Christ's grace or with Satan's condemnation?
  » Does that make sense? Do you have any questions?
  » Can we explore this level 2 stuff together and, as the Bible says, "take every thought captive to Christ"?

Share the Patterns and Themes That You Have Heard Using Their Language

After addressing any of Emma's and Logan's questions, I seek to summarize the level 2 marital story I have heard them telling. I do my best to use language that fits for them—that is unique to their marital story as they have been interpreting and sharing it.

- As you've been sharing, I've been praying for wisdom to capture what I'm hearing. Here's my best attempt, but what's most important is what you two think.

  » Logan, you're a mechanic. As you describe your marriage, it seems like you feel someone has given you an engine to work on but is withholding the tools you need. That someone is God. You see God holding back, holding out on you, not coming through for you. It's like, "God, if you want me to fix this, then at least provide the right equipment!" You *hate* not being able to fix things. So you're feeling like an incompetent mechanic—you despise that. One more picture. It's like Emma brought the car in, but no matter how many repairs you make, it's never enough, you're never good enough, there's always more you have to fix—you'll never measure up in her eyes. You're disappointed with God, despising yourself, and a disappointment to Emma. If I were to give your story a title, it might be *Judge, Jury, and Prosecutor: I'm My Judge, Emma Is My Jury, and God Is My Prosecutor.*

  » How am I doing?

Then we interact. Logan will tweak my version of his story. Emma will tweak my version of Logan's story. Then I share my take on Emma's earthly story interpretation and we work through the same process. The idea is to help them see any ways they are interpreting their marital story through a non-God, non-grace, non–resurrection power, non–eternal story lens. Where is Satan cropping out Christ and cropping in condemnation, doubt, division, and despair?

Explore the History of the Earthly Story Interpretation

Our view always seems like the only view. We fail to recognize our own interpretative grid, so we think we are stating reality and declaring truth when in fact we are putting our own spin on reality. Identifying the personal history and origin of our earthly story interpretations weakens the hold these eyeballs-only views have on couples. If they were learned, then they can be repented of, unlearned, and replaced with Christ's eternal story interpretation. Trialogues like the following can help spouses to recognize that there are other ways to view their situation.

- Have you always seen your marriage like this? Can you remember when you started interpreting your relationship through this lens?
- Where do you think this way of looking at things came from? Do you tend to always look at life through these same negative lenses?

- I'm wondering where you were recruited into this way of seeing God. From your family growing up? From past relationships? From the world? From past hurts?

Expose the Ultimate Source of the Earthly Story Interpretation

To put off the old lying narrative, we need to expose the source of the earthly story—the world, the flesh, and the devil.

- In what ways do you think the world's viewpoint is trying to creep into your thinking? Perhaps if we explored 1 John 4:1–6 together . . .
- How do you think the flesh, rather than the Spirit, may be dominating your viewpoint here? Perhaps if we looked at Galatians 5:13–21 compared to 5:22–26 . . .
- What role might Satan be playing in tempting you to misinterpret your marriage? Could we look at Ephesians 2:1–3 and 6:10–18 to explore this?
- In what specific ways might Satan be cropping Christ out of your wedding picture or marriage portrait?
- Let's contrast and compare your interpretation with God's interpretation in his Word.
- The way you're looking at your relationship, is it drawing you to greater dependence on Christ or greater self-sufficiency?

Maturing as a Biblical Marriage Counselor
Fighting Satan's Lying and Condemning Earthly Narrative

1. Recall Satan's condemning math equation: a horrible situation + a shrunken perspective + a shrunken Christ = despair.

   a. Think back to and write or share about a time in your life or marriage when you (like all of us) started to be trapped by this earthly story narrative.

   b. Write or share about a time either in a marriage you counseled or a marriage you know about when the couple was trapped in this condemning narrative.

---

2. Review the section titled "Identifying Satan's Condemning Narrative of God."

    a. When have you struggled against this lie of Satan?

    b. How did you fight this lie with the truth of God's good, generous, gracious heart?

3. Review the section "Identifying Satan's Condemning Marital Narrative."

    a. When have you struggled against this lie of Satan?

    b. How did you fight this lie with the truth of God's Word?

4. Review the section titled "Taking Every Thought Captive."

    a. In what situation have you experienced both level 1 and level 2 suffering? Describe the battle.

    b. Thinking back to that situation, review the bullet point trialogues under the heading "Expose the Ultimate Source of the Earthly Story Interpretation." Ask yourself several of those questions (reworded to fit your own situation and soul). How does asking those questions help you begin to put off the old lying narrative and start to put on God's truth and grace story?

We will turn couples off and be perceived as insensitive to their marital pain if all they hear from us is a steady stream of positives. That explains the need for sustaining and for compassionately listening as couples share their smaller-story situation and interpretation. However, we will leave couples in a casket without Christ and with his resurrection cropped out of their picture if we fail to listen with them to Christ's truth and grace larger-story reality. We unite these two stories by asking:

- How can we apply God's eternally real, infinite-sized story of resurrection hope, marital healing, and final victory so that it impacts, invades, and interprets this couple's very real, human-sized story of marital suffering, pain, and seeming defeat?

We want to help the couple develop a resurrection-hope mindset that communicates: "God's future vision is greater than our past baggage. God's healing is greater than our deep hurt. Christ's grace is greater than our suffering and sin."

Paul, who experienced tremendous suffering, says it like this: "I consider that our present sufferings are not worth comparing with the glory that will be revealed in us" (Rom. 8:18). "Consider" is a perspective/interpretation word. Paul does the spiritual math and weighs, compares, and computes his past and present suffering (the earthly story) against his future glory (the eternal story). Paul applies the end of the story to his current story.

Biblical counselors apply Christ's truth and grace narrative to a couple's earthly story by:

- Picturing life as a virtuous wedding and a victorious war
- Praying for open eyes to see
- Probing the two ways of viewing life and marriage

Picturing Life as a Virtuous Wedding and a Victorious War: Revelation 19:1–21

Hope starts in the counselor's heart before it enters the counselee's heart. Like the apostles Paul and John, have *we* read the end of the story? Have we allowed the end of the story to invade, impact, and interpret *our* life story?

What is the end of the Bible's story? To answer that question, we need to picture the Bible's grand drama of reconciliation and redemption.

The Bible is the story of a wedding and a war. The Bible is the greatest love story ever told set in the midst of the greatest war story ever told.

Life is a wedding. "For your Maker is your Husband—the LORD Almighty is his name—the Holy One of Israel is your Redeemer" (Isa. 54:5). The church is the bride of Christ (2 Cor. 11:2–3; Eph. 5:25–32; Rev. 19:7–10). Yet as we learn in Hosea and throughout God's redemptive drama, we are God's unfaithful spouse—guilty of spiritual adultery (Jer. 2:20–25). But God, rich in mercy, pursues and woos us back to himself—back to our marital vows (Hosea 2:14–20; John 3:16; 2 Cor. 11:2). Life is a reconciled marriage—the greatest love story ever told.

Life is a war. Satan is the false seducer, the great divorcer, who tempts us toward false love and false worship (Gen. 3:1–5). Life is a battle for our love and loyalty (Gen. 3:15; 2 Cor. 11:2–3). Satan seeks to deceive us and lead us astray from our pure devotion to Christ (2 Cor. 11:3). But God, rich in power, overpowers our adversary, the devil, and wins us back to himself (Gen. 3:15; Col. 2:13–15). Life is a redeemed people—the greatest war story ever told.

When we read the end of the story in Revelation 19, we learn that life on this earth ends with a virtuous wedding and a victorious war. Life as we know it will end with two suppers—a wedding feast and a war feast. One is the wedding supper of the Lamb, where we are adorned in Christ's righteousness (Rev. 19:5–10). The other is the great supper of God, where the King of Kings defeats all his enemies (Rev. 19:11–21).

So we ask ourselves and our counselees trialogue questions such as:

- When you feel defeated in your marriage, what difference does it make when you realize that in the end God wins, we win?
- How can you apply the truths of Revelation 19:5–21 about our final virtuous wedding and our final victorious war to your current marital situation?
- When you read passages like Ephesians 1:18–22 (Christ's resurrection power at work in us), Ephesians 6:10–18 (Christ's power over all evil forces), Colossians 2:13–15 (our victory in Christ over Satan), and Revelation 19:5–21 (our final victory with Christ), how does this impact your view of your marital situation? How does it provide you with resurrection hope?

Praying for Open Eyes to See: 2 Kings 6:13–23 and Ephesians 1:18–22

Prayer is a neglected topic in counseling. Very few counseling training manuals—even in the Christian world—list prayer as a counselor competency. Yet prayer ought to saturate every aspect of our counseling—including the aspect of applying Christ's truth-and-grace eternal narrative to marriage.

In 2 Kings 6:13–23, the King of Aram had surrounded the prophet Elisha with horses, chariots, and soldiers. When Elisha's servant awoke and saw the city surrounded, in terror he asked Elisha, "Oh no, my lord! What shall we do?" Elisha answered, "Don't be afraid. Those who are with us are more than those who are with them" (6:15–16). Elisha's servant likely thought his master needed his eyes checked or his mental state diagnosed, for this servant saw nothing but enemy armies. So Elisha prayed what every biblical marriage counselor should pray: "Open his eyes, LORD, so that he may see" (6:17). We might pray something like this:

> Open this hurting couple's eyes, Lord, so they may see. All they see now is defeat and despair. They're looking at their marriage with eyeballs only. Please open their eyes to see your hope, power, wisdom, and grace. Open their eyes to see their marriage with spiritual eyes.

What the Old Testament illustrates in Elisha's life, Paul prays in Ephesians 1:18–22. We could paraphrase this as a Marriage Counselor's Prayer for Resurrection Hope:

> Father, I pray that the eyes of the hearts of this eyeballs-only couple may be enlightened so they may know the hope to which you have called them and the riches of the glorious inheritance they have in Christ. Please open their eyes to see the incomparably great power they have through you. May they grasp that the power at work in their marriage is the same as the mighty strength you exerted when you raised Christ from the dead and seated him at your right hand in the heavenly realms, far above all rule and authority, power and dominion, and every name that is named. Help them in their marriage relationship to tap into your resurrection and ascension power.

Probing the Two Ways of Viewing Life and Marriage: 1 Samuel 17

I have been struck by the two vastly different ways of interpreting life that we find in 1 Samuel 17. Read the first twenty-five verses and detect what is absent—God. Those verses cover a period of forty days during which the inspired narrator never once mentions the name of the Lord. The Philistines do not speak of God and Goliath does not speak of God—and we expect that from them. But Saul does not mention God. David's brothers do not mention God. No one in the armies of Israel mentions God.

Then David, a young man—a boy—after God's own heart, is the first to utter the name of God. "Who is this uncircumcised Philistine that he should defy the armies of the living God?" (17:26). Every previous mention of the armies highlighted the armies of Israel, not the armies of the living God.

What are the results when the living (resurrection) God is absent from our interpretive narrative? Despair, fear, cowardice, dismay, terror, emotional paralysis—hopelessness (17:11, 24).

What are the results when the living (resurrection) God is the circumference, the center, the very environment of our interpretative narrative? Courage, not losing heart—hope (17:32).

David had spiritual eyes to see God in all of life. When he was performing the menial task of keeping the sheep and protected them by killing a lion and a bear, it was not by his power but Yahweh's. "The LORD who rescued me from the paw of the lion and the paw of the bear will rescue me from the hand of this Philistine" (17:37). David perceived God everywhere.

That is the same hope and nearly identical wording as Paul shares in 2 Corinthians 1:9–11. Trusting in the God who raises dead people (and dead marriages), Paul says, "He has delivered us from such a deadly peril, and he will deliver us again. On him we have set our hope that he will continue to deliver us" (1:10–11).

So you read 1 Samuel 17 with a discouraged couple, and you share trialogue questions such as:

- Are you seeing your marriage like the folks in the first twenty-five verses—without God? Or are you seeing your marriage through the eyes of the living God—the God who raises dead marriages?
- How will your view of your marriage be different from each perspective?
- How will each way of looking at life and your marriage impact your hope barometer?

Maturing as a Biblical Marriage Counselor
Applying Christ's Truth and Grace Eternal Narrative

1. How could the following summary question impact how you provide marital counseling?

   "How can we apply God's eternally real, infinite-sized story of resurrection hope, marital healing, and final victory so that it impacts, invades, and interprets this couple's very real, human-sized story of marital suffering, pain, and seeming defeat?"

2. Read these three sample trialogues and then respond using the questions below.

- "When you feel defeated in your marriage, what difference does it make when you realize that in the end, God wins; we win?"
- "How can you apply the truths of Revelation 19:5–21 about our final virtuous wedding and our final victorious war to your current marital situation?"
- "When you read passages like Ephesians 1:18–22 (Christ's resurrection power at work in us); Ephesians 6:10–18 (Christ's power over all evil forces); Colossians 2:13–15 (our victory in Christ over Satan); and Revelation 19:5–21 (our final victory with Christ), how does this impact your view of your marital situation? How does it provide you with resurrection hope?"

   a. How would you answer each question in a current situation in your own life or marriage?

   b. Rewrite each trialogue in your own words—for how *you* might use it with a couple.

-

-

-

3. Regarding prayer in counseling:

   a. What role does prayer currently play in your counseling? How could you increase the role of prayer in your counseling ministry?

b. Take either the 2 Kings 6:13–23 passage or the Ephesians 1:18–22 passage and write a prayer for a marriage counseling couple.

4. Concerning the trialogue questions from 1 Samuel 17:

   a. How would you answer each question in a current situation in your own life or marriage?

   b. Rewrite each trialogue question for how *you* might use it with a couple.

      •

      •

      •

NINE

Tuning into the Bible's Faith Story

Healing in Marriage Counseling, Part 2

Introduction: Hoping in Christ Alone

Angela and Carlos are two of the most judgmental spouses you could ever meet. When they entered marriage counseling, they had zero positives to say about each other. No matter what Angela would do, Carlos would question her motives. No matter what Carlos would try, Angela would question his integrity. Helping them move to any point of mutual empathy where they saw life from their spouse's perspective was a major *sustaining* work of God. Now, helping Angela and Carlos see their marriage, their spouse, and God from a resurrection-hope perspective will be a major *healing* work of God.

- Sustaining draws a line in the sand of retreat from God and each other; healing drives a stake in the heart of Satan's lies by encouraging couples to trust God's good heart.
- In sustaining, couples climb in the casket with each other; in healing, couples invite the resurrected Christ into their marital casket.
- In sustaining, couples tune into each other's earthly troubling story; in healing, couples unite to tune into Christ's eternal faith story.

Healing involves *mind* renewal, but even more than that it stresses *relationship* renewal—knowing Christ, the power of his resurrection, and the fellowship of his suffering so that we become like Christ (Phil. 3:10) and glorify Christ (Phil. 1:11). The Confessional Statement of the Biblical

Counseling Coalition captures the truth that we point people to a relationship with Christ:

> We point people to a person, Jesus our Redeemer, and not to a program, theory, or experience. We place our trust in the transforming power of the Redeemer as the only hope to change people's hearts, not in any human system of change. People need a personal and dynamic relationship with Jesus, not a system of self-salvation, self-management, or self-actualization (John 14:6). Wise counselors seek to lead struggling, hurting, sinning, and confused people to the hope, resources, strength, and life that are available only in Christ.[1]

Maturing as a Biblical Marriage Counselor
Hoping in Christ Alone

1. Imagine you are meeting with Carlos and Angela—and repeatedly hearing their negative perspective.

   a. How and for how long do you compassionately enter their pain (sustaining)?

   b. How would you attempt to crop Christ's hope into their picture—without coming across as ignoring their pain or being too heavenly minded to be of any earthly good?

2. We described marital healing as driving a stake in the heart of Satan's lies by encouraging couples to trust God's good heart; as couples inviting the resurrected Christ into their marital casket; and as couples uniting to tune into Christ's eternal faith story.

   a. For you, which of these summary descriptions best captures your calling as a biblical marriage counselor in the marital healing process?

   b. For each of these descriptions, what one or two passages would you go to when working with a couple toward each of those goals?

3. Reread the excerpt from the Biblical Counseling Coalition's confessional statement.

   a. How could this statement shape your approach to biblical marriage counseling through marital healing?

   b. What is the difference between pointing couples to a program, theory, or experience, versus pointing a couple to Jesus their Redeemer?

Inviting Couples to Crop the Life of Christ into Their Marital Life (1 Pet. 2:18–3:7)

In chapter 8, we introduced couples to Christ's truth and grace eternal narrative by sharing the end of God's story: *life is a virtuous wedding and a victorious war*. However, for Angela and Carlos, their marriage feels neither virtuous nor victorious. We do not pretend their current marriage is great. Nor do we swoop in with "the power of positive thinking," where we are so heavenly minded that we are of no earthly good. Instead, we journey with them, pivoting between their earthly suffering and Christ's eternal hope as we integrate God's eternal story into their earthly story. We are so heavenly minded that we are of great earthly good.

In 1 Peter 2:18–3:7, Peter serves as a biblical marriage counselor by connecting the life of Christ directly to marital life. Twice in 1 Peter 3:1–7, Peter says "in the same way" to wives and husbands. In the same way as what? In 1 Peter 2:18–25, Peter counsels his readers to face suffering (sustaining) face-to-face with the Father (healing) in the same way Jesus did.

First-century couples, especially wives, faced horrific marital suffering. In 1 Peter 3:1–2, Peter addresses wives of nonbelieving husbands. In the culture of the day, wives had few if any rights. Additionally, in that culture everyone expected the wife to follow the religion of her husband. A wife's conversion to Christ was seen as demeaning her husband—creating even greater tension in an already tense marital culture. Peter speaks into this marital suffering: *in the same way that Christ endured suffering, so wives endure suffering*. Peter says it even more pointedly: "To this you were called, because Christ suffered for you, leaving you an example, that you should follow in his steps" (1 Pet.

2:21). The famous "in his steps" passage applies directly to how to hope in God when handling marital suffering.

Cling to Christ by Facing Suffering Face-to-Face with the Father

In 1 Peter 2:23, Peter makes a direct correlation between how Christ handled suffering and how we handle suffering: "When he suffered, he made no threats. Instead, he entrusted himself to him who judges justly." The word "entrusted" pictures Christ taking his soul, his self, and his well-being and handing them over to his Father. This is what Jesus did on the cross when he commended his spirit into his Father's hands (Luke 23:46). Total trust. Total surrender. Total Father-sufficiency.

Why could Jesus do this? How can we? By having a biblical view of God—seeing our heavenly Father as the God who judges justly (1 Pet. 2:23). Satan tempts us to doubt the Father's good heart. Jesus models what we depicted in chapter 7—trusting in the God who is in caring control, the God who is affectionately sovereign, the God who is our Shepherd-King of Holy Love.

Slaves were also part of the household in ancient Near Eastern culture. In 1 Peter 2:18, Peter urges slaves to submit even to inconsiderate, harsh masters, "for it is commendable if someone bears up under the pain of unjust suffering because they are conscious of God." The phrase "conscious of God" conveys our idea of cropping Christ into the picture. It portrays the concept of *coram Deo* living—living all of life face-to-face with the Father, constantly aware of God and factoring him into every situation. Peter is saying that God makes a difference when others are indifferent. The Father is caring, compassionate, and protective when others are uncaring and harsh.

What might it sound like to walk through this passage with Angela and Carlos?

- First, Angela and Carlos, let's be clear that this passage is *not* a free ticket for verbally abusive marital behavior. Let's not take this section out of its larger scriptural context. Husbands are *not* to be harsh. Wives are *not* to be disrespectful. That sort of behavior must be eliminated, taken to Christ in repentance, and taken to a spouse by seeking forgiveness. Nor is this passage suggesting that abusive behavior is to be tolerated. Instead, it is saying, "Don't take matters into your own hands by returning evil for evil. Trust Christ and the body of Christ—and legal authorities when necessary—to address and deal with sinful marital behavior." Are we clear on this? Any questions, concerns, or fears we should address?
- Second, this passage is highlighting our thoughts and affections during marital suffering. When you're hypercritical of each other, the flesh tempts you to fight back, lash out, be self-protective, and be

hurtful. Jesus models being constantly aware of God (our mindset) and constantly entrusting ourselves to our good, good Father (our soul-set).

- So, let's go back to the mutually hurtful conversation you both just described. What difference could it have made, Carlos and Angela, if in the moment of suffering, each of you were *conscious of Christ*— focused on his goodness and glory?

- What difference could it have made if, instead of trusting in yourself, you made a conscious choice to *entrust yourself to your Father who judges justly*?

- You each felt like you had to verbally defend yourself against the other's criticism. What if you had surrendered to God and let him be your verbal defender, your advocate, your defense attorney, your Shepherd-King who cares and is in control?

- What could it look like for each of you to hope in God by being conscious of God and entrusting yourself to God in the midst of your suffering?

Imitate Christ by Shepherding Even When Suffering

When we talk about WWJD (What Would Jesus Do?) we rarely keep it in its original context: What would Jesus do in the midst of suffering? What would Jesus think (WWJT) in the midst of suffering? How would Jesus relate (HWJR) to God and others in the midst of suffering? Christ was not passive while suffering. If we are to walk "in his steps," it means imitating Christ by shepherding others even while suffering. Peter indicates we can do this in at least three ways:

- A Refusal to Harm (1 Pet. 2:23)
- A Decision to Heal (1 Pet. 2:24)
- A Demonstration of Hope in God (1 Pet. 2:25)

A Refusal to Harm

"When they hurled their insults at him, he did not retaliate; when he suffered, he made no threats. Instead, he entrusted himself to him who judges justly" (1 Pet. 2:23). Imagine how this could de-escalate most marital conflict! Jesus models the refusal to reciprocate in kind, the refusal to retaliate and take vengeance. No witty, cutting comebacks. No sharp, hurtful put-downs. No subtle (or not-so-subtle) cold shoulders. No defensive self-protection—because we consciously see the Father as our Protector, Shield, and Defender.

A Decision to Heal

"'He himself bore our sins' in his body on the cross, so that we might die to sins and live for righteousness; 'by his wounds you have been healed'" (1 Pet. 2:24). In the context, Jesus is healing the very people who are wounding him! That response would de-escalate a lot of marital conflict. "You're wounding me. That's wrong, and I will not simply be your verbal punching bag. However, I love you. How can I minister to you? I care about you. How can I help you?"

A Demonstration of Hope in God

"For 'you were like sheep going astray,' but now you have returned to the Shepherd and Overseer of your souls" (1 Pet. 2:25). The sheep who were going astray killed their Shepherd! Yet the Shepherd still shepherds and oversees the souls of his crucifiers. Amazing! This is what it means to walk *in his steps*—we so entrust ourselves to the Father and hope in him that we are willing to shepherd those who are crucifying us.

What might it sound like to walk through this passage with Angela and Carlos?

- Angela and Carlos, how could each of you tap into Christ's resurrection power *right when you are being criticized* and choose not to retaliate? If that seems impossible right now, are you willing to work with me toward that level of maturity in Christ?
- What would it take, in the middle of a fight, for one of you to say, "I love you. How can I minister to you? How can I help you?"
- Jesus was willing to shepherd those who were crucifying him. What would it look like for one or both of you to make that choice?

Maturing as a Biblical Marriage Counselor
Inviting Couples to Crop the Life of Christ into Their Marital Life

1. When counseling a spouse not to retaliate, we never communicate that this means they are to passively accept abusive behavior. In marriage counseling, how do you balance these truths: entrust yourself to Christ and the body of Christ rather than retaliating, yet do not accept abusive behavior?

---

2. Picture a couple in marital crisis. How could you use 1 Peter 2:18 and 2:23 to help each spouse cling to Christ by facing suffering face-to-face with the Father? What would it look like to help them be conscious of God and entrust themselves to the God who judges justly?

3. Picture a couple in marital crisis.

    a. How could you use 1 Peter 2:23 to explore how to imitate Christ in his refusal to harm?

    b. How could you use 1 Peter 2:24 to explore how to imitate Christ in his decision to heal?

    c. How could you use 1 Peter 2:25 to explore how to imitate Christ in his demonstration of hope in God, which led to a commitment to shepherd those who were crucifying him?

4. In the trialogue vignettes with Carlos and Angela, you read, "If that seems impossible right now, are you willing to work with me toward that level of maturity in Christ?" We will further explore the maturity process in chapters 12 and 13 under biblical guiding. With what you know now, how would you help a couple like Carlos and Angela to grow in grace (sanctification, spiritual maturity, spiritual formation) so that their marital life would reflect more of the life of Christ?

Trialoguing about Christ's Truth and Grace Eternal Narrative

I have written about trialogues in at least half a dozen books. In each book, I wrestle with how best to communicate the essence of trialogues. In book form, trialogues can come across as a series of questions. That's too stilted and non-relational an image. Trialogues are relevant, relational discussion prompters suited for a specific couple, where together we apply the truth of a particular biblical passage or scriptural principle to their unique situation and soul issues.

I like the idea communicated by the phrase "gospel conversations." Biblical marriage counseling involves personal, relational conversations where we seek to relate the gospel (the good news of Christ's life, death, burial, resurrection, ascension, and return) to marital life today—trialogues.

In this section, we illustrate gospel conversation trialogues with Angela and Carlos, using Romans 8 to apply relevant biblical truths to their marital struggles. Any of these sample gospel conversations could easily lead into interactions taking most of a counseling session.

> BOB: So, Angela and Carlos, last week I asked you both to spend the week meditating on Romans 8:1–39 and specific biblical application to your marriage situation—especially focusing on where you see Christ's resurrection hope and power relating to your marriage. I also spent the week focused on this passage for you. There are several directions I think we could head. But where would each of you prefer we start?
>
> ANGELA: Carlos encouraged me to share first. He and I both were struck by the first verse. "Therefore, there is now no condemnation for those who are in Christ Jesus." You won't be surprised, Pastor Bob, to hear that we spend a lot of time condemning each other. With your help and the Spirit's help, we're gradually changing. But the memory of the shaming words sticks with us. So it's been wonderful to be reminded that the God of the universe never condemns us because of Christ. (*Angela pauses tearfully. I wait.*)
>
> BOB: I can see how powerfully this is impacting you, Angela. You mentioned that you both have been encouraged by this truth of your acceptance in Christ. I'd love to hear how each of you is applying this eternal truth right in the moment when you're being criticized by your spouse.
>
> CARLOS: We both talked about that, Pastor Bob. We've both noticed a growing ability to catch ourselves and stop the verbal battle. For me, it's been like, "I hate the pain of Angela's rejection, but since the Father accepts me in Christ, I'm not running on empty." I think I used to use Angela to fill me up so I felt good about myself—and that never worked. Now I'm clinging to Christ and asking him to help me fill up Angela.
>
> BOB: That's a great point, Carlos. Remember when we talked about Jeremiah 2:13 and our choice to turn either to broken cisterns that hold no water or to God, the Spring of Living Water? What I hear you saying is that increasingly you're in awe of God and you're turning to him more and more. I love the fact that you're not doing it "just to

feel good." You're doing it to be filled *so* you can fill Angela. That's great growth! What do you think of that, Angela? Have you seen Carlos making these changes?

As another example, consider how we might use Romans 8:17–39 as a hope-giving gospel conversation trialogue for Angela and Carlos.

BOB: (*After wrapping up our conversation on Romans 8:1 by collaboratively discussing a homework assignment, I shift us to Romans 8:17–39.*) That's great stuff, Angela and Carlos, from just one verse—Romans 8:1. Let's at least start thinking through how a longer section—Romans 8:17–39—might apply to your marriage. How about we each take turns reading one verse until we've read all of 8:17–39?

(*We read the passage together.*)

BOB: As we read, did you notice how several times this passage moves back and forth from suffering to hope?

ANGELA: Yeah, I did. I couldn't help but think about the picture you drew for us of the casket and the empty tomb. As we read, I kept picturing the resurrected Jesus climbing in our casket.

CARLOS: I agree. When we read about the groaning and the frustration and the wordless groans or moaning in grief and pain, I thought about what you've taught us—Jesus gives us permission to grieve and Jesus invites us to lament to the Father. That's been so helpful, because I've started doing less complaining to and about Angela and more lamenting to God . . .

BOB: I'm sure Angela appreciates that! But seriously, that's another sign of great growth. Angela, have you noticed that?

ANGELA: Yes, but no. I'm not going to go there. The "yes but" isn't fair. I *have* noticed Carlos biting his tongue . . .

BOB: Angela, maybe instead of telling me about it, share with Carlos what you've noticed and what it's meant to you. Oh, I really appreciate how you caught yourself with the "yes but." So, Carlos, when Angela is done, maybe it would be helpful for you to share with her what it meant to you that Angela did catch herself . . .

Now consider a final trialogue sampler, this one from Romans 8:31–32.

BOB: As I read this passage this week, there were two verses that I wanted to be sure we discussed and applied—8:31–32. "What, then, shall we say in response to these things? If God is for us, who can be against us? He who did not spare his own Son, but gave him up for us all— how will he not also, along with him, graciously give us all things?"

I know the two of you have been against each other at times. Paul is saying that no one—including your spouse—can be against you *in a way that defeats you*—if you truly believe that *God is for you.* I think that's huge for the two of you—for all of us. We know *theologically* that God is for us. We know, as Paul says, that the Father once-for-all proves his "for-ness" by not sparing his Son but giving him up for Bob, Carlos, and Angela. But personally, do you view God as being for *you*, Carlos? As being for *you*, Angela? Let's make this really practical. I'd like each of you to think about a recent time when it felt like your spouse was against you. But don't stop there. Now I want you to think about how you could have brought this truth into that situation: *God is for you—he demonstrated it by not sparing his own Son . . .*

Think about the practice we are illustrating: trialoguing about Christ's truth and grace eternal narrative. Then consider the practice of fighting Satan's lying and condemning earthly narrative. We are using Romans 8 to help Angela and Carlos reinterpret life from Christ's perspective. With Christ cropped out, they kept turning to each other as broken cisterns that hold no water. With Christ cropped in, they still feel the pain and emptiness of their fallen, finite spouse. However, now Christ's resurrection hope is beginning to empower them to minister to each other.

Maturing as a Biblical Marriage Counselor
Trialoguing about Christ's Truth and Grace Eternal Narrative

1. Notice in the trialogue vignettes that even when there are teaching and explaining times, they never stop there. They always bring the gospel conversation back to Angela and Carlos and ask them to ponder, apply, and interact.

   a. What is your style as a marriage counselor? Are you more directive—more of a teacher/teller? Or are you more collaborative—teaching and then drawing out the couple?

   b. If you tend to be less collaborative, what could you do to develop more of a gospel conversation mode where you take advantage of the personal ministry of the Word to be sure that the couple ponders, applies, and interacts?

---

2. In the trialogue interaction about Romans 8:17–39, notice how Carlos and Angela were directed to interact with each other rather than just talking to their counselor.

   a. What is your style as a marriage counselor? Do your sessions tend to focus more on each spouse talking individually to you? Or do you work to help the couple talk to each other?

   b. If you tend to have each spouse talk mainly to you, how could you help the couple in the session talk more to each other as they relate God's truth to their marriage?

3. Think about Carlos and Angela and their pattern of hyper-condemnation of each other. Choose any two sections of Romans 8 and craft one trialogue gospel conversation for each section, where you help them apply the truth of that passage to their specific marital issue.

   Trialogue Gospel Conversation #1

   Trialogue Gospel Conversation #2

Healing Individually and Together in Christ

Biblical healing is *not* the removal of all pain. It is not fixing every feeling. It is not changing my circumstances. Those are fine areas to pray about and legitimate desires to have. However, God does not promise there will be no more pain, crying, sorrow, loss, and suffering this side of heaven.

Healing Defined: "Our Marriage Is All about Him"

What then is biblical healing? Healing is not about fixing me but about fixing my eyes on Christ. Healing is not about my happiness but about my·

holiness in Christ. Healing is not about my immediate good but about God's ultimate glory. A healed or healing couple lives out Ephesians 1:3–14 by saying, "More than anything else, we want our marriage to be to the praise of God's glorious grace. We want people to realize that our marriage was not resurrected by our power but through Christ's grace." A healed or healing couple lives out Ephesians 3:9–11 by saying, "We want our resurrected marriage to make known to the watching world the manifold wisdom and infinite grace of Christ."

Healed Couples Pictured: "Our Lives Are All about Reflecting Him"

What does a maturing (healing) couple look like? What are marks of a Christ-like couple?

- *Circumstantial/Situational*: The ability to remain under suffering without giving in to sin, without giving up hope, and with a commitment to glorify God (Rom. 5:3–5; 1 Cor. 10:13; Eph. 3:10).
- *Emotional*: Experiencing God's comforting, caring, compassionate presence (2 Cor. 1:3–7) in such a way that we are hard pressed but not crushed, perplexed but hopeful (2 Cor. 4:7–9), grieving but not without hope (1 Thess. 4:13).
- *Volitional* (Will/Choices/Motivation): Desiring a change in circumstances or feelings but choosing, like Christ, that not our will but God's will be done (Matt. 26:39).
- *Rational*: Cropping the cross of Christ (Rom. 8:32–33) and Christ's resurrection power into our picture (Rom. 8:37–39) so that we interpret life from God's eternal, end-of-the-story perspective (2 Cor. 4:16–18; Heb. 10:24–26; Rev. 19:1–21).
- *Relational/Social*: Being so conscious of God as our just Judge that we choose to shepherd each other even in our suffering (1 Pet. 2:18–25).
- *Relational/Self-Aware*: Experiencing God's shalom (peace, wholeness) regardless of how others see me or what others think of me (Rom. 12:3; 1 Cor. 4:3–5) because my identity is embedded in who I am *in* Christ and *to* Christ (Rom. 8:1, 14–15, 31–39).
- *Relational/Spiritual*: Worshiping God—exalting and enjoying God—by living for the praise of his glorious grace (Eph. 1:3–14) and by enjoying him even in the midst of suffering (1 Pet. 1:7–10).

Saying "Our marriage is all about him" and "Our lives are all about reflecting him" are *drastically* different descriptions of healing than what most couples focus on when they enter marriage counseling. Chapters 8 and 9 have been about journeying with couples from the world's healing focus to the Word's healing focus. Scriptural explorations and spiritual conversations help couples make this transition and transformation.

Healing, Hope-Giving Scriptural Explorations

In scriptural exploration trialogues you examine a relevant biblical passage and explore couple-specific applications. Here is a sample pattern for hope-giving trialogues:

- Based on this passage, how would the two of you envision God working your story out for his glory?
- What biblical images of God from this passage will be vital for the two of you as you seek God's wisdom for your marriage?
- Based on this passage, how would the two of you envision God working your story out for good?
- Based on principles from this passage, how would you see God giving you resurrection power in your marital story?
- What timeless principles from this passage could you apply to your marriage today?
- What in this passage would you like to add to your marital story? How could you do that?

Since we want to empower couples, rather than always directing them to a particular passage we think is relevant, we can ask:

- What passages have deepened your relationship to and trust in Christ?
- What passages have the two of you found helpful in gaining God's perspective on your marriage?
- What Scriptures have the two of you found helpful in gaining encouragement as you experience this?

Healing, Hope-Giving Spiritual Conversations

Recall the essence of spiritual conversation trialogues. We interact with couples about how they can apply broad biblical principles to their marriage.

God-Glorifying Spiritual Conversations

Here we help couples shift their focus from themselves to God.

- In Ephesians 3:7–11, Paul teaches that the universe—the angelic host—is watching our lives. They want to see whether God is trustworthy. What message is your marriage sending?
- In Ephesians 1:3–14, Paul says that everything in life is to be for the praise of God's glorious grace. How could your marriage relationship bring praise to God's grace?
- In Job 1–2, Satan claimed that Job served God only because of the blessings he received. Job's trials were an opportunity to reveal that he loved the Giver more than the gifts. In your marital trials, how could you live for God's glory even when life is hard?

Cross-Focused Spiritual Conversations

Here we explore how Christ's death for us impacts our hope in God in the midst of marital discouragement.

- What difference could it make in your view of God if every time Satan tempted the two of you to doubt God, you reflected on passages about the cross of Christ such as John 3:16, Romans 5, Ephesians 1, or Colossians 1?
- When everything seems darkest and your doubts are the strongest, what passages could you turn to regarding the cross of Christ and God's grace-love for you?
- When everything seems aligned against you and your marriage, what difference could it make to know that the cross forever proves that God is for you?

Resurrection-Hope Spiritual Conversations

We can co-author *resurrection-hope* narratives that unite our helplessness in ourselves with God's power at work within us through Christ (2 Cor. 1:8–11; 12:7–10).

- In your suffering, how has Christ's strength been made perfect in your weakness?
- Paul says that the same power that raised Christ from the dead is in *you* (Eph. 1:15–23). What difference does it make in your response to your marital suffering when you live according to Christ's resurrection power?
- Paul says in Philippians 3:10 that he wants to know the power of Christ's resurrection. How can each of you tap into Christ's power at work in you?

- In Romans 8:37, Paul calls us "more than conquerors" in Christ. How could that truth impact how you respond to each other during your marital conflict?

Heroes-in-Christ Spiritual Conversations

We can co-author *heroes-in-Christ* narratives. Satan attempts to blind us to Christ's past and current work in our lives. Helping a couple to see Christ at work in their marriage gives them confidence in his ongoing and future work. David was confident that God would empower him to defeat Goliath because *previously* God had empowered him to defeat a lion and a bear.

- How has Christ already been giving you some victory in this area of your marital relationship?
- Tell me about some times when, through Christ's strength, the two of you are already defeating some of these problems.
- Have the two of you ever struggled with anything like this before? How did you overcome it together through Christ then? What could you take from that past victory and use now?

Celebration Spiritual Conversations

We can co-author *celebration* narratives. When couples share a recent time of victory, we can respond with:

- What do these recent times of victory say about the two of you and Christ?
- If you each applied what you learned from those victorious times this past week, what would you do to work through this new issue?
- In light of that time of marital victory, what will you two do differently this week?

Healing-through-Christ Spiritual Conversations

Resurrection hope does not eliminate all problems and pain, so we co-author narratives focused on healing through Christ.

- Tell me how it impacts each of you to know that Christ is suffering with you right now. That he's praying for you.
- What would it look like for each of you to rest in God right now?
- How is all of this helping you cling to Christ?
- What would it be like for each of you to worship God in the middle of this?

Maturing as a Biblical Marriage Counselor
Healing Individually and Together in Christ

1. On page 172, you read a list of seven marks of a maturing, Christlike couple.

   a. On a scale of 1–10, with 10 being the most Christlike, assess your current level of Christlikeness in each of those seven areas.

   _____ Circumstantial/Situational

   _____ Emotional

   _____ Volitional

   _____ Rational

   _____ Relational/Social

   _____ Relational/Self-aware

   _____ Relational/Spiritual

   b. Which of those seven areas would you most like to keep maturing in? How could you do that?

2. On page 173, you read a sample pattern for healing, hope-giving scriptural explorations. Take an issue, struggle, or relationship in your own life, select a relevant passage, and work through the scriptural exploration.

3. On pages 174–76 you read sample patterns for healing, hope-giving spiritual conversations.

   a. Craft three sample glorifying-God conversations.

b. Craft three sample cross-focused conversations.

c. Craft three sample resurrection-hope conversations.

d. Craft three sample heroes-in-Christ conversations.

e. Craft three sample celebration conversations.

f. Craft three sample healing-through-Christ conversations.

Transitioning

Chapters 5–9 focused on *parakaletic* marriage counseling to help suffering couples comfort one another (sustaining) and hope in God together (healing). As a biblical marriage counselor, the thirteen marriage counseling competencies you have learned thus far will further equip you to help couples to:

- Empathize with each other by climbing in the casket together (sustaining).
- Encourage each other by celebrating the empty tomb and experiencing Christ's resurrection power and hope in their marriage (healing).

Chapters 10–13 shift our focus to *nouthetic* marriage counseling, which will help couples to address sin in their lives by receiving Christ's grace (reconciling) and to grow in grace in their marriage (guiding). You will learn nine marriage counseling competencies to further equip you to help couples to:

- Enlighten each other to apply the truth that it's horrible to sin against Christ and each other, but through Christ it's wonderful to be forgiven and to forgive (reconciling).
- Empower each other to apply the truth that in Christ, it's supernatural to love each other like Christ (guiding).

TEN

Dispensing Grace

Reconciling in Marriage Counseling, Part 1

Introduction: Whatever Happened to Sin . . . and Grace?

You know I believe the fall and sin are crucial aspects of marriage counseling (see chapter 2). You know that our marriage counseling model includes nouthetic counseling for marital sin and sanctification (see chapter 4). Still, as we journeyed through parakaletic counseling for suffering couples in chapters 5–9, you may have been thinking, "Whatever happened to sin?" Fair question. Consider three responses.

First, the fact that we spent five chapters on suffering in marriage does not mean that we start with suffering for every couple we counsel. In book form it might seem like a linear approach, where we always address suffering first and only start tackling sin later. No. Not at all. Remember our image of marriage counseling as spaghetti relationships. Every couple is different. *Each marriage counseling case involves a different starting place & different emphasis.* All biblical marriage counseling will move all over the place, from suffering to sin, from sin to suffering, a little sustaining here, some guiding there, reconciling now, healing then. My purpose is to teach a comprehensive biblical approach. Your focus is to apply various aspects of that marriage counseling model in whatever order or combination is biblically most appropriate for a specific couple.

Second, while I am not suggesting a straitjacket approach where you must start with suffering, there is biblical precedence for assuring couples that you *At the same time, we must demonstrate we care about ppl's pain & sorrows.* care about their hurt—as a foundation for lovingly confronting couples about their sin. Ponder Jesus and the Pharisees.

Jesus clearly supported the Pharisees' right to address sin. "The teachers of the law and the Pharisees sit in Moses' seat. So you must be careful to do everything they tell you" (Matt. 23:2–3). However, Jesus confronted their lack of compassionate care. "They tie up heavy, cumbersome loads and put them on other people's shoulders, but they themselves are not willing to lift a finger to move them" (Matt. 4:4). The Pharisees were skilled sin spotters and sin confronters. They were lousy casket climbers and resurrection-hope givers.

Yes, there are times in marriage counseling when I lead with confrontation of sin, especially in crisis situations involving marital abuse. Yet I want to be careful never to counsel like a heartless Pharisee who coldly confronts sin without ever stopping to identify with suffering.

My reason for this is both relational and theological. Relationally, when a suffering husband knows I care about his hurt, he is much more apt to listen when I expose his sin. Theologically, the Christian couples I am counseling, in their core identity in Christ, are saints and sons/daughters who endure suffering and battle against sin as they pursue sanctification. I do not look at a sinning wife primarily through the grid of sinner. I look at that Christian wife first through the grid of saint and daughter of God. This always impacts *how* I confront sin; it often impacts *when* I confront sin.

while a Christian is still a sinner, they are first & foremost a saint. Thus, this should influence the how and when of sin confrontation.

Third, in addition to asking, "Whatever happened to sin?" we should also be asking, "Whatever happened to *grace*?" Some of us are good at exposing sin. Are we even better at magnifying grace? We should be, because where sin abounds, grace superabounds (Rom. 5:20). This is why our image for reconciling is of marriage counselors as dispensers of grace.

Biblical counselors are there to not just expose sin, but magnify the grace present in the gospel of Jesus Christ.

Consider Jesus's words to the Pharisees: "Woe to you, teachers of the law and Pharisees, you hypocrites! You give a tenth of your spices—mint, dill and cumin. But you have neglected the more important matters of the law—justice, mercy, and faithfulness" (Matt. 23:23). The Pharisees were good at insisting on the external letter of the law; they were horrible at the gospel and matters of the heart. They got the law; they did not grasp grace.

This is why marital reconciling does not stop with "It's horrible to sin against Christ and each other . . ." Exposing sin is vital. However, magnifying grace is essential. This is why marital reconciling continues with ". . . but through Christ it's wonderful to be forgiven and to forgive."

In marital reconciling, sinning spouses must see the plank in their own eye (Matt. 7:3–5). But having identified that plank, we do not beat spouses over the head with it. Instead, we gently and humbly carry their burden, fulfilling Christ's law of love (Gal. 6:1–2). Unlike the Pharisees, we direct spouses to Christ's gospel of grace and forgiveness (1 John 1:8–10). Then Christ's great forgiveness in their life motivates each spouse to be forgiving (Luke 7:47).

spouses do not just identify each other's sin or even their own sin and beat themselves upon it. They are to carry one another's burdens and to direct each other to the gospel.

Seeing & reflecting on our own forgiveness should drive us to forgive others in love of God.

Sadly, couples rarely come to us with grace as their main focus. Instead, they come with sin, shame, and guilt that lead to separation. Lacking shalom, couples desperately need peace with God and with each other—reconciliation. So biblical marriage counselors follow a PEACE plan in the reconciling process:

P Probing Theologically: Taking a Biblical MRI of the Marital Heart (chap. 10)

E Exposing Marital Heart Sins: Care-Fronting Marital Heart Sin Humbly, Gently, Lovingly, and Wisely (chap. 10)

A Applying Truth Relationally (chap. 11)

C Calming the Conscience with Grace (chap. 11)

E Enlightening Couples about Biblical Marital Reconciliation (chap. 11)

Maturing as a Biblical Marriage Counselor
Whatever Happened to Sin . . . and Grace?

1. Several times you have encountered the image of marriage counseling as "spaghetti relationships"—a relational process where we move back and forth between suffering and sin, sustaining and healing, reconciling and guiding.

   a. How much should marriage counseling be a science—structured so you identify a biblical process and follow it vigilantly? How might this approach impact your marriage counseling?

   b. How much should marriage counseling be an art—a process that guides you, but you follow it creatively in a way that fits each couple and situation? How might this approach impact your marriage counseling?

2. Have you been thinking, "Bob, whatever happened to sin?" If so, how well or poorly does this chapter's introduction address your question? What further questions or concerns might you have?

3. I state the following: "All biblical marriage counseling will move all over the place, from suffering to sin, from sin to suffering, a little sustaining here, some guiding there, reconciling now, healing then." Agree or disagree? Why or why not?

4. "The Pharisees were skilled sin spotters and sin confronters. They were lousy casket climbers and resurrection-hope givers." How might those descriptors impact how you provide biblical marriage counseling?

5. "Whatever happened to *grace*? Some of us are good at exposing sin. Are we even better at magnifying grace? We should be, because where sin abounds, grace superabounds (Rom. 5:20)." In what specific ways might those sentences impact your approach to biblical marriage counseling?

Preliminary Crisis Intervention Stage:
Interrupting Destructive Marital Patterns—Protecting Spouses

Before exploring the PEACE Plan of reconciling in marriage counseling, we need to consider a preliminary stage that is at times necessary. Some couples come to us for counseling and we begin to detect that one spouse is demonstrating a pattern of abuse. Other couples come to counseling without abuse issues but with a high level of mutual disdain. What do we do in such cases?

Contacting Authorities in Abuse Situations

When there is suspicion of abuse or accusations of abuse, appropriate authorities must be contacted. At times it may mean police or child protective services. At other times it may mean contacting legal authorities for a restraining order. Spouses (and children) must be protected.

Also in abusive marital situations, church leaders need to be contacted. The situation has expanded beyond marriage counseling to church discipline and restoration.

Crisis Intervention in Abuse Situations

In marital abuse, the focus shifts from marriage counseling to crisis intervention and individual counseling. The abused spouse is counseled with a focus on providing protection, support, empathy, comfort, care, consolation, guidance, and wisdom. The perpetrating spouse is counseled individually with a focus on identifying heart issues, coming to a place of true repentance, demonstrating ongoing fruit of repentance (see 2 Cor. 7:7–13), putting off old patterns, and putting on new patterns.

While there are varying opinions in the Christian world related to separation, it is my biblical conviction that for the protection and well-being of a spouse, at times separation must occur. Within this context, depending on the nature of the situation, the heart issues of the perpetrator, the readiness of the victim, the support structures in place, and timing issues, you may want to develop a specific separation plan. You collaboratively create with the couple, with extended family members, with an intervention support team, and with legal authorities a Restorative Separation Agreement. This spells out the reasons for the separation, parameters of the separation (including if, when, and under what conditions and in what places the couple will see each other), the timeline of the separation, necessary steps that *must* occur *over time* for the separation to end, accountability structures, and the details of the treatment plan (individual counseling, other church-related discipleship structures, legal accountability structures, etc.).[1]

Contracting with Couples in Situations of High Levels of Mutual Disdain

At other times, couples come to us without abuse issues but with high levels of mutual disdain. Depending on the nature of their relational interactions, the couple may be able to continue in marriage counseling. If so, it is wise to collaboratively develop a written contract. The nature of the contract varies depending on the nature of the relationship. The contract requires whatever stipulations, safeguards, and guarantees are necessary to disrupt mutually hurtful behavior. It could include an agreement not to discuss controversial issues for the time being except in your presence. It might include a commitment to contact you or another trusted individual if a conflict arises.

Changing Patterns in Situations of High Levels of Mutual Disdain: Doing Something Different

When the relational issues are serious, but are not deemed to be crisis-oriented or a danger to a spouse, you can create shorter-term intervention plans. Follow the premise: "If what you are doing is not working, then do something different." For example:

- When do most of your disagreements occur? Change the time and setting.
- What are most of your disagreements about? For the time being, do not discuss those issues except during counseling.
- Let's identify what you each tend to do to start and inflame the discussion . . . Now, let's agree that for the next week, Becky, you will *not* do ____. James, you will *not* do ____. Keep track, because I'm going to keep you accountable . . .

The goal is not to absolve either spouse of responsibility; it is not to deny problems. Our goal is to interrupt harmful patterns. The plan is temporary and crisis-oriented. When the relationship stabilizes, then teach and institute principles of conflict resolution and healthy communication.

Conflict Resolution and Communication Principles in Situations of High Levels of Mutual Disdain

Biblical marriage counseling is much more than teaching communication skills and conflict-resolution principles. However, there is a place for both of these relational competencies—especially when given to couples who are addressing their heart issues. You can discuss a document you created (with scriptural passages and principles), or you can assign a book or booklet on communication principles or conflict-resolution processes. Give them as a homework assignment and as ground rules that govern how the couple interacts.

Counseling Separately in Situations of High Levels of Mutual Disdain

When the relationship is so tense that joint marital counseling is unfruitful, it is often wise to temporarily counsel the spouses separately. Address individual maturity issues and help each spouse put off old sinful patterns and put on new Christlike patterns. Even when couples are not in crisis, I often do joint marital counseling along with individual biblical counseling.

Maturing as a Biblical Marriage Counselor
Preliminary Crisis Intervention Stage

1. Review the six crisis intervention recommendations: contacting authorities, crisis intervention, contracting with couples, changing patterns, conflict resolution and communication principles, and counseling separately.

    a. Which have you used? When? How? Which would you like to add to your marriage counseling ministry? Why? How?

    b. Which do you perhaps disagree with? Why? What would you do instead?

    c. What other crisis intervention responses do you recommend for marriage counseling?

2. Regarding abuse in marriage:

    a. Is your church a safe place for abuse victims? On what do you base your answer? How could your church become a safe or safer place for abuse victims?

b. How equipped do you believe you and your church are to address abuse issues in a marriage? What written resources could you and your church learn from in this area? What experts—either locally, regionally, nationally, or internationally—could you and your church learn from?

3. Reread the section on restorative separations.

   a. What is your view on couples temporarily separating? Support your convictions biblically.

   b. If you were to develop a Restorative Separation Agreement, what elements would you include? How would you word each element?

4. Review the section about "Confliction Resolution and Communication Principles in Situations of High Levels of Disdain."

   a. What are your go-to Scriptures when teaching about conflict resolution and communication?

   b. What are your go-to books or booklets you recommend for couples for conflict resolution and healthy communication?

Probing Theologically: Taking a Biblical MRI of the Marital Heart

Before we can lovingly expose marital sin, we need a biblical understanding of marital heart sin. What does a healthy marriage look like? What is the essence of an unhealthy marriage? What does the Bible say about the core marital heart sin of a husband? Of a wife? Chapters 1, 2, and 3 provided us with biblical answers to those questions through their examination of a creation-fall-redemption theological understanding of marriage.

- *Creation*: God's Ultimate Purpose for Marriage—God's Marital Design
- *Fall*: Our Core Problem in Marriage—Our Marital Heart Disease
- *Redemption*: Christ's Central Prescription for Marital Healing—Christ's Death for Sin and Our Death to Self

As we sit with a couple, we are not left to guess what is healthy or unhealthy, holy or unholy marital relating. We have a standard—God's standard. Our task is to turn our academic theology into a practical theology of marriage relationships. We do that by having relevant biblical diagnostic questions going through our mind as we counsel.

Marital Diagnostic Questions about the Gospel-Centered Foundation of Marriage

All *secular* models of marriage counseling reduce marriage to a set of principles and procedures designed to help couples better manage life without God. All *truly Christian* models of marriage counseling expand marriage to God's eternal perspective to help couples realize they cannot live by bread alone but by every word that comes from the mouth of God. So based on the book of Ephesians and on chapter 1 of this book, we ponder gospel-centered diagnostic probes as we listen to each spouse.

Marital Diagnostic Questions about the Purpose of Marriage

Based on the biblical purposes of marriage, we ponder these diagnostic probes as we listen to each spouse:

- To what extent is this couple thinking about how their marriage could reflect the intimacy within the Trinity? Or are they each focused on their own pain or happiness?
- To what extent is this couple considering that their marriage is meant to reflect the relationship between Christ and the church? Or are they each looking to the other to make them whole and happy?
- To what extent is it in this couple's mindset that a major purpose of their marriage is mutual discipleship in which they nurture each other to become more like Christ? Does this husband see himself as a shepherd who seeks to help his wife increasingly reflect Christ? Does

this wife see herself as her husband's encourager who seeks to help him increasingly reflect Christ?

Marital Diagnostic Questions about Marital Leaving, Cleaving, Weaving, and Receiving

Based on Genesis 2, we ponder these gospel-centered diagnostic probes as we listen to each spouse:

- *Leaving*: How well is this couple shifting their core loyalty from their parents to their spouse? Which of the following are they saying by their actions?

  » "Finally, I'm free from Mom and Dad! It's all about me and my freedom!"

  » "Our core loyalty to each other displays our core loyalty to Christ. Our marriage relationship is ultimately about showing the world how Christ and his bride are faithfully devoted to each other."

- *Cleaving*: How well is this couple demonstrating a loyal love and lifelong commitment to honor Christ in their marriage? Which of the following represents their heart attitude?

  » "Finally! I can feel loved. Someone will be devoted only and always to me!"

  » "Lord, may our loyal love be a reflection of your loyal love to us in Christ. When folks marvel at our commitment, help us point them back to your eternal commitment and our eternal security in Christ."

- *Weaving*: How well is this couple becoming interdependent and intertwined in one beautiful tapestry? Which of the following best represents their heart attitude?

  » "Finally! Someone will love me and complete me, and my self-esteem will blossom!"

  » "Thank you, Lord, for the marital joy of oneness in body, soul, and spirit. May I bring my spouse pleasure in every way, and may our mutual oneness reflect the eternal unity of Father, Son, and Holy Spirit."

- *Receiving*: How well is this couple communicating grace-knowing—awareness of sin without rejection, plus awareness of uniqueness without jealousy? Which of the following is the goal of their heart?

» "I demand that you wink at my sins."

» "I invite you to speak into my heart with exposure and encouragement."

Marital Diagnostic Questions about Marital Heart Disease

In chapter 2, we explored Genesis 3, Matthew 7, and James 4 as core passages exposing marital heart sin. Out of the heart the mouth speaks (Prov. 4:23; Matt. 12:34; Luke 6:45). If we relate intimately and listen intently and theologically, we will hear marital heart disease.

- *Shame*: In what ways are they shaming each other by attacking and questioning their spouse's character?
- *Blame*: In what ways are they failing to take responsibility and instead blaming their spouse for their emotions, actions, motivations, beliefs, and affections?
- *Claim*: To what degree am I sensing controlling behavior where they are trying to manipulate the other into meeting their needs?
- *Maim*: To what degree do they express an attitude of retaliation? "You've hurt me, now I'm going to make you pay!"
- *Plank and speck*: How aware is each spouse of their own role in their marital conflict? Are they saying, "The problem in our marriage is *you*"? Or are they able to recognize, "The problem in our marriage is *me*—my heart issues"?
- *Demandingness and illegitimate desires*: In what ways are they sinfully corrupting good desires into illegitimate demands?
- *Mishandling unmet legitimate desires*: In what ways are they responding sinfully to the unmet desires of their soul?
- *Idolatry*: How does each spouse answer the following questions: When I feel empty and powerless in my marriage, do I go to God or to myself? Do I acknowledge that I'm impoverished and poor in spirit? Is God my ultimate source of life?
- *Carnality*: Am I sensing any evidence of a carnal, self-serving attitude rather than an other-centered and God-glorifying mindset?
- *Spiritual adultery*: In what ways are they worshiping the creature instead of the Creator by turning from God as their Spring of Living Water and turning to their spouse as a broken cistern that can hold no water?

Marital Diagnostic Questions about the Husband's Ministry Calling: An Empowering Shepherd Who Loves Sacrificially

In chapter 3, we examined the husband's and wife's redeemed ministry callings. We probe these theologically by asking ourselves diagnostic questions about how the husband is living out his role.

- How well or poorly is this husband being an initiator who starts the chain of love?
- How well or poorly is this husband being a sacrificial shepherd who loves his wife passionately?
- How well or poorly is this husband being a sanctifying pastor who offers his wife impacting love?
- How well or poorly is this husband being the head who offers his wife nourishing, cherishing, and honoring love?
- How well or poorly is this husband being a servant leader who offers his wife empowering love?

Marital Diagnostic Questions about the Wife's Ministry Calling: An Encouraging Intimate Ally Who Loves Respectfully

We probe theologically by asking ourselves diagnostic questions about how the wife is living out her ministry role.

- How well or poorly is this wife living out her role as a suitable helper who offers her husband responding/corresponding love?
- How well or poorly is this wife being vulnerably submissive as she openly receives her husband's loving headship?
- How well or poorly is this wife being an encourager who offers her husband respectful love?
- How well or poorly is this wife being a refuge-giver who offers her husband loving, gentle strength?

The marital diagnostic questions you just read may reveal a great deal of sinning. However, they may also reveal much potential maturity. In *guiding*, when you see maturity, you spur it on and fan it into flame. In *reconciling*, when you see immaturity, you expose it gently, patiently, humbly, and lovingly—so that no spouse is hardened by sin's deceitfulness.

Maturing as a Biblical Marriage Counselor
Probing Theologically

1. You read, "All *secular* models of marriage counseling reduce marriage to a set of principles and procedures designed to help couples better manage life without God. All *truly Christian* models of marriage counseling expand marriage to God's eternal perspective to help couples realize they cannot live by bread alone but by every word that comes from the mouth of God." In what specific ways could you apply these truths to your marriage counseling ministry?

2. Of the thirty marital diagnostic questions:

    a. Which ones most convict you in your life? If you are married, which ones most convict you in your marriage?

    b. Which ones strike you as most important to have in mind as you listen to spouses interacting with you and with each other?

    c. Which ones have you seen the most in couples you have counseled? If you have yet to do marriage counseling, which of these have you seen the most in couples you know?

3. Review the five questions related to the husband's ministry calling.

   a. If you are a husband, assess yourself in each of these five areas and map out a personal growth plan.

   b. What specific words, attitudes, actions, and ways of relating would you look for in a husband you were counseling that would help you discern how well or poorly he was living out each calling?

4. Review the four questions related to the wife's ministry calling.

   a. If you are a wife, assess yourself in each of these four areas and map out a personal growth plan.

   b. What specific words, attitudes, actions, and ways of relating would you look for in a wife you were counseling that would help you discern how well or poorly she was living out each calling?

Exposing Marital Heart Sins: Care-Fronting Marital Heart Sin Humbly, Gently, Lovingly, and Wisely

Some sinning spouses come to us aware of and repentant over their sin. Paul teaches that for folks like this, calming the conscience is needed (see 2 Cor. 2:5–11 and our next chapter).

Other sinning spouses come to us blind to the plank in their eye (Matt. 7:3–5), hardened by sin's deceitfulness (Heb. 3:13), or ensnared, trapped, and taken captive by the devil (2 Tim. 2:24–26). For a husband or wife like this,

God calls us to confront. Or, as I like to say it, God calls us to "care-front"—to expose marital heart sin humbly and gently (Gal. 6:1), lovingly (Eph. 4:15), and wisely (2 Tim. 2:24–26).

The Heart of the Marital Care-Fronter: Confronting out of Caring Concern

If you enjoy confronting others, you may not be very good at it. Enjoying confrontation may indicate some hubris, pride, and anger. In 2 Corinthians 7:8–9, Paul describes the tension he experiences as a result of having to confront the Corinthians: "Even if I caused you sorrow by my letter, I do not regret it. Though I did regret it—I see that my letter hurt you, but only for a little while—yet now I am happy, not because you were made sorry, but because your sorrow led you to repentance." Paul does not enjoy making others sorrowful with words of confrontation. The only joy he takes is in the result—repentance.

Paul preaches what he practices. As he mentors young Pastor Timothy, Paul writes in the context of confronting sin, "The Lord's servant . . . must be kind to everyone, able to teach, not resentful. Opponents must be gently instructed" (2 Tim. 2:24–25). When we confront/care-front in biblical marriage counseling, could a couple say of us, "Though you needed to confront us, you were kind and gentle, not harsh and resentful"?

Paul preaches the same message to the Galatians in the context of a brother or sister being caught in a sin and needing restorative confrontation. "Brothers and sisters, if someone is caught in a sin, you who live by the Spirit should restore that person gently. But watch yourselves, or you also may be tempted" (Gal. 6:1). Could a couple say of us, "Though you needed to confront us, you did it gently and humbly; you made it clear that you were not above being tempted or beyond sinning"?

The Goal of the Marital Care-Fronter

If we are honest, sometimes our hidden agenda when we confront someone is to put them in their place. God's Word has no place for that—not in our personal relationships and not in our biblical marriage counseling. Instead, we care-front so that:

- The marriage can be restored to spiritual health and relational maturity (Gal. 6:1).
- Spouses can turn back to a trusting heart that returns to the living God (Heb. 3:12–14).
- Spouses can each repent, come to the knowledge of the truth, come to their senses, and escape the devil's snare (2 Tim. 2:24–25).

- Spouses can grow up together in Christ and build each other up in love (Eph. 4:15–16).
- Spouses experience godly sorrow leading to repentance and the demonstration of the ongoing fruits of repentance (2 Cor. 7:10–11).
- Spouses return to God, who runs to them, throws his arms around them, celebrates with them, and dresses them in the Father's family attire (Luke 15:17–24).

The Power/Person behind Effective Care-Fronting: Leave the Conviction to God

God is the person and the power behind effective care-fronting. I love the way Paul describes this to Timothy. "Opponents must be gently instructed, *in the hope that God will grant them repentance* leading them to a knowledge of the truth, and that they will come to their senses and escape from the trap of the devil, who has taken them captive to do his will" (2 Tim. 2:25–26).

Biblical marriage counselor, leave the conviction to God. Lovingly and humbly present truth. Then step out of the way.

Those who train counselors talk about power struggles between the counselor and the counselee. Power struggles occur in marriage counseling when I feel the need to make the husband or wife change. My motivation becomes more about me than about them. "You're making me look bad by not responding to my counsel. Change *for me!*"

Power struggles also occur when I think it is in my power to change anyone. Rather than empowering people, such an arrogant attitude has the opposite effect and is seen as being overpowered, forced, and even abusive.

God and God's Word are the change agents. Not me. Not you.

Rather than a husband or a wife entering into a power struggle with me, I step aside so they can enter into a power struggle with the all-powerful God of the universe. I tell them:

- Susie, here's God's truth as best as I see how it relates to you and Devon. I've shared it in several ways from several passages related to several ways you've related to Devon. All I would ask is that you prayerfully explore the passages we've discussed and ask God's Spirit to reveal to you anything that applies . . .

The Focus of Marital Care-Fronting: Patterns of Relational Heart Sin

While I am neither a mind reader nor a heart reader, God is (Jer. 17:9–10). Because we are easily blinded and self-deceived, God calls us to expose heart sins as we encourage one another daily so that no one has a heart that is hardened by sin's deceitfulness (Heb. 3:11–15). What God calls us to do he equips us to accomplish. He gives biblical marriage counselors his Word, which is "alive and active. Sharper than any double-edged sword, it penetrates even to dividing soul and spirit, joints and marrow; it judges the thoughts and attitudes of the heart" (Heb. 4:12).

What reveals the heart? Our *words*—out of the heart the mouth speaks (Luke 6:45). So we listen carefully to the pattern of the words a husband and wife say to us and to each other.

Our *actions* also reveal our heart (1 Sam. 24:12–13). The Bible talks about our walk, our conversation, or our way of living. Paul commands us to "no longer walk as the Gentiles do" (Eph. 4:17 ESV). "You used to walk in these ways" (Col. 3:7), he says, but now we are to "walk in the way of love" (Eph. 5:2). The verb "walk" is often in the present tense in Greek, referring to a continued pattern of behavior and an ongoing course of life or conduct that flows out of the heart (Col. 3:5–10; 1 John 1:6; 2:1).

As we listen theologically and prayerfully for patterns of relating revealed by a spouse's words and actions, we might say:

- Susie, have you noticed that when you talk to Devon, sometimes you tend to cut him off? At other times you correct him or almost put him down. I've jotted down a few examples from today. I'm wondering if you've noticed this tendency and if you're aware of the impact it has on Devon. I'm curious what it might say about your heart toward Devon . . .

- Devon, how aware are you of the way you often respond to Susie? At times even your body language seems to be dismissive. I have some examples if you'd like to hear them. Then maybe we could explore what this pattern could be saying about your heart attitude . . .

The Process of Marital Care-Fronting: Softening Hardness by Confronting Discrepancies

In 2 Timothy 2:25, Paul commands Timothy to "gently instruct [confront, correct] those who oppose themselves" (author's translation). The phrase "oppose themselves" is from the Greek word for "antithesis"—a contrary position. It means to set oneself against God's moral order. In 2 Timothy 2:25, the verb is in the middle tense and means to stand opposed to oneself. Paul is saying to care-front people when you detect a pattern of inconsistency between their calling from God and their lifestyle. Care-front when you detect a discrepancy between who they are in Christ and how they actually relate to others.

Because of this biblical idea of confronting discrepancies, I find it helpful to use the wording "on the one hand . . . on the other hand."

- Susie, on the one hand, I hear you saying you have a deep, abiding trust in God's grace. On the other hand, I sense that your perfectionistic demands on Devon and even on yourself are lacking in grace . . .

Then we encourage Susie to confront her own discrepancies:

- Susie, how does this appear to you? What do you make of this? How do you put these two together?

There is no single formula for care-fronting and speaking God's truth in love. Here are additional samples of spiritual conversations and scriptural explorations designed to help a spouse become aware of their sinful pattern of relating and soften sin's grip on them.

- What passages from Scripture could we look at that might clarify God's position on this way of relating to your spouse?
- Devon, what do you think a perfect way of relating to Susie might have been in those two situations? [This can help him see the contrast between how he related and how he could have related.] What do you think a more Christlike way of relating to Susie might have been?
- Susie, how would you have felt if the shoe had been on the other foot? [Empathy for a spouse is another way to soften heart stubbornness.]
- Devon, could we explore any times others may have felt intimidated by you like Susie has felt? [This is designed to enlarge Devon's vision by identifying relational patterns so Devon can't say, "Even if this were true, it's just an isolated incident."]
- Devon, for me it's hard to admit when I've been intimidating. But I have been guilty of that. I wonder about you also . . . [By sharing your own spiritual defeats, you encourage spouses to be willing to do the same.]
- Susie, I'm no prophet, but I will make a prediction about what's likely to happen if you don't take a serious look at this potential pattern . . .
- Devon, how would you characterize your speech with Susie? In what ways do your words give life? In what ways do they kill? Have you asked Susie how your words impact her?
- When the two of you are in conflict, do you tend to heighten the battle, flee the argument, or seek a solution?
- Devon, as a husband, are there times when you fail to be sacrificial? Empowering? Shepherding?
- Susie, as a wife, are there times when you fail to be encouraging? A refuge-giver? An intimate ally?

Maturing as a Biblical Marriage Counselor
Exposing Marital Heart Sins

1. What are the different ways you counsel a sinning spouse blind to their sin versus a sinning spouse repentant of and overwhelmed by the guilt of their sin?

2. Perhaps I gained your attention by saying, "If you enjoy confronting others, you may not be very good at it." What do you think about that? How do 2 Corinthians 7:8–9; 2 Timothy 2:24–25; and Galatians 6:1 speak to the issue of your heart as a care-fronter?

3. You read six goals of the marital care-fronter. Which of those goals surprise you? Which encourage you?

4. How could 2 Timothy 2:25–26 help you avoid power struggles in your counseling?

5. Craft four sample trialogue scriptural explorations or spiritual conversations designed to care-front sinful relational patterns.

Sample Trialogue #1

Sample Trialogue #2

Sample Trialogue #3

Sample Trialogue #4

ELEVEN

Superabounding Grace

Reconciling in Marriage Counseling, Part 2

Introduction: Sin and Grace

As I begin chapter 11, my mind is reflecting back on three marriage counseling situations. In each case the husband was admittedly a plank-size sinner. Through the process of care-fronting (chap. 10) and applying truth relationally (chap. 11), each man confessed the guilt of significant sin in his marital calling as a husband. Each husband began seeking God's strength to show fruits of repentance. Each husband willingly placed himself under substantial accountability through various ministries and leaders in our church and community.

In each of these counseling relationships, I co-counseled with a female counselor. This is always helpful, even recommended. In these situations it was especially wise, as each wife needed the empathetic care of both a male *and* female biblical counselor. We spent a meaningful amount of time patiently working through each wife's pain, suffering, and healing—parakaletic sustaining and healing.

As each wife moved through her own healing process, they experienced two similar struggles. First, they each had a difficult time seeing themselves as even a speck-size sinner. We were consistently careful never to communicate that the wife's sin caused or motivated or was responsible for her husband's sin. Yet none of the six spouses were sinless saints—none of us are. If these marriages were to be restored, in each situation we needed to first address the husband's plank-size sins *and* over time address the wife's speck-size sins. (Note: The female counselor and I did not assess any of these three situations as cases of an abuser and an innocent victim, and none of the wives accused their husbands of abuse.)

The husband's sinfulness in each case was more overt, external, and identifiable. The wife's sinfulness in each case was more covert, internal, and concealed in heart attitudes. And while these three cases had the husband on one end of the spectrum and the wife on the other, I have counseled couples where the wife's sins were more overt and the husband's more hidden.

Second, each wife had serious difficulty granting forgiveness, even when there was evidence of ongoing fruits of repentance and heart and behavioral change. Each wife struggled with what appeared to be a graceless, harsh, condemning, perfectionistic, pharisaical attitude toward her husband.

As you read this, I suspect your mind is racing. You want more info to assess these three marriage counseling situations and our approach. Unfortunately, space and confidentiality issues preclude that. However, I trust you will have enough information to ponder how these situations relate to the three marriage counseling competencies discussed in this chapter.

- *Applying Truth Relationally*: When care-fronting is not enough to lead a counselee to recognition and repentance of sin, how does applying truth relationally move us forward?
- *Calming the Conscience with Grace*: When a spouse confesses sin and shows fruits of repentance, how does calming the conscience with grace minister to this spouse?
- *Enlightening Couples about Biblical Marital Reconciliation*: What does the Bible teach about the marital process of confession, fruits of repentance, forgiveness, comfort, and reaffirmation of love?

Maturing as a Biblical Marriage Counselor
Sin and Grace

1. Have you counseled any couples like those described in the introduction—where one spouse is more overtly and clearly sinful but the other is not guiltless, though his or her sin may be more subtle and hidden?

   a. What unique difficulties does this combination add to the marriage counseling process?

---

b. How did or could you approach each spouse in unique ways in such situations?

2. What are your thoughts on the potential benefits of co-counseling? In what ways might those benefits be changed when the co-counseling includes a male and a female counselor?

3. How could you respond when a spouse is showing fruits of repentance but is so over-whelmed with guilt that he or she is ready to give up hope?

4. When one spouse shows fruits of repentance and the other spouse struggles to forgive and grant grace, how could you work through the process of forgiveness?

5. What does biblical marital reconciliation look like?

   a. Should a person forgive before their spouse repents, or should they wait until there is confession and fruits of repentance? Where would you go in Scripture to address this question?

   b. Is there a difference between forgiveness and reconciliation? Can a person forgive yet still hold their spouse accountable for ongoing change before there is a full restoration of the marital relationship? Where would you turn in the Bible to address these questions?

We are all tempted toward a stubborn inclination to continue in self-sufficient attitudes that lead to self-centered relationships maintained by self-protective suppression of the truth (Rom. 1:18–32). The beach ball of guilt pops to the surface, but we force it back down under the water. How do we handle such resistance to repentance? We apply truth relationally. In biblical marriage counseling we do this in three ways:

- Connecting couples intimately
- Catching spouses red-handed
- Confessing sin personally

Connecting Couples Intimately: Sinning in Front of You

In *sustaining*, there is great power when the couple empathizes with each other. In *healing*, there is great encouragement when the couple hopes together in Christ. In *reconciling*, there is clear exposure of sin when the couple relates intimately with each other in the counseling room as you observe.

I like to call it "keeping the relationship in the room." Couples become histrionic—telling and retelling their story of being hurt and sinned against by their spouse. If you have counseled at least one couple, then you have experienced this "he said, she said" dynamic. Who do you believe since you were not there? Many times I have thought, "Wow, to be a fly on the wall and witness what *really* happened last week between this couple!"

Keeping the relationship in the room does exactly that. Picture Candi and Mitch retelling their version of what happened last week. You move them back to the present moment by having them relate to each other right now.

- Candi, what do you want to say *right now* to Mitch about what happened last week?
- Mitch, share with Candi *right now* what you wish you had done differently last week.
- Mitch and Candi, I'd like each of you to take turns sharing what you're feeling *right now* as you think about what happened last week.

Because you are watching, they may be on their best behavior at first. However, if you get them talking to each other about each other, they are going to sin against each other in your presence.

Keep them in the present moment by inviting them to interact about what is happening right now as they relate.

- Mitch and Candi, how are each of you experiencing your relationship *right now*?

- Could we discuss what's happening between the two of you *as you talk*?
- Candi, what's going on inside you *right now*?
- Mitch, how are you feeling as you think about what Candi *just said* to you?

As they talk, observe and listen for patterns. Listen theologically by pondering the marital heart probes you read in chapter 10.

Next, explore the current interaction with the couple, seeking to identify heart patterns and styles of relating.

- Mitch and Candi, is this how things *usually* turn out when you talk?
- Based on what I just witnessed, is that a *typical* pattern of how you two relate?
- Is this what *normally* occurs?

Most couples will say something like, "If we're honest, it's usually worse than this. We were trying to behave and be civil since you were watching. But we still didn't do so well, did we?"

Now, seek to identify and expose sinful heart patterns in one of two ways. First, you can share what you witnessed.

- I appreciate your honesty, Candi and Mitch. Here's what I observed. Mitch, you tend to race right to defending yourself. I'm wondering if you see that . . . And I'm wondering if we could explore why you might do that . . .
- Candi, you're tenacious. You won't relent until Mitch repents. You have a sharp eye to his faults, but I'm wondering if your vision is blurred some to your heart attitude in this . . .

Second, you can expose sinful styles of relating by helping the couple explore the impact they are having on each other.

- Mitch, as Candi was giving you her feedback just now, how did you feel? Invited in? Pushed away? Respected? Intimidated? As you shared, do you think Candi felt cared about? Put down? Encouraged? Discouraged?
- Candi, as Mitch responded to you, did you feel and sense warmth? Sarcasm? Acceptance? A judgmental spirit? As you shared, do you think Mitch sensed teamwork? Faultfinding? Trust? Emotional withdrawal?

The point is not to beat them up with how bad they are. Our goal is to expose what is already going on in their heart and in their relationship *so that* they can own the mote or speck in their eye. We want to help them to see that "It's horrible to sin against Christ and my spouse when I _____."

Catching Spouses Red-Handed: Sinning against You

Blindness to sin and hardness of heart die hard. Spouses will often claim, "But I only respond like this to *her*!" "*He* instigates all of this!" "I'm not like this in any other relationship!" When being caught *sinning in front of you* is not enough, then perhaps being caught *sinning against you* will soften a hard heart.

It can be rare for biblical counselors to focus on how a counselee relates to us or sins against us. So consider some descriptors:

- *Relating in the Moment*: Face-to-face relating with our counselee about our counseling relationship with a view toward implications for their relationship with their spouse.
- *Immediacy*: Dealing with what is taking place in our counseling relationship at the present moment and interacting about the counselee's way of relating to us as a snapshot of how they relate to their spouse.
- *Staying in the Room*: Discussing the here-and-now between the counselor and the counselee as a core sample of how they relate to and impact their spouse.

Throughout 1 and 2 Corinthians, Paul models intimate connecting as he uses his relationship with the Corinthians as a catalyst to expose their relational immaturity. Witness a beautiful and powerful example from 2 Corinthians 6:11–13: "We have spoken freely to you, Corinthians, and opened wide our hearts to you. We are not withholding our affection from you, but you are withholding yours from us. As a fair exchange—I speak as to my children—open wide your hearts also."

Paul understands a foundational principle: *how people relate intimately to us mirrors how they relate intimately to others.* We can only hide ourselves for so long. Eventually our words either reveal or betray us in significant relationships, for out of the abundance of the heart the mouth speaks. Whatever is central to our style of relating will reflect itself in all our meaningful relationships.

This principle holds true *only if* our marriage counseling relationships are truly and purely intimate. If our biblical counseling relationships are shallow and merely academic, then we cannot expect to detect significant relational patterns.

I fear turning something so personal into a process. Applying truth relationally involves our commitment to connect deeply. We refuse to maintain some aloof professional image or distant pastoral stiffness. Instead, we:

- Taste the horrors of sin
- Stay in the room
- Paint the person a picture
- Connect the relational style to their marriage relationship

In *tasting the horrors of sin*, I allow Mitch to impact me. I found with Mitch that every interaction became a deeply defensive debate—that *he must win*. He moved from meek and mild to angry and hostile. So I was thinking, "Hmm, at this stage of my life, winning debates and making interactions a competition is not my style. But with Mitch I feel pulled to debate and I feel pushed away. I wonder what's going on between us and within Mitch. I wonder how this style of relating impacts Candi."

Staying in the room required that I keep my relationship with Mitch current. Instead of focusing on Mitch's angry, defensive patterns in the past, I shared ways that he became defensive with and hostile toward me in the moment. "Mitch, people typically give me feedback that I'm a positive encourager whose acceptance and vulnerability make it rather easy for them to receive confrontation from me. Yet right now it seems like you're biting my head off at the slightest implication that there might be something you need to look at . . ."

Mitch became defensive when I wondered if he was becoming defensive. So I continued to stay in the room. "It's happening right now, Mitch."

"What's happening right now?" Mitch said with more than a twinge of exasperation.

"Even as I try to share where you may be defensive with me, you're getting more defensive and upset . . ."

Staying in the moment, searching my heart, praying for wisdom, I *painted Mitch a picture* by using imagery that fit our current relationship, "So, Mitch, help me to understand if this is your picture of our relationship. Rather than seeing me as a brother or even a father figure who cares about you and has your best interests at heart, you see me as an enemy who is against you and out to get you. And in response you become an angry enemy . . ."

By God's grace, Mitch melted. He had an "Aha!" moment.

Mitch's pattern of angry defensiveness became so clear to him that I barely needed to move toward *connecting his relational style to his marriage relationship*. But we did explore this together. "Mitch, is it possible that this is how you see Candi—as an enemy out to get you, even in those times when she really does have your best interests at heart? If so, how might your angry, defensive responses to Candi be impacting her and your relationship?"

Confessing Sin Personally

As powerful as it can be to be caught red-handed, nothing is as powerful as confessing our sin to God. Second only to that is the power of confessing our sin to our spouse.

By exploring God's story of sin, Mitch was able to face God's perspective on his way of relating. Together we discussed biblical diagnostic questions such as:

- What does God's Word say concerning your current way of relating—to me and to Candi?
- How would you compare and contrast your way of relating and Christ's way of relating?
- How would you compare your way of relating to Candi with the love chapter in 1 Corinthians 13?

As Mitch came to a place of conviction, we then explored God's story of confession and repentance using scriptural explorations from Hosea 14.

- Mitch, I respect your integrity in facing the ways you have harmed Candi. Could we look at Hosea 14 to see how God wants you to respond to your sin? First, God tells us that the hallmark of repentance and confession is *relational return* (14:1). What would it be like for you, right now, to return to God? To turn face-to-face with him?
- Mitch, Hosea 14:2 teaches that we are to "take words with us" when we return to God. Confession means we describe specifically what our sin has been, not because God doesn't know, but so we can come clean before God. What words of confession would you take to God?
- Hosea 14:2 also teaches that it's not enough to say "I'm sorry." We need to have the brokenness to ask God to forgive us. What will this sound like for you, Mitch?
- In Hosea 14:3 we learn that true confession admits our false hopes and false gods. In true confession we acknowledge to God what false gods we were clinging to. Mitch, what have you been trusting in that you want to confess to God?

With Mitch, addressing issues of sin, repentance, and confession, and asking for forgiveness required several sessions. We also needed to address these issues with Candi, whose sins were more subtle than Mitch's.

Maturing as a Biblical Marriage Counselor
Applying Truth Relationally

1. We are all tempted toward a stubborn inclination to continue in self-sufficient attitudes that lead to self-centered relationships maintained by self-protective suppression of the truth.

   a. Are there times in your life where you have recognized this type of stubborn resistance to God's conviction? How did the Spirit break through to you?

   b. If you experience this stubborn resistance in marriage counseling, how can you work with God's Spirit, God's Word, and your counselee to break through?

2. This chapter is not the first time you have seen an emphasis on having the husband and wife talk to each other. Previously it was to comfort and encourage each other. Now it is to keep their relationship current and in the room so you and they can see their sin in action.

   a. How hard do you think it will be for you to move from having each spouse talk to you about their past conflict to having them talk to each other about their current conflict?

   b. How helpful do you think it will be in identifying and exposing spousal sin to have the couple interact in front of you?

3. Applying truth relationally through catching a spouse red-handed requires a lot of us.

   a. How new or different were these concepts about applying truth relationally through catching a spouse red-handed?

   b. How easy or hard would it be for you to relate with a counselee with this level of connection and openness?

4. Using the scenario with Mitch and catching him red-handed, write trialogues that you might use for each of the following relational competencies.

   a. Taste the horrors of sin

   b. Stay in the room

   c. Paint the person a picture

   d. Connect the relational style to their marriage relationship

Calming the Conscience with Grace

The Puritans were skilled at loading the conscience with guilt. Think "Sinners in the Hands of an Angry God." The Puritans were even more skillful at lightening the conscience with grace. Think "Sons and Daughters in the Palms of a Forgiving Father."

In chapter 8, we examined 2 Corinthians 2:5–11 and Satan's scheme to overwhelm the repentant sinner with excessive sorrow and guilt. Read that again—overwhelm the *repentant* sinner. In 2 Corinthians 2:5–6, Paul indicates that a sinning brother was confronted by the church (many commentators link this passage to 1 Corinthians 5:1–5 and the man who sinned by having sexual relations with his stepmother). "The punishment inflicted on him by the majority is sufficient" (2 Cor. 2:6). Church discipline worked! The person repented. What should the church do now?

Now instead [of continuing to load his conscience with guilt], you ought to forgive and comfort him [lighten his conscience with grace], so that he will not be overwhelmed by excessive sorrow [loading the conscience with guilt]. I urge you, therefore, to reaffirm your love for him [lighten his conscience with grace]. (2 Cor. 2:7–8)

It is beautiful to watch a spouse come to a place of repentance. It is terrible to watch Satan torment that repentant believer with his condemning lie that says, "God may possibly forgive you, but he will never welcome you home!"

The prodigal son believed this lie. He came to his senses, left his life of sin, repented, and returned to his father. Yet, before he arrived at his father's house and even after his father ran to meet him and receive him home, this younger son twice repeats the mantra, "I am no longer worthy to be called your son; make me like one of your hired servants" (Luke 15:19, 21).

In marriage counseling, I regularly see husbands and wives come to a place of deep repentance before God and their spouse. Yet I often find the sinned-against spouse unable or unwilling to grant forgiveness even after the sinning spouse has demonstrated the fruits of repentance (2 Cor. 7:8–13). Rather than forgiving, comforting, and reaffirming their love like Paul commands, the injured spouse heaps guilt on the repentant spouse, who then becomes overwhelmed by sorrow, swallowed up by Satan's scheme, and ensnared in Satan's condemning trap.

What is a biblical counselor to do with a struggling spouse like this? First, we address the issue with the repentant spouse—*calming the conscience with grace*. Second, we address the issue between the couple—*enlightening couples about biblical marital reconciliation* (our next counseling competency).

Having exposed sin, we magnify grace. We show a repentant spouse that where sin abounds, grace superabounds (Rom. 5:20). We never leave a spouse with sin exposed but grace ignored. We dispense grace. We apply the gospel to a spouse's troubled heart, encouraging him or her to return home to the forgiving heart and loving arms of our gracious Father. We direct repentant spouses to Christ's gospel of grace—calming their conscience with grace. We do this through:

- Providing tastes of grace
- Sharing gospel conversations about grace
- Penning psalms of homecoming

Providing Tastes of Grace

There is tremendous power when a biblical counselor, speaking from God's Word, affirms to a struggling husband or wife, "God has graciously forgiven you in Christ!" This becomes even more powerful when that biblical counselor has related in the loving, caring, gentle ways depicted in chapters 1–11.

Providing tastes of grace means we live out 2 Corinthians 2:5–8. Like Paul, we become an advocate for the repentant spouse, urging the other spouse to reaffirm their love. When we see this brother or sister drowning in guilt and despairing of ever receiving the Father's grace, we become ambassadors of reconciliation (2 Cor. 5:20).

We share biblical words of forgiveness, speaking graciously to our repentant counselees and reminding them that when we confess our sins, God is faithful and just to forgive us our sins (1 John 1:8–10). We comfort our overwhelmed counselees, consoling them, pointing them to Jesus Christ their Advocate (1 John 2:1–2). We reaffirm our love for them—demonstrating and confirming that we value and respect them.

As I write these words, I am picturing a husband whose wife struggled to forgive him. With tears in his eyes, he shared, "Pastor Bob, humanly speaking, your gracious acceptance of me has saved my life as you've pointed me back to Christ's saving and forgiving grace. I was at the end of my rope; your grace words have given me hope."

Martin Luther thoroughly rejected the notion of any human being as the mediator between God and man, pointing people instead to Christ alone. However, Luther consistently emphasized the value of believers confessing sin to one another and speaking God's gracious forgiveness into one another's lives.

> When we have laid bare our conscience to our brother and privately make known to him the evil that lurked within, we receive from our brother's lips the word of comfort spoken by God himself. And if we accept this in faith, we find peace in the mercy of God speaking to us through our brother.[1]

Sharing Gospel Conversations about Grace

In his letters of spiritual counsel, Luther models grace-saturated gospel conversations.

> For who is able to express what a thing it is, when a man is assured in his heart that God neither is nor will be angry with him, but will be forever a merciful and loving Father to him for Christ's sake? This is indeed a marvelous and incomprehensible liberty, to have the most high and sovereign Majesty so favorable to us.[2]

Our grace words flow from God's Word. Consider some sample scriptural explorations and spiritual conversations:

- Speaking to repentant sinners, Hosea 14:1–4 tells us that God forgives all your sins and receives you graciously. In God, the fatherless find compassion. His anger is turned away. He heals your waywardness and loves you freely. How do these truths impact you?

- In Luke 15, Jesus presents God as a Father who longs for his son, rushes out to meet him, embraces him, and celebrates with him. What difference would it make if you saw God as a Father willing to forgive you and longing to celebrate with you?
- Let's explore 1 John 1:8–10. What does this promise mean to you?
- What Scripture passages could we explore about the riches of Christ's grace and forgiveness?
- Where were you recruited into this idea that God rejects you when you sin? Where was this idea modeled for you? Does it square with Scripture? How do Paul's words in Romans 8:1–39 speak to this?

Penning Psalms of Homecoming

One of my favorite homework assignments is to encourage a repentant counselee to pen their own psalm of homecoming. I ask them to read and meditate on Psalms 32 and 51. Both psalms powerfully express heartfelt repentance and returning home. They each magnify God's grace in receiving us to himself and restoring to us the joy of our salvation.

I then ask them to pen their own paraphrased Psalm 32 or 51—from their heart to God's heart. I encourage them to craft not only words of repentance but also words reflecting God's gracious reception of them as they return home to the Father's forgiving and reconciling heart.

Maturing as a Biblical Marriage Counselor
Calming the Conscience with Grace

1. During times of overwhelming shame and condemning guilt, who has been a 2 Corinthians 2 spiritual friend for you? How did they express God's forgiveness to you, comfort you, and reaffirm their love for you?

2. For *sustaining*, our word picture is *climbing in the casket*. For *healing*, it is *celebrating the empty tomb*. For *reconciling*, our word picture is *dispensers of grace*. Having read this section on calming the conscience with grace:

   a. Rate yourself on a scale of 1 to 10, with 10 being highest, on how well you dispense grace and calm people's conscience with grace.

---

b. How could you keep growing as a dispenser of grace?

3. Reread the two quotes from Martin Luther. Like Luther, how could you provide tastes of grace and share gospel conversations about grace to struggling spouses?

4. Reread the section titled "Sharing Gospel Conversations about Grace." Craft several grace-based scriptural explorations and spiritual conversations.

Gospel Conversation #1

Gospel Conversation #2

Gospel Conversation #3

Gospel Conversation #4

5. An additional aspect of dispensing grace and calming the conscience with grace is penning psalms of homecoming. Ponder an issue of sin, confession, repentance, and returning home. Then pen your own (private/confidential) psalm of homecoming.

Enlightening Couples about Biblical Marital Reconciliation

We have arrived at yet another delicate surgical procedure. Theologians debate it. Couples live it. *What is the connection between sin, confrontation, repentance, forgiveness, and reconciliation?* To address this imperative question, we return to three passages we have previously linked together: 1 Corinthians 5:1–5; 2 Corinthians 7:8–13; and 2 Corinthians 2:5–11.

Picture again Candi and Mitch. Mitch has a sin issue with angry defensiveness. Candi has a sin issue with pharisaical perfectionism, a non-grace response to Mitch, and a legalistic, judgmental spirit.

Through biblical counseling (probing theologically, exposing marital heart sin, and applying truth relationally), each one is beginning to own their sin. Each one is repenting before God (applying truth relationally). Each one is beginning to grasp and receive God's gracious fatherly forgiveness (calming the conscience with grace).

They are experiencing all but the last three words of our reconciling summary sentence:

> It's horrible to sin against Christ and each other, but through Christ it's wonderful to be forgiven *and to forgive.*

How do we help Candi and Mitch forgive each other and reconcile with each other? This is an immensely personal question fraught with a long relational and emotional history for Candi and Mitch (and all couples). If you have done any marriage counseling, then you have heard sentences and pushback like:

- But you don't understand. He's quick to mouth words about change and confession, but he never really changes.
- Don't you see how she's just manipulating me? It's just words. I want to see real change over time before I'll trust her again!
- What? I'm supposed to just wink at her sin and pretend everything's fine just because she's apologized *again?*
- What? I'm supposed to forgive and forget before he's ever confessed and repented?

These are real and raw ways of asking the theological question, What is the connection between sin, confrontation, repentance, forgiveness, and reconciliation?

Numerous books have been written to address these questions (see the resource list at the end of this book). In marriage counseling, I require couples to read at least one of those books. Then I give them a one-page handout with the words of 1 Corinthians 5:1–5 on the left, 2 Corinthians 7:8–13 in the middle, and 2 Corinthians 2:5–11 on the right. After reading and explaining those passages, here is a snapshot of our ongoing interaction.

- Mitch and Candi, notice how Paul artfully weaves together everything we've been addressing over the past two months. First, on the left, in 1 Corinthians 5, Paul never winks at sin. He confronts the Corinthians about their failure to confront this sinning brother. You and I have not winked at sin. We've confronted/care-fronted sin you each needed to address. Neither of you has been let off the hook.

- For just a moment, notice what's on the right—2 Corinthians 2, where Paul talks about forgiveness. We're not focusing there just yet. Like Paul, we need to address what's in the middle—2 Corinthians 7, where Paul focuses on fruits of repentance. Anyone can give lip service to repentance. Anyone can mouth words of confession. Neither of you wants to be conned or manipulated. You each want to see real change. Paul gets that. That's why he writes about worldly sorrow that does *not* result in heart repentance and lasting change. It's also why he shares seven marks of repentance. It's why we've spent several weeks talking about how to identify real change— change from the heart that leads to change in relational behavior. This middle section is vital. There's no way you can rebuild relational trust unless each of you, through God's power, continues to put off the old sinful ways of relating and keeps putting on the new Christlike ways we've been discussing. [We then spend some time reviewing the fruits of repentance demonstrated by each of them.]

- As we start to move to what's on the right—2 Corinthians 2—let's quickly review. We don't wink at sin; we confront sin. We don't just mouth words of confession; we show fruits of repentance over time. As this happens—imperfectly, because none of us is glorified yet— Paul insists on starting the reconciliation process. In 2 Corinthians 2:5–6, he's saying, "Corinthians! Enough already. I asked you to confront and now you're stuck on confrontation. Don't you see? It worked! You confronted. He's changing. If you don't let up, he's going to give up!" What does it mean to let up? Let's explore these three phrases together: forgive, comfort, and reaffirm your love. [We'll spend a good amount of time dissecting what these three phrases mean for Candi and Mitch.] Let's also remind ourselves, Mitch and Candi, what happens if we refuse to reconcile like this. We're aiding and abetting Satan's scheme of overwhelming us with excessive sorrow by refusing to grant grace. [Now we'll spend more time discussing what this looks like.]

- Candi, I've heard you say, "How can I forgive when Mitch's sin has been such a pervasive pattern?" To answer that, we need to go to another of Paul's passages—Ephesians 4:30–5:2. [We may spend several weeks on this forgiveness process—our forgiveness of others being motivated by Christ's great grace to us.]

- Mitch, I've heard you say that you're afraid that easy or quick forgiveness will enable Candi to keep sinning against you. And that you can't trust Candi until you see further, ongoing evidence of change. We need to separate two categories: heart forgiveness and relational trust. I'd suggest that you start with heart forgiveness. In your heart, keep forgiving Candi as Christ has forgiven you. But trust . . . that takes time. And ultimately it means you first and foremost trust God. He is the only one who is fully trustworthy. And as you see incremental steps—fruits of repentance—in Candi's relationship with you, you trust her more as you keep entrusting yourself to God. Remember when we talked about that from 1 Peter 2? [We will spend several weeks wrestling through heart forgiveness versus relational trust and vulnerability.]

- Through my years of providing marriage counseling, I've detected three practical steps that we can start taking to launch this process of relational reconciliation. First, you guys have confessed and repented to God—to use Hosea's image, you've taken words with you. Now you need to spend some time—in our sessions and between our meetings—to "take words with you," specifically confessing your sins against each other *and* specifically asking forgiveness from each other. [We'll start exploring this together . . .]

- Second, let's look more closely at Paul's seven marks of repentance. Let's use them to outline specifically what it will look like for each of you to demonstrate true, ongoing change . . . [We'll start exploring this together . . .]

- Third, we've just started talking about Paul's three phrases: forgive, comfort, and reaffirm your love. Are you each at a place where you can take words to your spouse and offer words of forgiveness? What will it look like to comfort the very spouse who has hurt you but is now repentant? What will it look like to reaffirm your love for your sinful but repenting spouse? [We'll start exploring this together . . .]

Maturing as a Biblical Marriage Counselor
Enlightening Couples about Biblical Marital Reconciliation

1. Recall our question for this section: What is the connection between sin, confrontation, repentance, forgiveness, and reconciliation?

   a. To what passages of Scripture do you turn to answer this question biblically?

   b. What Christian books or other resources do you use and recommend to help you and couples think through this question?

2. In the reconciling work of biblical marriage counseling, the last three words of this statement are often the most difficult to achieve: "It's horrible to sin against Christ and each other, but through Christ it's wonderful to be forgiven *and to forgive*." How do you help couples to work through that last part—how do you help them to forgive one another?

3. On page 213, you read four examples of how spouses often push back when you begin talking about forgiveness. Have you heard these or similar sentences? How do you address these concerns?

4. I use 1 Corinthians 5:1–5; 2 Corinthians 7:8–13; and 2 Corinthians 2:5–11 (in that specific order) to address the biblical connection between sin, confrontation, repentance, forgiveness, and reconciliation. How could you use these three passages to help couples think through and live out biblical reconciliation?

5. Imagine some Christian ministry has asked you to craft a blog post (five hundred to one thousand words) addressing how you help struggling couples think through sin, confrontation, repentance, forgiveness, and reconciliation. Ready? Write your blog post!

TWELVE

Discipling Disciple-Makers

Guiding in Marriage Counseling, Part 1

Introduction: Have Fun!

Most couples enter counseling hurt and hurting (sustaining), hopeless and helpless (healing), and sinning and unforgiving (reconciling). Be honest. Entering that mess is *not* fun. We do it because God calls us to it. We share in the mess because we care about the marriage.

For me, biblical guiding is the most fun part of marriage counseling. *Sustaining* is vital but exhausting, as we encourage the couple to climb into each other's casket. *Healing* is encouraging as we help couples crop Christ into their picture as they celebrate his empty tomb. *Reconciling* is essential, but care-fronting sin is not enjoyable, though it is beneficial, especially when the couple dispenses grace to each other. But *guiding* is fun because in it God calls us to disciple spouses to disciple each other. This is what we live for—discipling disciple-makers.

A review will help us sense just how much fun guiding is. Recall from chapter 1 that every marriage is meant for couples to nurture each other to become more like Christ. God intends the husband-wife relationship to be the most fertile ground for growth in grace. God calls every husband and wife to be each other's best biblical counselor. Fun!

Recall the summary of biblical guiding from chapter 4: "It's supernatural to love each other like Christ, through Christ, for Christ." Uniting chapters 1 and 4 we get, "Through Christ, it's supernatural to empower each other to become more like Christ for Christ's glory." God calls couples to fan into flame the gift of God within each other. Fun!

Many approaches to marriage counseling stop prematurely. I can understand why. If you have really helped couples to sustain, heal, and reconcile, God has done a lot. They care about each other now (sustaining). They hope in God together now (healing). They have forgiven and reaffirmed their love for each other now (reconciling). What more could be left?

What is left is continued growth—biblical progressive sanctification (guiding). In guiding, we point couples to Christ, to each other, and to the body of Christ as we work ourselves out of a job. But our job is not finished until we have started them on the journey of mutual discipleship.

In guiding, they equip each other to put off the old and put on the new. They envision together their identity in Christ. They empower each other to tap into Christ's resurrection power. They encourage each other to put Jesus first. Fun!

In chapter 4, we identified the guiding question that helps us have all this fun discipling couples: How can I help this couple to discover and apply gospel wisdom from Christ and his Word so they can discern together what is best and pure and glorifying to Christ (Phil. 1:9–11)? We worded our summaries of relational competencies for sustaining, healing, and reconciling with a focus on the *counselor's* competencies. Since guiding is so focused on coaching the couple, our wording now focuses more on the *couple's* relational competency to LOVE:

L Leaving the Past Behind: Equipping Each Other to Put Off the Old and Put On the New (chap. 12)

O Ongoing Gospel Growth: Envisioning the Marriage with Gospel Lenses (chap. 12)

V Victorious Together through Christ: Empowering Each Other to Tap into Christ's Resurrection Power (chap. 13)

E Exalting Christ Together: Encouraging Each Other to Keep Putting Jesus First, Keep Loving Jesus Most (chap. 13)

Maturing as a Biblical Marriage Counselor
Have Fun!

1. Have you ever thought of counseling as fun?

   a. How could viewing the biblical guiding process as fun give you resilience and persistence during the not-so-fun aspects of marital counseling?

---

b. We are all wired differently by God. For you, which aspect of biblical marriage counseling do you think will be most fun—sustaining, healing, reconciling, or guiding?

2. Consider two summaries of biblical guiding: (a) In Christ, it's supernatural to love each other like Christ; (b) Through Christ, it's supernatural to empower each other to become more like Christ. How do these two descriptors shape your thinking about and cast a vision for biblical guiding in marriage counseling?

3. Too many approaches to marriage counseling stop prematurely.

   a. What is your end goal in marriage counseling? What is your final stage in marriage counseling?

   b. How do you know when you are ready to wrap up marriage counseling with a couple?

4. Review our guiding question: How can I help this couple to discover and apply gospel wisdom from Christ and his Word so they can discern together what is best and pure and glorifying to Christ (Phil. 1:9–11)?

   a. How can this question shape your approach to guiding in marriage counseling?

   b. What other summary question or statement shapes your approach to the final stage of marriage counseling?

Leaving the Past Behind: Equipping Each Other to Put Off the Old and Put On the New

With Mitch and Candi, we launched the guiding process by discussing my paraphrase of Ephesians 4:22–24 and linking it to Romans 6.

- Mitch and Candi, through God's grace, you've made such great progress. I'd like to see your growth continue by talking in specifics about what the Bible describes as "putting off" and "putting on." Take a look at this handout where I've paraphrased Ephesians 4:22–24: "Now put off in practice what Christ has already put off when he saved and cleansed you—continually put off your former way of relating to each other. Christ has made you new in the spirit of your mind—in the deepest core of your being. Now put on in practice what Christ has already put on when he made you a new creation—continually put on your new Christlike way of relating to each other." What questions, thoughts, or comments do you have about this passage or about how it connects to your relationship?

- Here's what's so exciting and empowering about this, Candi and Mitch. You don't have to change your heart. Christ already did that when he regenerated you—when he saved, cleansed, and made you a new creation. You are, however, responsible for choosing—in Christ's strength—to live out the new you. This is what Paul teaches in Romans 6. [We read together Romans 6:1–14, explaining and discussing as we go.] You are each dead to sin and alive to Christ. Therefore, you can stop living the old, fleshly, self-centered way, and you can start offering yourselves to God as living sacrifices who love each other like Christ loves each of you. [We also read Romans 12:1–2.] What questions, thoughts, or comments do you have about these passages or about how they connect to your marriage?

All biblical counselors help couples think through and apply passages like these. We fine-tune this process by following the principle of relating in the moment—relating to each other in the room. I had Mitch and Candi apply the put off/put on principles in specific ways during our meetings—staying in the present moment in my presence.

Relating Maturely in the Present Moment

In guiding relational interactions, assign one or both spouses the task of shifting from their old self-focused way of relating to a new ministry way of connecting. The key is coaching spouses to shift from their specific characteristic sinful style of relating to a new other-centered way.

One of Mitch and Candi's major ways of hurtful relating is for Candi to play the "Perfect Pharisaical Mommy" to Mitch's "Prodigal Little Boy." So, in the midst of a relational interaction, I provided specific put off/put on coaching for each of them.

- Candi, I really respect how you've owned the way you sometimes play the role of Mitch's mom or, as you've even confessed, his "Holy Spirit." You've been able to identify some ways you respond with a bitter, biting tone, with something of a pharisaical judgmentalism, and treat Mitch more like your child than your respected spouse. So just before we continue this interaction, let's do a couple of things. First, share with us what you see as the new Christlike way you'll relate instead. Second, how about praying and asking God's Spirit to fill you so you can put off the old and put on the new *right now* . . .

- Mitch, you have a major role in this also. This is a perfect opportunity for you to step up like we've been discussing. You want to put off the two extremes you say you tend to go to—either playing the helpless, overpowered little boy, or being the angry, defensive, overpowering opponent. *Right now*, I want you to move toward Candi with loving adult strength and compassion. As with Candi, just before you two interact, tell us what mature love for Candi will look like in this conversation, and pray for God's strength to do that . . .

Before we provide some structure for these relational interactions, consider another example—this one focused more on the two of them working together.

- Mitch and Candi, we've talked about the "Mother Knows Best" story the two of you often play out. You both have expressed your distaste for it. You even worked together to craft a story title you prefer—"Adam and Eve: The Sequel." By that you meant the idea of a new Adam and Eve where Adam wasn't in the background passively listening and Eve wasn't in the forefront—in your case by caustically criticizing. Well, time for the sequel! I'm going to sit back. The only time I'm going to comment is when I see the two of you falling back into that ugly old black-and-white movie. When I see the two of you passionately enjoying the new colorized version of your relationship, I'm gonna munch some popcorn and enjoy!

Shepherding Relational Interactions: Structure and Principles

Several overlapping concepts are at work as you shepherd these in-session relational interactions.

- *Let them talk to each other in your presence.* It won't go perfectly. Give them some space and time. Prayerfully ponder when to step in with a word of feedback and when to be quiet. If it gets messy, go back to sustaining or healing or reconciling—whichever is most needful in the moment.
- *Coach . . . but do not over-coach.* Avoid enabling sinful behavior, yet also avoid mothering or smothering the couple. Allow their interaction to play itself out enough so that you can observe and provide feedback on the good and the not-quite-so-good.
- *Explore and apply God's Word to hungry hearts.* If it does get messy, what a wonderful opportunity to teach hungry hearts. Now interact about passages like Ephesians 4:25–32 and what it looks like when two maturing people communicate in love.
- *Fan into flame the gift of God.* When it goes well, what a wonderful opportunity to fan into flame the good that you observe. Encourage them. Affirm them. Celebrate with them.
- *Guide them to evaluate themselves and to encourage each other (mutual coaching).* Mitch should point out where Candi did a great job. He should assess what he did well and not-so-well and what he would do better next time.
- *Highlight renewed thinking patterns.* Right in the middle of putting off (Eph. 4:22) and putting on (4:24), Paul highlights being renewed in the spirit of our minds—in our heart of hearts (4:23). Help the couple—in the moment—dismantle the old ways of thinking and remind them of new, biblical ways of perceiving life (as you did in sustaining, healing, and reconciling). Then call on them to act on their renewed beliefs.
- *Draw out renewed Christlike love.* Help the couple verbalize *specific* old ways to put off and new relational styles to put on. Then coach them to coach each other to live these out in the present moment.
- *Strengthen communication.* Urge the couple to interact out of their new, godly style of relating. Since the mouth speaks out of the overflow of the heart, this new style will reveal itself in their interactions—especially their intense interactions.
- *Cement commitment.* Relational interactions have the potential to cement commitment. They encourage the couple to live out their new life in Christ—their new co-created joint marital relational narrative.

- *Send them home with relational interaction homework.* First they live out their newness in Christ in front of you. Then they do it without your help but with the Spirit's help throughout the week. Co-create with them the specifics of their relational interaction assignment. When you next meet, plan to discuss how it went, what they learned, and how they can keep depending on Christ to continue growing up together in him.

Maturing as a Biblical Marriage Counselor
Leaving the Past Behind

1. All biblical counselors address the put off/put on principle.

   a. How have you seen this addressed in marriage counseling? How have you addressed it in marriage counseling?

   b. We highlighted putting off and putting on as relational interactions in the present moment in the presence of the counselor. Is this a new idea for you? What do you make of it? How could this practice impact your counseling ministry?

2. We tend to apply truth generically: put off the old sinful way. But what *specific* old sinful way? The power of guiding relational interactions depends upon reconciling—where you have identified specific heart sins and relational patterns.

   a. In your Christian life, have you detected that you tend to apply put off/put on truth generically? If so, how does that hinder your growth in grace? How would specific put offs and put ons impact further growth in grace?

---

b. In biblical marriage counseling, have you detected a tendency to apply put off/put on truth generically? If so, how does that hinder a couple's growth in grace? How would specific put offs and put ons impact a couple's further growth in grace?

3. In the section on shepherding relational interactions, you read ten principles.

a. How hard or easy do you think it will be to apply these principles so you can shepherd these relational interactions?

b. What principles or structure would you add? Why? How?

Ongoing Gospel Growth: Envisioning the Marriage with Gospel Lenses

As Mitch and Candi start leaving their past behind, we want them to keep experiencing ongoing gospel growth. This requires gospel vision.

In chapter 5, I explained that infusing hope begins with counselors who hope in God. Similarly, whenever I teach about couples envisioning their marriage through gospel eyes, I first start with the counselor praying for spiritual eyes to see the couple's redeemed potential in Christ. Messed up marriages and messy couples can tempt counselors to see only the couple's problems and be blinded to who they are individually and jointly in Christ.

The Counselor's God-Given Gospel Vision

If I start to struggle with a negative attitude toward a spouse or couple, I recall Paul's words in 1 Thessalonians 2:17–20. When Paul was torn away (Paul chose a phrase that means bereaved or orphaned) for a short time from the believers in Thessalonica, he said that "out of our intense longing we made every effort to see you" (2:17). So we pray, "Father, help me have such a depth of love and concern for this couple that between meetings I have an intense longing to see them again."

Paul not only wanted to see them; he wanted to see them with God's vision. "For what is our hope, our joy, or the crown in which we will glory in the presence of our Lord Jesus when he comes?" (2:19). If I were reading this passage for the first time, I would never guess that Paul's answer would be, "Is it not you? Indeed, you are our glory and joy" (2:19–20). Paul uses the language of a conquering general who is awarded the highest honor by the king—the victor's crown. Paul's highest honor and greatest joy are the people he shepherds. We pray, "Father, help me have your eternal vision of this couple—your vision of them as victors in Christ."

Having God's vision never means pretending or being blind to reality. God clearly sees us as we are *and* as we will become in Christ (Rom. 5:6–8; Phil. 1:6).

God helps us catch his gospel vision by reminding us of the truth we highlighted several chapters ago: every Christian is a saint and a son or daughter of God who faces suffering and struggles against sin on their sanctification journey. We can also remind ourselves of the biblical truth of our comprehensive salvation.

- *Justification*: Our New Pardon—The Judge Declares Us "Not Guilty! Forgiven!"
- *Reconciliation*: Our New Peace—The Father Says to Us, "Welcome Home, Son, Daughter!"
- *Regeneration*: Our New Person—The Creator Calls Us "Saint! New Creation in Christ!"
- *Redemption*: Our New Power—The Victor Says to Us, "Victor! More than a Conqueror!"

So I pray, "Father, help me see Mitch and Candi as they truly and eternally are in Christ. When their current way of relating tempts *me* to despair, by your Spirit speak Scripture truth about them to my spirit. Mitch and Candi are forgiven! Son! Daughter! Saints! Victors!"

The Couple's God-Given Gospel Vision

Our task is to help couples apply *gospel* reality to their *daily* reality. Spouses have seen each other at their worst—their most hateful and hurtful, their most broken and sinful, their most hopeless and helpless, their most selfish and egotistical. So spouses need to pray that God would enlighten the eyes of their hearts. I typically see it happen like this: I catch God's vision for each spouse individually and for the couple jointly. I then cast this vision to the couple. They then slowly catch and own the vision. As biblical counselors, God calls us to plant the seeds of gospel envisioning through:

- Anticipating gospel growth
- Affirming gospel growth
- Expecting the gospel to keep changing couples

Anticipating Gospel Growth

If we believe our theology, then we believe that God has given every redeemed couple all they need for marital life and godliness (2 Pet. 1:3–4). So, as we illustrated in chapter 5, we create an expectant attitude from our first contact.

- How will each of you know that our counseling has been successful?
- In your thinking, what does the Bible say successful marital counseling will produce?
- What will each of you be doing/thinking/relating differently after successful biblical counseling?
- After you have heard their concerns, ask: What would you like to change about this? About yourself as you go through this?

Throughout counseling, keep expecting the gospel to change the marriage and each spouse.

- As the two of you leave here today and you are on track toward applying God's truth as we discussed today, what will you be doing differently? How will you be thinking differently? How will you be relating differently?
- As you put off the old way of relating, what will you be doing instead? Specifically, how will you be doing this?

Affirming Gospel Growth

A couple envisions each other with gospel eyes as we become their number one fan—jointly and individually. When we see gospel change, we affirm it.

- Wow! I'm amazed. I've seen such great growth in your relationship in just the past three weeks. What do you attribute this to?
- How have the two of you learned to overcome your old style of relating?
- That's terrific, Candi! How did you manage to do that? What do you think of that, Mitch? What would you want to say to Candi about that?
- How awesome, Mitch! How do you explain that? What do you think of that, Candi? What would you want to say to Mitch about that?
- What words of affirmation and encouragement could you share with each other right now? What would it be like to keep cheering each other on in Christ throughout the week?
- How have you managed to stay on top of all these things as much as you have? [Said when things have been tough but the couple has been resourceful.]

Expecting the Gospel to Keep Changing Couples

The core passage behind infusing hope is the same passage underlining gospel change: "Now to him who is able to do immeasurably more than all we ask or imagine, according to his power that is at work within us" (Eph. 3:20).

Couples are not in this alone, and neither are we as biblical marriage counselors. God is our hope. He is *the* Change Agent. He has been, is, and will continue to be at work in this couple's marriage (2 Cor. 1:10–11). They do not have to start from a dead stop. In guiding, we explore how God has empowered past and current change—and how that gives them hope for ongoing, future growth. But because couples come to us squinty-eyed, we need to open their eyes.

- How is God already making some of this happen now?
- When isn't this problem happening? When is it a little bit less? What do you think God is up to in those times?
- Tell me about some times when God is already helping the two of you to fulfill his calling in your marriage. What is different in your relationship at these times? What are you each doing or thinking differently?

We also can use future-focused questions, like those we used in infusing hope.

- What will it look like when God does exceedingly, abundantly above all you could ask or imagine? In you, Mitch? In you, Candi? In the two of you together?

- Imagine that God answered your prayers for your own heart, for your spouse, and for your marriage. What would you be praying? What are you praying? How would you be different as a result of those answered prayers? How would your marriage be different?
- Our counseling will come to an end at some point. How can each of you use Ephesians 3:20 to be each other's ongoing biblical counselor?

Maturing as a Biblical Marriage Counselor

Ongoing Gospel Growth

1. Consider the following prayers. How could it impact your marriage counseling and your vision of couples if you prayed these types of prayers? Is there a couple you want to or need to pray these prayers for?

   - Father, help me to have such a depth of love and concern for this couple that between meetings I have an intense longing to see them again.
   - Father, help me have your eternal vision of this couple—your vision of them as victors in Christ.
   - Father, help me to see this couple as they truly and eternally are in Christ. When their current way of relating tempts me to despair, by your Spirit speak Scripture truth about them to my spirit. This couple is forgiven! Son! Daughter! Saints! Victors!

2. In your life, how could God use these four comprehensive gospel truths to change how you see yourself in Christ?

   a. Justification: Your New Pardon—The Judge Declares You "Not Guilty! Forgiven!"

   b. Reconciliation: Your New Peace—The Father Says to You, "Welcome Home, Son, Daughter!"

   c. Regeneration: Your New Person—The Creator Calls You, "Saint! New Creation in Christ!"

   d. Redemption: Your New Power—The Victor Says to You, "Victor! More than a Conqueror!"

3. Craft trialogue gospel conversations for each of the following aspects of ongoing gospel growth:

   a. Anticipating gospel growth

   b. Affirming gospel growth

   c. Expecting the gospel to keep changing couples

A Parenthesis: Homework That Works—Keeping the Change Going

In this chapter and the next, we address biblical counseling homework. In chapter 12 we focus on the *counselee's* homework, while in chapter 13 we will focus on the *counselor's* homework (something we think about less but should think about more). Homework is vital in sustaining, healing, reconciling, and guiding. So these principles fit throughout the biblical counseling journey.

- *Cast a vision for 24/7 gospel application.* From the onset of counseling, communicate that there is no magic counseling hour that cures all human ills. Instead, the counseling hour prepares the couple for the other 167 hours in their week. Communicate the following: "Here's what we've focused on today. What will it look like for the two of you to apply these biblical truths in love with each other this week?"

- *Collaboratively create Scripture-focused, couple-unique, situation-specific homework.* On the basis of what you focused on in the current session, discuss with the couple what would be the best homework assignment during the week: "Of all the passages we explored today, which ones will be most important for you to study and apply this week? How will you each go about doing that?" "Out of all the biblical principles we discussed today, what stands out as most important that you want to focus on and apply this week?" Couples learn what they can expect to hear at the end of each session. After a few sessions, I no longer need to ask. Throughout our meeting they have been thinking about what homework assignment they will give themselves—they are co-coaching each other in their marital discipleship.

- *How and when to use specific passages for specific situations.* We all have our go-to passages for various issues. Often *during* the session I will direct us toward those verses or ask the couple what passages they see as relevant to a particular issue. These passages become fair game for homework. However, I want to avoid a canned, one-size-fits-all approach. Keeping homework assignments collaborative strikes a good balance here.

- *How to use your own time in God's Word.* I avoid trying to apply to every couple or counselee the passage that has impacted me that day or week. My life situation may require different biblical wisdom than their life situation. However, when God works in my heart, I want to be open to the possibility that this passage may have some specific application to the couple.

- *How to use extrabiblical resources.* Collaboratively decide with the couple on which pertinent Christian booklets, books, videos, discussion guides, or workbooks to use. Resources that have questions for couples to work on together are especially beneficial. I typically do not cover this homework in detail during sessions, as if counseling is a class and they are being graded. Instead, I ask basic accountability questions: "How is the study going? What are a couple of main points you've been gleaning and applying?"

- *Keep couples connected to their local church.* We want couples to understand that marriage counseling is a subset of the ongoing one-another discipleship ministry of their local church. Require couples to be in Sunday morning worship and part of a small group. If the church has redemption or recovery ministries that fit a couple's specific issues, the couple should be regularly participating. They should have an advocate or spiritual friend who is building into their life and marriage and who knows specifically about their marriage counseling—perhaps even being a part of the sessions.

- *How to follow up.* Follow-up and accountability are vital. So I typically start with, "Last week the three of us agreed that you would focus on _____ throughout the week. Let's talk about how that's going . . ." Notice I said I *typically* start with that. There are times when it is obvious that the couple has had a horrible week and they are in distress. The problem of the moment may trump homework follow-up.

Maturing as a Biblical Marriage Counselor
Homework That Works

1. What has been your experience—homework given out by the counselor, or homework collaboratively created by the counselor and counselees? What are the pros and cons of each approach?

2. You read several principles of homework that works.

   a. Which one, if any, surprises you? How?

b. Which one, if any, do you disagree with? Why? What would you do differently?

c. What principles would you add?

3. Between meetings, how do you keep couples connected to

   a. The Word of God?

   b. The people of God (their local church)?

4. What are some best practices for following up on homework and keeping couples accountable?

CHAPTER

THIRTEEN

Growing in Grace

Guiding in Marriage Counseling, Part 2

Introduction: Infusing Helplessness and Hopelessness

In chapter 5 we emphasized infusing hope. Now we highlight infusing help-lessness and hopelessness. What a way to start our final chapter!

Recall how we started our first chapter by observing that solution-focused marital therapy encourages self-sufficiency. Biblical marriage counseling urges Christ-sufficiency. Our guiding goal is for couples to repeat after Paul:

> But [Christ] said to me, "My grace is sufficient for you, for my power is made perfect in weakness." Therefore I will boast all the more gladly about my weak-nesses, so that Christ's power may rest on me. . . . For when I am weak, then I am strong. (2 Cor. 12:9–10)

We infuse helplessness by coaching couples to be victorious together through Christ, empowering each other to tap into Christ's resurrection power and not their own strength.

But what about infusing *hopelessness*? Marriage counseling is hopeless if the goal is the couple's *happiness*. God does not guarantee happiness. But what if, as Gary Thomas reminds us, God designed marriage to make us holy more than to make us happy?[1] That is hopeful because God promises ongoing holiness (Rom. 6:1–18; 2 Pet. 3:18). We call it progressive marital sanctification (Eph. 5:21–6:18).

And what if marriage is more about God and less about us? Peter power-fully coalesces our growth in holiness and God's glory: "But grow in the grace

233

and knowledge of our Lord and Savior Jesus Christ. To him be glory both now and forever!" (2 Pet. 3:18).

The dangerous part of our ideal marital love story is that we are the god in our story. The story centers on us. Everyone else, including God, is a supporting actor.[2]

But God, in his holy love, thwarts our attempts to make life all about us. Not only is self-sufficient marriage helpless; self-centered marriage is hopeless. We help couples turn from that hopeless marital goal by traveling with them on a very different path—the path of exalting Christ together. We seek to help them apply the truths taught in Matthew 22:34–40 to their marriage.

> Love God most with your most: with all your heart, soul, mind, and spirit. Repent of anything you put on the throne above Jesus. Put Jesus before yourself. Put Jesus before your marriage, your children, your work, your ministry. Put Jesus before your need to be right. Put Jesus first. Love Jesus most.

Maturing as a Biblical Marriage Counselor
Infusing Helplessness and Hopelessness

1. What might it look like in your marriage counseling ministry to make it your goal to repeat after Paul? How might it impact your marriage counseling if you prayed this marriage counselor's version of 2 Corinthians 12:9–10?

   Lord, you have said to me, "My grace is sufficient for you, for my power is made perfect in your weakness." Help me to gladly recognize my incompetency as a biblical marriage counselor apart from your resurrection power at work in me and apart from your Spirit filling me. Help me enter every marriage-mentoring session with palms open to you so that your power rests on me. When I acknowledge my weakness as a counselor, then I am strong.

2. "But [Christ] said to me, 'My grace is sufficient for you, for my power is made perfect in weakness.' Therefore I will boast all the more gladly about my weaknesses, so that Christ's power may rest on me. . . . For when I am weak, then I am strong" (2 Cor. 12:9–10). The guiding goal is for couples to repeat after Paul. How could this goal impact the way you biblically guide couples?

3. Marriage is not about our happiness but our holiness.

    a. How does this provide hope for couples?

    b. How could you help couples to move from a happiness goal to a holiness pursuit?

4. Marriage is not about us and our glory but about God and his glory. How does this provide hope for couples? How could you help couples to move from a self-centered focus to a focus on God's glory like in 2 Peter 3:18?

A Parenthesis: The Counselor's Homework— Five Actions a Counselor Can Take between Meetings

Before we explore how to help couples live through Christ and for Christ, I want to insert another parenthesis. In chapter 12 we discussed the counselor collaborating with the couple to develop homework. We less frequently discuss the *counselor's* homework. So now we ask, What could I be doing during the week as the counselor to prepare for my next meeting with the couple?

Action #1: Pray—Be Christ-Dependent

Pray Philippians 1:9–11 over your marriage counseling and over the couple. Pray for wisdom to discern what is best in their situation so they can grow like Christ and glorify Christ.

Pray specific prayers based on previous and upcoming sessions. "Lord, please help John and Rose to . . ." Pray for strength from above. "Father, empower me and empower John and Rose to apply your Word to their marriage."

Action #2: Ponder—Be Curious

Review your marriage counseling notes—sometimes just the previous session and sometimes many or all of the preceding meetings. Seek to identify important themes and patterns. What are the heart issues? What are the reoccurring relational struggles? Do not think of this simply in technocratic terms. Instead, be *curious*.

- Who is this person? Who is this couple?
- What is their joint story? What is Christ up to in their story?
- What's the key to his heart? To her heart? What is the unique DNA of this person's soul as designed by God?

Action #3: Probe Passages and Principles

As you pray for them and ponder patterns, also probe biblical passages and theological concepts that relate to the issues you have been highlighting. Explore the Scriptures for person-specific, couple-specific, and situation-specific wisdom.

- What biblical principles most specifically apply to this couple?
- What biblical passages could provide the greatest wisdom, encouragement, and conviction for this couple with this marital struggle?

Action #4: Prepare

Based on prayer, pondering, and probing passages, begin to identify specific goals, directions, and areas of focus for your next meeting together.

- What should my goals be as their marriage counselor?
- How could we journey together to help them with _____?
- Of everything going on in this couple's marriage, what one or two areas are most vital for us to discuss this week?

Action #5: Provide Private Communication

In the past decade, perhaps the most important addition I have made to my counseling practice is communicating with my counselees between sessions via email or text messages. First, a caution—use wisdom and discretion. Before emailing or texting a counselee about counseling, obtain their written permission. Determine what email address or text number they prefer. Explore who, if anyone, sees or has access to their email. There are also simple programs to password protect emails. Use safeguards to keep your communication as confidential as possible, but realize that anything you send could eventually enter the public domain.

Second, be careful what you write—focus on positives. As with any relationship, remember the rule of thumb: save difficult or negative interactions for in-person meetings. Use email and texts for positive communication.

Third, if I am communicating with someone of the opposite sex via email or text, then I am copying her husband, an advocate, or a co-counselor.

Fourth, consider these areas of communication via email or text:

- Empathize and comfort (sustaining).
- Affirm and encourage (healing).
- Share positive summaries of the previous meeting: "Wow! I'm amazed at how you two have been able to . . ."
- Paint positive word pictures about their progress: "When I think of the progress God is producing in your marriage, the picture that keeps coming to my mind is . . ."
- Check in to see how the spouse or couple is doing: "We shared some hard stuff. You guys were honest with each other. How are you doing this week? How are you feeling?"
- Write and send them a prayer of request, supplication, thanks, or praise specifically related to your most recent meeting.
- Share additional biblical passages and scriptural wisdom principles or follow up on passages and principles you discussed.
- Ponder together possible directions and next steps for the spouse or couple.
- Ask stretching questions.

  » In our meeting, the two of you mentioned _____. How do you think you can address that using heart communication principles from Ephesians 4:25–32?
  » When we met, you committed to _____. What will it be like for the two of you to tap into Christ's strength to continue that this week?

- Keep them accountable for their homework: "How's it going in following through on _____?"

Counselees love this! They cannot believe that you are thinking about them, praying for them, and caring about them between meetings.

When it comes time to check in on their homework, they are motivated. They know that you have been spending time between meetings thinking about them. So if you are doing homework, they feel some godly pressure to be sure they are also completing their homework.

Maturing as a Biblical Marriage Counselor
The Counselor's Homework

1. To what extent is this a new idea for you—that the *counselor* is actively working on the marriage counseling and working with the couple during the week?

2. If it is not new, what do you typically do between sessions to follow up and to prepare for the next session?

3. What do you typically do in terms of communication with the couple between sessions?

4. From the five action steps, what might you want to add in terms of what you do between sessions to follow up on the past session and to prepare for the next session?

5. What might you want to add in terms of communication with the couple between sessions?

6. Written communication with spouses and couples is helpful but needs to be done wisely and carefully. What cautions might you add related to written communication with counselees? What safeguards might you put into place to maintain confidentiality?

Victorious Together through Christ: Empowering Each Other to Tap into Christ's Resurrection Power

Our first two guiding relational competencies focused on coaching couples to love like Christ. They learn to leave the past behind by putting off the old unloving ways and putting on Christ's new loving style of relating. Then they learn to keep Christlike love growing through ongoing gospel growth. We commonly and correctly take couples to Ephesians 5:22–33 to equip them to love each other with Christlike love. Our final two relational competencies place this goal into its proper biblical context. We love each other supernaturally *through* Christ's resurrection power—victorious together *through* Christ. We also love each other *for* Christ—exalting Christ together. Taken together, our four guiding relational competencies seek to coach spouses to live out the truth that it's supernatural to love each other *like* Christ, *through* Christ, *for* Christ.

A Biblical Vignette: The Power of Our New Affections

Consider how Paul weds these guiding concepts in Colossians 3:18–19, which is a two-verse synopsis of Ephesians 5:22–33. Two verses? On marriage? Surely that is too brief. Talk about short-term therapy!

But wait . . . Paul marries these two verses on marriage to the preceding seventeen verses on Christian living (Col. 3:1–17) *and* embeds them in the preceding two chapters on glorifying Christ through Christ's redemptive power (Col. 1:1–2:23).

The pivot verse is 3:1: "Since, then, you have been raised with Christ, set your hearts on things above, where Christ is, seated at the right hand of God."

"Since then": Therefore, base your marriage counseling and build your marriage on God's glory and Christ's power discussed in Colossians 1–2.

"You have been raised with Christ": How do marriages change? Christ changes spouses through co-resurrection with himself—through his resurrection power that saves *and* sanctifies spouses. Couples are victorious through Christ.

"Set your hearts on things above, where Christ is, seated at the right hand of God": Focus on the exalted Christ and on exalting Christ together in your marriage.

What a monumental transformation in mind and heart. Very few couples enter marriage counseling confessing, "Both of us are sinfully focused on ourselves instead of on exalting Christ in our marriage." Few spouses complete their Marital Personal Information Form by writing, "Yes, we are deeply hurt.

However, our main concern is not our pain but the shame we are bringing to Christ's name. We're coming to you for help with our number one goal: exalting Christ together in our marriage."

And as counselors, we are unlikely to achieve such a change of mind and heart if in the first ten seconds of our initial meeting with a couple we say, "I don't care about your pain. We're here only to hear about how you can start glorifying Christ." However, if we patiently hear their pain (sustaining), direct them to hope in Christ (healing), and gently expose their sin and Christ's grace (reconciling), then God will have used us to till fertile soil for heart change.

When couples finally gain a glimpse of their calling to exalt the Trinity through their marriage, they are amazed by the human impossibility of that calling. Now they are prepared to hear about Christ's resurrection power. They are ready to explore what it means to "put to death, therefore, whatever belongs to your earthly nature: sexual immorality, impurity, lust, evil desires and greed, which is idolatry" (Col. 3:5).

A Marital Vignette: Through Christ Alone

A wife shares with you, "My affair just about killed John, my husband. And now I see how it is shaming Christ. I've confessed it. I've repented of it. But it seemed so enslaving. Help me never go back to that sin."

A husband shares his heart. "I want to keep putting off my impurity, lust, and my past enslavement to pornography. It was killing my wife, Rose. It's shaming Christ. I've confessed it. I've repented of it. But its tentacles still surround me. Help me never go back to that sin."

This is where we shock our counselees by introducing a massive mindset shift.

"I can't help you."

"What! You're our pastor. If you can't help us, then who in the world can?"

"No one in *this* world can help you change. But Christ already changed you, Rose and John. Notice a key word in verse 5: '*therefore*.' 'Therefore, put to death . . .' Paul is pointing you back to the reality that you have *already* been raised with Christ (3:1). You are dead to sin and alive to God. 'For you died, and your life is now hidden with Christ in God' (3:3). Paul sends you the same message a couple of verses later. 'You have taken off your old self with its practices, and have put on the new self, which is being renewed in knowledge of its Creator' (3:9–10).

"John and Rose, you're both *already* new—changed by Christ to be like Christ. You're both already new creations in Christ—made new in Christ. That's your *regeneration*.

"As amazing as this is, that's not all! You're also victors in Christ, empowered by Christ. The same power that raised Christ from the dead is at work within you so that the new you can progressively keep having victory over sin. You are more than conquerors in Christ. That's your *redemption*."

"But we don't *feel* changed or victorious. At least most days we don't."

"I get that. But I'm thankful that all three of us can know by faith that Christ has already transformed us—given us a new heart with new power over sin. As your counselor, I'm immensely thankful that I don't have to try to change you. That would be helpless and hopeless. Instead, God calls me to help you believe by faith that you are already changed—co-resurrected with Christ, and then to help you help each other tap into Christ's resurrection power. Can we explore what it looks like for you to help each other put off what's already been put to death by Christ and put on what's already been made alive in Christ?"

Marriage Counseling Vignettes: Progressive Marriage Sanctification Conversations

When a couple is hungry for progressive sanctification truth, then marriage counseling is like giving candy to a baby. Explore and apply Scripture to their marriage. Think of what follows as sample progressive marriage sanctification conversations.

Progressive Marriage Sanctification Conversations about Mutual Edification

Consider these your "Kellemen Samplers" of scriptural explorations and spiritual conversations about mutual edification.

- Rose and John, God has already done the work in you. I want to help you tap into the victory you already have. More importantly, I want to get the two of you started in helping each other live out your victory in Christ. Let's begin right here in the passage we've been exploring. "Let the word of Christ dwell in you richly, teaching and admonishing one another in all wisdom, singing psalms and hymns and spiritual songs, with thankfulness in your hearts to God" (Col. 3:16).

  » For the specific besetting sins you're each fighting against, what would it look like for the word of Christ to dwell in you richly? What passages are most relevant to each of you in your fight for victory in Christ over these temptations?
  » What would it look like for you to teach and admonish each other with all wisdom? Is your relationship ready for that? If not, what needs to happen to get there? What humility would it require to

learn from each other? What passages would you go to? Could we try some of this teaching and admonishing together now?

> » The last part of the verse highlights edifying worship—singing psalms, hymns, and spiritual songs with gratitude in your hearts to God. *The greatest power over a sinful desire is defeating it with a greater holy desire.* The greatest affection in the universe is worshiping God. How can you help each other to grow in your awe for God and in your sense of wonder at God's holy love? How could mutual worship empower each of you?

- Rose and John, let's look at some additional passages about the two of you discipling each other.

  > » What might it look like for the two of you to fan into flame the gift of God within each other (2 Tim. 1:5–7)?
  > » How could you encourage each other daily so that neither of you is hardened or blinded by sin's deceitfulness (Heb. 3:11–15)?
  > » How could you stir up love and good deeds in each other (Heb. 10:24–25)?

Progressive Marriage Sanctification Conversations about Christ's Resurrection Power

Here are some Kellemen Samplers about couples tapping into Christ's resurrection power and the victory they already have in Christ.

- Rose and John, we've talked before about the bookends surrounding Ephesians 5:22–33.

  > » What would it be like for the two of you to study together and apply the biblical teaching on being filled with the Spirit?
  > » What would it look like for the two of you to put on each piece of the marital armor of God? How could you study what this means? How could you help each other apply this?

When you have affirmed already existing evidence of God's victory in their individual spiritual life or in their marriage relationship, you can explore:

- How will you tap into Christ's resurrection power to keep this change going?
- How can the two of you keep cooperating with God to keep this growth going?

- How can the two of you keep being filled with the Spirit so these changes in you and in your marriage will keep happening?

You can co-author a victorious marital narrative by trialoguing about:

- As you're on this journey together of growth in Christ, what unique gifts does your spouse bring?
- As you battle against Satan, how can you fight together in Christ's power? How can you grow together?
- Who are your other comrades in arms in the church who can join you in this battle?
- Who are your fellow pilgrims at church who can walk with you?
- What dead things do you anticipate Christ resurrecting in your marriage?
- What will your marriage look like when Christ resurrects it—when his resurrection power does its work in your relationship?

Progressive Marriage Sanctification Conversations That Fan into Flame Our Maleness and Femaleness

God created us male and female (Gen. 1:26–28), so biblical marriage counseling is gender specific. In guiding, we help couples ponder, "What do you have to offer each other out of your maleness and femaleness?" We fan into flame a husband's God-designed capacity to offer his wife empowering strength and a wife's God-designed capacity to offer her husband encouraging nurture (see chapter 3). Some samplers include:

- John, as Rose battles this temptation and seeks to tap into her victory in Christ . . .

  » What strength do you sense she needs from you right now?
  » How could you empower Rose?
  » How could you pastor and shepherd Rose toward growth in grace in this area?
  » How could you guard Rose?
  » What would it look like to move into Rose's world, even when it seems confusing and risky?

- Rose, as John fights for victory in Christ in this area . . .

  » What encouragement do you sense John is needing from you right now?
  » How could you nurture John?

» How could you build him up, edify him, and affirm him?

» What would it look like for you to open your heart to John, even in the midst of things that are painful? How could you receive John's pain right now?

» What support could you offer John at this time in his life?

Maturing as a Biblical Marriage Counselor
Victorious Together through Christ

1. In chapter 12 we focused on the first part of our guiding summary statement: "It's supernatural to love each other *like* Christ . . ." In chapter 13 we are focusing on the last part: ". . . *through* Christ, *for* Christ."

   a. How do those last four words impact your goal(s) as a biblical marriage counselor?

   b. How could those last four words shape your practice of biblical marriage counseling?

2. Read Colossians 3:18–19. Then read Colossians 3:1–17. Now read verses 18–19 again, this time consciously placing them into the context of the first seventeen verses.

   a. How does reading 3:18–19 in context change how you would apply these verses to your marriage?

   b. How could reading 3:18–19 in context reshape how you help a couple apply these verses to their marriage?

3. Reread the section titled "A Marital Vignette: Through Christ Alone."

    a. We often struggle with gospel amnesia. This is why Peter keeps reminding believers of the gospel in 2 Peter 1:12–21. How could the reminders in the marital vignette about our gospel victory in Christ impact your personal progressive sanctification journey?

    b. How could the reminders in the marital vignette about our gospel victory in Christ impact how you guide couples in their progressive sanctification journey?

4. You read about a dozen trialogues under the heading "Marriage Counseling Vignettes."

    a. Which three or four of these trialogues stand out to you as most important? Why? How?

    b. Craft half a dozen of your own progressive marriage sanctification conversations.

We frequently quote Colossians 3:17. We rarely quote it in connection with the two marriage verses directly following it. If we did, we might paraphrase Paul's marriage message in context like this:

> Wives, whatever you do in God's calling on your marriage to submit to your husband as is fitting in the Lord, whether you do it in word or deed, do all your vulnerable respecting of your husband in the name of the Lord Jesus, giving thanks to God the Father through him—exalt God as you submit to your husband. Husbands, whatever you do in God's calling on your marriage to love your wife and never be harsh with her, whether you do it in word or deed, do all your sacrificial shepherding of your wife in the name of the Lord Jesus, giving thanks to God the Father through him—exalt God as you love your wife.

The Wonderful Counselor: It's All about Him

The church where I am serving as pastor of counseling ministries has a sign at the main exit from the sanctuary. The preacher sees it as he preaches, the worship team views it as they lead in worship, and every attendee passes under it as they depart. It is a simple yet profound reminder of the purpose of our lives.

IT'S ALL ABOUT HIM!

Those four words capture the message of our final marriage counseling relational competency. Our counseling is all about him—Father, Son, and Holy Spirit. When couples transition from counseling with us, they may say, "What a great counselor you are!" But our deepest desire is to hear them say, "What a Wonderful Counselor Jesus is!" As biblical marriage counselors, our attitudes and actions should communicate, "It's all about him!" We are incompetent marriage counselors pointing to the Wonderful Marriage Counselor.

It is our prayer that the couples we counsel come to the realization that marriage is all about Jesus. Easier said than done. Hurt tempts us to focus on ourselves, and nothing hurts more than marital hurt. So we patiently, gently, and humbly walk with hurting and hurtful spouses, helping them to glimpse the glory of the Father who compassionately cares about their pain (2 Cor. 1:3–4), the Son who sympathetically shares in their pain (Heb. 4:14–16), and the Spirit who bears their pain (John 14:15–18; Rom. 8:12–17, 26–27).

Keep guiding them to biblical images of God's holy love—images like Isaiah 40:10–11, which we explored in chapter 7. "It's all about him" does not mean that God cares *only* about his glory. It means he cares *ultimately* about his glory, because he is the most glorious being in the universe. His shining glory is that though he does not need us, he chooses to love us. It's all about him, and our infinite God cares about finite us!

Gospel-Centered Marriage Counseling: It's All about Him

How do we help couples progress to this point? First, like most of life, it is something more caught than taught. Do they see us as their counselor making life all about Christ?

Second, discuss marriage counseling passages in their biblical context. The three primary New Testament passages about marriage all have a gospel-centered context.

Working backward, 1 Peter 3:1–7 is all about husbands and wives. Or in context is it all about him—about Christ's gospel of grace?

> Praise be to the God and Father of our Lord Jesus Christ! In his great mercy he has given us new birth into a living hope through the resurrection of Jesus Christ from the dead, and into an inheritance that can never perish, spoil or fade. This inheritance is kept in heaven for you, who through faith are shielded by God's power until the coming of the salvation that is ready to be revealed in the last time. (1 Pet. 1:3–5)

Colossians 3:17–19 is all about husbands and wives. Or in context is it all about him—about Christ's gospel of grace?

> The Son is the image of the invisible God, the firstborn over all creation. For in him all things were created: things in heaven and on earth, visible and invisible, whether thrones or powers or rulers or authorities; all things have been created through him and for him. He is before all things, and in him all things hold together. And he is the head of the body, the church; he is the beginning and the firstborn from among the dead, so that in everything he might have the supremacy. For God was pleased to have all his fullness dwell in him, and through him to reconcile to himself all things, whether things on earth or things in heaven, by making peace through his blood, shed on the cross. (Col. 1:15–20)

Ephesians 5:22–33 is all about husbands and wives. Or in context is it all about him—about Christ's gospel of grace?

> Praise be to the God and Father of our Lord Jesus Christ, who has blessed us in the heavenly realms with every spiritual blessing in Christ. For he chose us in him before the creation of the world to be holy and blameless in his sight. In love he predestined us for adoption to sonship through Jesus Christ, in accordance with his pleasure and will—to the praise of his glorious grace, which he has freely given us in the One he loves. (Eph. 1:3–6)

IT'S ALL ABOUT HIM!

Maturing as a Biblical Marriage Counselor
Exalting Christ Together

1. It's all about Jesus!

   a. How does this theology of life play itself out in your life? Where is God already helping you to live out the truth that it's all about Christ? What areas of your life do you need to make more about him?

   b. How does this theology of life play itself out in your ministry as a marriage counselor?

2. How could you help couples come to a greater realization that their marriage is all about Christ?

3. How does it impact your marriage counseling when you examine 1 Peter 3, Colossians 3, and Ephesians 5 in the context of 1 Peter 1, Colossians 1, and Ephesians 1, respectively?

4. As we near the end of our journey, pen a psalm or a prayer of praise to God titled "It's All about Him!"

Commencement

We all love commencements! Graduations. "Pomp and Circumstance"—the graduation march. Moving forward.

We will be using the word "commencement" in two ways. First, we will discuss commencement in the sense of the final marriage counseling session and what follows. Second, we will use commencement in the way other authors end their book with a conclusion.

Marriage Counseling Commencement: Moving Forward with Hope

I encouraged you to launch your marriage counseling meetings by infusing hope. Now you want to wrap up your formal meetings by moving forward with hope. We help couples to commence well through:

- A Marriage Counseling Commencement Meeting
- A Marriage Counseling Commencement Plan
- A Marriage Counseling Commencement Letter

A Marriage Counseling Commencement Meeting

A marriage counseling commencement meeting is hope-filled. It pictures the ongoing fresh start a couple has initiated in Christ. It communicates how proud of them you are as their counselor. It also communicates that there is more growth on the horizon—marital progressive sanctification.

How do you know when it's nearing time to wrap up ongoing marriage counseling? When the couple is making consistent (not perfect) progress toward the goals they set when they completed their Marriage Counseling Goals and Focus Form (see fig. 5.1).

You will find it helpful to give the couple some advance notice that you think they are well on their way to keeping the change going without regular meetings with you. Most couples will be both encouraged and scared by this because they have come to appreciate your ministry in their marriage. One way to address their fears is to start spreading out the time between your meetings—perhaps meeting every other week or every third week. This begins to wean them away from dependence on you and toward ongoing dependence on Christ and the body of Christ.

At least one week before a commencement meeting, provide the couple with some commencement questions specific to their marriage and the issues they have been addressing. Help them to ponder their current and future growth. Ask them to respond to the commencement exercises first individually and then together. When you meet, discuss their responses further.

Every couple will be different, but some sample commencement exercises could include:

- Before we started counseling, you each identified the top two or three areas in your heart, actions, attitudes, and way of relating to your spouse that you wanted help changing so that you could be more Christlike and your marriage could be more Christ-honoring.

  » In each area, describe the progress you have made through Christ's strength.
  » Write out a prayer of thanks and celebration for the work Christ has been doing in your heart.
  » Begin to map out a biblical plan in each area to keep the growth going.

- Before we started counseling, you each identified the two or three aspects of your marriage that you wanted help changing so that your marriage could be more Christ-honoring.

  » In each area, describe the progress you have made together through Christ's strength.
  » Write out a prayer of thanks and celebration for the work Christ has been doing in your marriage.
  » Begin to map out a biblical plan in each area so the two of you can keep the growth going.

- Before we started counseling, you each identified a vision for your marriage from Ephesians 3:14–21. You thought ahead three months about God doing exceedingly, abundantly above all that you could ask or imagine in your heart and in your marriage. And you identified two or three amazing changes you were envisioning, praying for, and hoping for.

- » Looking back on the time since we began marriage counseling, what amazing work has God already done in your marriage?
- » Looking ahead another six months, what is your God-given vision for ongoing change and growth in your marriage?
- » What ongoing goals do you have for your marriage? Be prepared to share these with each other and to share specific ways the two of you can move toward these goals.

- Before we started counseling, you each identified the top two or three strengths that you saw in your spouse that you wanted to affirm.

- » How have you seen your spouse use these gifts and strengths to bring healing and growth to your marriage?
- » What additional words of affirmation, encouragement, and thanks would you like to share with your spouse as you reflect on the past several months of your marriage?

- *Sustaining Commencement Exercises*: You have climbed in the casket with each other—empathizing with each other. What are your spouse's burdens, hurts, sorrows, suffering, and pain? How can you continue to comfort your spouse in these areas?
- *Healing Commencement Exercises*: What aspects of your marriage has Christ resurrected? How can you celebrate that resurrection together? You have celebrated together Christ's resurrection of your marriage. How can you praise Christ together?
- *Reconciling Commencement Exercises*: Where have you seen, appreciated, and benefited from your spouse's gracious forgiveness? What will it look like for you to continue to forgive, comfort, and reaffirm your love for your spouse in those areas where you have forgiven your spouse?
- *Guiding Commencement Exercises*: In what ways has your relationship with your spouse changed for the better? How has your spouse influenced you to reflect God's glory more clearly? In what ways have you and your spouse been weaving your lives together? How can you both work on weaving your lives together even more? Discuss times when your weaving of stories has brought you intimacy. What are some of the most beautiful and wonderful characteristics of your spouse? What vision do you have for how Christ will continue to work in your spouse's life? How could Christ use you to help your spouse continue to grow in grace?

A Marriage Counseling Commencement Plan

During your commencement meeting(s), discuss the couple's answers to your commencement questions. This discussion will allow you to collaboratively craft your commencement plan. The plan seeks to address the question, How can we continue to tap into Christ's resurrection power and the resources of the body of Christ to keep this biblical change going and growing?

As you develop their plan together, be specific—make it actionable, measurable, and unique to them. Connect them to the body of Christ. What ministries in your church (small groups, marriage groups, discipleship groups, marriage classes, men's or women's groups) and in the parachurch (marriage retreats, marriage mentoring) could the couple participate in to keep growing? What resources (books, booklets, study guides, video series) could the couple use together?

Then schedule a follow-up meeting six to eight weeks in the future. This expresses your ongoing concern for them. This keeps them accountable to continue working on their marriage—they are going to be checking in with you. It also addresses the potential embarrassment they may experience if they backslide. Couples sometimes feel guilty about marital failures after concluding counseling. This can lead them to not contact you when they need additional counsel. So say something like:

- Let's look at our schedules now and let's plan a follow-up meeting in six to eight weeks. By the way, if you find yourself in a crisis before then, you know I'm here for you. Let's be honest, every marriage has its ups and downs. So scheduling this meeting now will make it easier if there are some difficulties that we need to address. Or maybe it's a meeting where we spend most of our time celebrating. Either way, let's plan to meet again on __.

A Marriage Counseling Commencement Letter

After your commencement meeting, write and send a marriage commencement letter (or email). If you have been communicating with the couple between sessions, then this will not come as a surprise to them. Focus on specific areas of growth and strength that you have observed in their marriage. Use language from your meetings. Perhaps it might sound something like this:

Shannon and Dex,

You've come a long way by God's grace! And in such a short time too. In the twelve weeks we've been counseling, both of you have shown intense commitment to your marriage and to our marriage counseling.

Dex, I've seen you move from rather passive in how you responded to Shannon's concern to downright confident. Over the last few weeks you have shed the excess weight of excuse making and "dodging" (as we humorously called it). I've seen you turn those extra pounds into abs of steel! Your honesty with Shannon, both about yourself and about her, is rebuilding her trust. Shannon is responding—because she can trust you to lift the weights off of her, she no longer has the need to carry the load for the two of you. Dex, you're like an Olympic weight-lifting champion in my book!

Shannon, "softening" is the word that keeps coming to mind when I think about how you've allowed your trust in God to reshape your responses to Dex. I know that there were times when you and I went toe-to-toe, but I also sense your softness toward what God was wanting to do in your life through our interactions. Lately I've really appreciated how you've been Dex's number one fan. Have you noticed how encouraged he's been by this?

When I picture your marriage, I think of the three Rs.

Resilience. You two are persistent. You have a fight in you—not fighting each other but fighting Satan together. Never give up!

Respect. Over the last six weeks I've heard you share so much growing mutual respect. Keep it up!

Resurrection. You guys realize that this change is all through Christ and all for Christ. You keep tapping into his resurrection power. Way to go!

Of course, we all face occasional setbacks in our relationships. When those come your way, how will the two of you work together to maintain your newfound teamwork?

Along with this letter, I'm sending you our Marriage Commencement Exercise Form. I'll be excited to hear how the two of you respond to these questions.

I'm praying for you. I really am. And I'm also praising for you—I'm praising God for how his grace has reconnected the two of you.

> In Christ's grace,
> Pastor Bob

Maturing as a Biblical Marriage Counselor
Marriage Counseling Commencement

1. What is your final marriage counseling session typically like? How might this section on commencement shape or reshape your final session(s)?

2. You read an extensive list of sample commencement exercises.

   a. Which ones do you think would be most important and helpful in your final session(s) with couples? Why? How?

   b. What other commencement exercises or questions would you add?

3. What would your marriage counseling commencement plan contain? What areas would you focus on? How could you make it couple-specific?

4. If you were to craft a marriage counseling commencement letter, what areas would you cover? How would you make it couple-specific?

Gospel-Centered Marriage Counseling Commencement

Marriage Counseling Prayer and Praise

I started our journey by discussing my incompetence without Christ. In Christ, we can all become competent biblical marriage counselors (Rom. 15:14). Just as with marriages, counselor growth is a lifelong progressive sanctification process. Christ works in us as we work through his power.

I am repeating our summary of the twenty-two gospel-centered marriage counseling relational competencies in figure C.1. Use figure C.1 to respond to our final Maturing as a Biblical Marriage Counselor exercises and questions.

My concluding words to you come from Ephesians 3:20–21, the same passage as my first words to marriage counseling couples.

The Biblical Marriage Counselor's Commencement Prayer and Praise

Now, biblical marriage counselor,
depend upon him alone and give glory to him alone
who is able to do immeasurably more than all we ask or imagine
through our marriage counseling and in our marital counseling couples,
because our ministry of marriage counseling is according to his resurrection power
that is at work within us and within the couples we counsel,
to him—the Divine Counselor, the Wonderful Counselor—be glory in the church
and in Christ Jesus throughout all generations, for ever and ever!
Amen.

Figure C.1

Overview of Biblical Marriage Counseling

22 Gospel-Centered Marriage Counseling Relational Competencies

Infusing Hope

H Having Hope as a Marriage Counselor (chap. 5)
O Offering Hope to Hurting Couples (chap. 5)
P Promoting God's Perspective (chap. 5)
E Enlightening Couples (chap. 5)

Parakaletic Biblical Marriage Counseling for Suffering Spouses

- **Sustaining**: Like Christ, we care about each other's hurts.
    C Coupling with the Couple (chap. 6)
    A Assisting the Couple to Become Intimate Allies (chap. 6)
    R Renewing the Couple's Trust in the God of All Comfort (chap. 7)
    E Engaging the Couple through Empathetic Encouragement (chap. 7)

- **Healing**: Through Christ, it's possible for us to hope in God together.
    F Fighting Satan's Lying and Condemning Earthly Narrative (chap. 8)
    A Applying Christ's Truth and Grace Eternal Narrative (chap. 8)
    I Inviting Couples to Crop the Life of Christ into Their Marital Life (chap. 9)
    T Trialoguing about Christ's Truth and Grace Eternal Narrative (chap. 9)
    H Healing Individually and Together in Christ (chap. 9)

Nouthetic Biblical Marriage Counseling for Sinning Spouses

- **Reconciling**: It's horrible to sin against Christ and each other, but through Christ it's wonderful to be forgiven and to forgive.
    P Probing Theologically (chap. 10)
    E Exposing Marital Heart Sins (chap. 10)
    A Applying Truth Relationally (chap. 11)
    C Calming the Conscience with Grace (chap. 11)
    E Enlightening Couples about Biblical Marital Reconciliation (chap. 11)

- **Guiding**: It's supernatural to love each other like Christ, through Christ, for Christ.
    L Leaving the Past Behind (chap. 12)
    O Ongoing Gospel Growth (chap. 12)
    V Victorious Together through Christ (chap. 13)
    E Exalting Christ Together (chap. 13)

Maturing as a Biblical Marriage Counselor
Gospel-Centered Marriage Counseling Commencement

1. Review figure C.1.

   a. Which of the twenty-two relational competencies are you strongest in? Is that due more to natural giftedness and how God has wired you, or is it due more to hard work in developing that area?

   b. Which of the twenty-two relational competencies do you need to work on the most? How could you develop those areas? Why do you suppose those areas are not your strengths?

2. Reflect back on your time reading and working through this equipping manual.

   a. What truths will you take with you for your life and for your marriage (if married)?

   b. What truths will you take with you for your marriage counseling ministry?

3. If you have worked through this equipping manual in a lab small group:

    a. What has been most rewarding for you in the group process?

    b. What words of encouragement and affirmation would you like to share with specific members of your small group?

4. As you commence . . .

    a. What will you do to keep the change going and growing in your life?

    b. What will you do to keep the change going and growing in your marriage counseling ministry?

Notes

Chapter 2 Marriage My Way . . . or the Highway!

1. Paul Tripp, *What Did You Expect?* (Wheaton: Crossway, 2015), 1–24.

Chapter 3 Marriage Christ's Way

1. Ray Ortlund, *Marriage and the Mystery of the Gospel* (Wheaton: Crossway, 2016), 100.
2. Ortlund, *Marriage and the Mystery of the Gospel*, 100.
3. Tim and Kathy Keller, *The Meaning of Marriage* (New York: Penguin, 2013), 44.
4. Paul Tripp, *Instruments in the Redeemer's Hands: People in Need of Change Helping People in Need of Change* (Phillipsburg, NJ: P&R, 2002).

Chapter 4 Mapping Biblical Marriage Counseling

1. Frank Lake, *Clinical Theology: A Theological and Psychiatric Basis to Clinical Pastoral Care* (London: Darton, Longman, & Todd, 1966), 21, italics in original.
2. See Jay Adams, *Competent to Counsel, The Christian Counselor's Manual*, and *A Theology of Christian Counseling*.
3. For a comprehensive development of sustaining, healing, reconciling, and guiding, see Bob Kellemen, *Gospel Conversations* (Grand Rapids: Zondervan, 2015).

Chapter 6 Comforting Each Other with Christ's Comfort

1. Warren Wiersbe, *On Being a Servant of God* (Nashville: Thomas Nelson, 1993), 20.

Chapter 9 Tuning into the Bible's Faith Story

1. Drawn from the Biblical Counseling Coalition Confessional Statement, updated July 2018, http://biblicalcounselingcoalition.org/about/confessional-statement/.

Chapter 10 Dispensing Grace

1. Abuse counseling is beyond the scope of this book. However, readers are strongly encouraged to read and apply materials such as the eight resources listed in the bibliography under Domestic Abuse and Marriage.

Chapter 11 Superabounding Grace

1. Quoted in Bob Kellemen, *Counseling Under the Cross* (Greensboro, NC: New Growth, 2017), 165.
2. Quoted in Kellemen, *Counseling Under the Cross*, 160–61.

Chapter 13 Growing in Grace

1. Gary Thomas, *Sacred Marriage: What If God Designed Marriage to Make Us Holy More Than to Make Us Happy?* (Grand Rapids: Zondervan, 2015).
2. Brad Hambrick, *Creating a Gospel-Centered Marriage* (Durham, NC: The Summit Church, 2013), 25.

Resources for Marriage
and Marriage Counseling

I have designed this bibliography for the practical use of marriage counselors and couples. By organizing the bibliography into categories, counselors and counselees can select resources appropriate for the unique couple and their specific situation. Many of these resources are in booklet or discussion/study guide format or have workbooks associated with them—making them excellent for marriage counseling homework and small group use.

Dating and Pre-Engagement

Baker, Ernie. *Marry Wisely, Marry Well: A Blueprint for Personal Preparation.* Wapwallopen, PA: Shepherd, 2016.

James, Joel. *Help! I'm Confused about Dating.* Wapwallopen, PA: Shepherd, 2017.

Lane, Tim. *Sex before Marriage: How Far Is Too Far?* Greensboro, NC: New Growth, 2009.

Perron, Sean, and Spencer Harmon. *Letters to a Romantic: On Dating.* Phillipsburg, NJ: P&R, 2017.

———. *Letters to a Romantic: On Engagement.* Phillipsburg, NJ: P&R, 2017.

Powlison, David, and John Yenchko. *Pre-Engagement: Five Questions to Ask Yourselves.* Phillipsburg, NJ: P&R, 2000.

Priolo, Lou. *Danger Signs of an Unhealthy Dating Relationship.* Sand Springs, OK: Grace and Truth, 2016.

Reju, Deepak. *She's Got the Wrong Guy: Why Smart Women Settle.* Greensboro, NC: New Growth, 2017.

Segal, Marshall. *Not Yet Married: The Pursuit of Joy in Singleness and Dating.* Wheaton: Crossway, 2017.

Smith, William. *Should We Get Married?: How to Evaluate Your Relationship.* Greensboro, NC: New Growth, 2008.

Thomas, Gary. *The Sacred Search: What If It's Not about Who You Marry, but Why?* Colorado Springs: David C. Cook, 2013.

Premarital Counseling and Premarital Relationships

Green, Rob. *Tying the Knot: A Premarital Guide to a Strong and Lasting Marriage.* Greensboro, NC: New Growth, 2016.

Henderson, John. *Catching Foxes: A Gospel-Guided Journey to Marriage.* Phillipsburg, NJ: P&R, 2018.

Mack, Wayne. *Preparing for Marriage God's Way: A Step-by-Step Guide for Marriage Success Before and After the Wedding.* Second edition. Phillipsburg, NJ: P&R, 2013.

Parks, Catherine. *A Christ-Centered Wedding: Rejoicing in the Gospel on Your Big Day.* Nashville: B&H, 2014.

Piper, John. *Preparing for Marriage: Help for Christian Couples.* Revised and expanded edition. Minneapolis: Desiring God, 2018.

Marriage: Biblical Meaning and Purpose

Ash, Christopher. *Married for God: Making Your Marriage the Best It Can Be.* Wheaton: Crossway, 2016.

Hambrick, Brad. *Creating a Gospel-Centered Marriage, Part V: Intimacy.* Durham, NC: The Summit Church, 2013.

Keller, Tim, and Kathy Keller. *The Meaning of Marriage: Facing the Complexities of Commitment with the Wisdom of God.* New York: Penguin, 2013.

Ortlund, Ray. *Marriage and the Mystery of the Gospel.* Wheaton: Crossway, 2016.

Piper, John. *This Momentary Marriage: A Parable of Permanence.* Wheaton: Crossway, 2012.

Thomas, Gary. *Sacred Marriage: What If God Designed Marriage to Make Us Holy More Than to Make Us Happy?* Grand Rapids: Zondervan, 2015.

Marital Relationships

Adams, Jay. *Solving Marriage Problems.* Grand Rapids: Zondervan, 1986.

Harvey, Dave. *When Sinners Say "I Do": Discovering the Power of the Gospel for Marriage.* Wapwallopen, PA: Shepherd, 2007.

Lane, Tim, and Paul Tripp. *Relationships: A Mess Worth Making.* Greensboro, NC: New Growth, 2008.

Mack, Wayne. *Strengthening Your Marriage.* Phillipsburg, NJ: P&R, 1999.

Mack, Wayne, and Carol Mack. *Sweethearts for a Lifetime: Making the Most of Your Marriage.* Phillipsburg, NJ: P&R, 2006.

Smith, Winston. *Marriage Matters: Extraordinary Change through Ordinary Moments.* Greensboro, NC: New Growth, 2010.

Tripp, Paul. *What Did You Expect? Redeeming the Realities of Marriage.* Wheaton: Crossway, 2015.

Marriage Counseling and Marriage Homework

Holmes, Jonathan D. *Counsel for Couples: A Biblical and Practical Guide for Marriage Counseling*. Grand Rapids: Zondervan, 2019.

Mack, Wayne. *A Homework Manual for Biblical Living: Family and Marital Problems*. Phillipsburg, NJ: P&R, 1980.

———. *A Homework Manual for Biblical Living: Personal and Interpersonal Problems*. Phillipsburg, NJ: P&R, 1979.

Roles in Marriage: Both Husbands and Wives

Miller, Keith, and Patricia Miller. *Quick Scripture Reference for Counseling Couples*. Grand Rapids: Baker Books, 2017.

Piper, John, ed. *Rediscovering Biblical Manhood and Womanhood*. Wheaton: Crossway, 2012.

Roles in Marriage: Women and Women's Issues

Fitzpatrick, Elyse. *Helper by Design: God's Perfect Plan for Women in Marriage*. Chicago: Moody, 2003.

———, ed. *Women Counseling Women: Biblical Answers to Life's Difficult Problems*. Eugene, OR: Harvest House, 2010.

Fitzpatrick, Elyse, and Carol Cornish. *Women Helping Women: A Biblical Guide to Major Issues Women Face*. Eugene, OR: Harvest House, 1997.

Hotton, Glenda. *Help! I Want to Model Submission in Marriage*. Wapwallopen, PA: Shepherd, 2016.

Miller, Patricia. *Quick Scripture Reference for Counseling Women*. Grand Rapids: Baker Books, 2013.

Peace, Martha. *The Excellent Wife: A Biblical Perspective*. Bemidji, MN: Focus, 1999.

Street, John, and Janie Street. *The Biblical Counseling Guide for Women*. Eugene, OR: Harvest House, 2016.

Roles in Marriage: Men and Men's Issues

Miller, Keith. *Quick Scripture Reference for Counseling Men*. Grand Rapids: Baker Books, 2014.

Priolo, Lou. *The Complete Husband: A Practical Guide for Improved Biblical Husbanding*. Phillipsburg, NJ: P&R, 2017.

Scott, Stuart. *The Exemplary Husband: A Biblical Perspective*. Bemidji, MN: Focus, 2002.

Street, John, ed. *Men Counseling Men: A Biblical Guide to the Major Issues Men Face*. Eugene, OR: Harvest House, 2013.

Marriage Communication and Conflict Resolution

Baker, Ernie. *Help! I'm in Conflict*. Wapwallopen, PA: Shepherd, 2015.

Jones, Robert. *Pursuing Peace: A Christian Guide to Handling Our Conflict*. Wheaton: Crossway, 2012.

Lane, Tim. *Conflict: A Redemptive Opportunity*. Greensboro, NC: New Growth, 2006.

Powlison, David. *Renewing Marital Intimacy: Closing the Gap between You and Your Spouse*. Greensboro, NC: New Growth, 2008.

Sande, Ken. *The Peacemaker: A Biblical Guide to Resolving Personal Conflict*. Grand Rapids: Baker Books, 2004.

Sande, Ken, and Kevin Johnson. *Resolving Everyday Conflict*. Grand Rapids: Baker Books, 2015.

Sande, Ken, with Tom Raabe. *Peacemaking for Families*. Colorado Springs: Focus on the Family, 2002.

Scott, Stuart. *Communication and Conflict Resolution: A Biblical Perspective*. Bemidji, MN: Focus, 2005.

Tripp, Paul. *War of Words: Getting to the Heart of Your Communication Struggles*. Phillipsburg, NJ: P&R, 2001.

Sexual Intimacy in Marriage

Chandler, Matt, with Jared Wilson. *The Mingling of Souls: God's Design for Love, Marriage, Sex, and Redemption*. Colorado Springs: David C. Cook, 2015.

Green, Rob. *"Not Tonight, Honey": Handling Your Wife's Sexual Rejection*. Greensboro, NC: New Growth, 2012.

Piper, John, and Justin Taylor, eds. *Sex and the Supremacy of Christ*. Wheaton: Crossway, 2005.

Sexual Purity in Marriage

Black, Nicholas. *What's Wrong with a Little Porn When You're Married?* Greensboro, NC: New Growth, 2012.

Coyle, Rachel. *Help! She's Struggling with Pornography*. Wapwallopen, PA: Shepherd, 2017.

Croft, Brian. *Help! He's Struggling with Pornography*. Wapwallopen, PA: Shepherd, 2014.

Lambert, Heath. *Finally Free: Fighting for Purity with the Power of Grace*. Grand Rapids: Zondervan, 2013.

Powlison, David. *Making All Things New: Restoring Joy to the Sexually Broken*. Wheaton: Crossway, 2017.

Reju, Deepak. *Pornography: Fighting for Purity*. Phillipsburg, NJ: P&R, 2018.

Street, John. *Passions of the Heart: Biblical Counsel for Stubborn Sexual Sins*. Phillipsburg, NJ: P&R, 2019.

Tiede, Vicki. *Your Husband Is Addicted to Porn: Healing after Betrayal*. Greensboro, NC: New Growth, 2013.

Tripp, Paul. *Sex in a Broken World: How Christ Redeems What Sin Distorts*. Wheaton: Crossway, 2018.

Marital Unfaithfulness

Eyrich, Howard, with Cheryl Blackmon. *After an Affair: Rebuilding Your Trust, Rebuilding Your Marriage*. North Charleston, SC: CreateSpace, 2018.

Ganschow, Julie. *Living Beyond the Heart of Betrayal: Biblically Addressing the Pain of Sexual Sin*. Kansas City, MO: Pure Water, 2013.

Gembola, Michael. *After an Affair: Pursuing Restoration*. Phillipsburg, NJ: P&R, 2018.

Jones, Robert. *Restoring Your Broken Marriage: Healing after Adultery*. Greensboro, NC: New Growth, 2009.

Smith, Winston. *Help! My Spouse Committed Adultery: First Steps for Dealing with Betrayal*. Greensboro, NC: New Growth, 2008.

Summers, Mike. *Help! My Spouse Has Been Unfaithful*. Wapwallopen, PA: Shepherd, 2014.

Domestic Abuse and Marriage

Dryburgh, Anne. *Debilitated and Diminished: Help for Christian Women in Emotionally Abusive Marriages*. North Charleston, SC: CreateSpace, 2018.

Hambrick, Brad. *Self-Centered Spouse: Help for Chronically Broken Marriages*. Phillipsburg, NJ: P&R, 2014.

Henderson, John. *Abuse: Finding Hope in Christ*. Phillipsburg, NJ: P&R, 2012.

Holcomb, Lindsey, and Justin Holcomb. *Is It My Fault? Hope and Healing for Those Suffering Domestic Violence*. Chicago: Moody, 2014.

Moles, Chris. *The Heart of Domestic Abuse: Gospel Solutions for Men Who Use Control and Violence in the Home*. Bemidji, MN: Focus, 2015.

Newheiser, Jim. *Help! Someone I Love Has Been Abused*. Wapwallopen, PA: Shepherd, 2014.

Strickland, Darby. *Domestic Abuse: Help for the Sufferer*. Phillipsburg, NJ: P&R, 2018.

Welch, Ed. *Living with an Angry Spouse: Help for Victims of Abuse*. Greensboro, NC: New Growth, 2008.

Sexual Abuse and Marriage

Holcomb, Justin, and Lindsey Holcomb. *Rid of My Disgrace: Hope and Healing for Victims of Sexual Assault*. Wheaton: Crossway, 2011.

Kellemen, Bob. *Sexual Abuse: Beauty for Ashes*. Phillipsburg, NJ: P&R, 2013.

Nicewander, Sue, and Maria Brookins. *Treasure in the Ashes: Our Journey Home from the Ruins of Sexual Abuse*. Wapwallopen, PA: Shepherd, 2018.

Marriage, Grieving, Healing, Forgiveness, and Reconciliation

Brauns, Chris. *Unpacking Forgiveness: Biblical Answers for Complex Questions and Deep Wounds*. Wheaton: Crossway, 2008.

Kellemen, Robert W. *God's Healing for Life's Losses: How to Find Hope When You're Hurting*. Winona Lake, IN: BMH, 2010.

———. *Grief: Walking with Jesus*. Phillipsburg, NJ: P&R, 2018.

Lane, Tim. *Forgiving Others: Joining Wisdom and Love*. Greensboro, NC: New Growth, 2005.

MacArthur, John. *The Truth About Forgiveness*. Nashville: Thomas Nelson, 2012.

Newcomer, Jim. *Help! I Can't Forgive*. Carlisle, PA: Day One, 2012.

Priolo, Lou. *Bitterness: The Root That Pollutes*. Phillipsburg, NJ: P&R, 2008.

Viars, Steve. *Putting Your Past in Its Place: Moving Forward in Peace and Forgiveness*. Eugene, OR: Harvest House, 2011.

Marriage, Separation, Divorce, and Remarriage

Adams, Jay. *Marriage, Divorce, and Remarriage in the Bible*. Grand Rapids: Zondervan, 1986.

Grissom, Steve. *Divorce Care: Hope, Help, and Healing During and After Your Divorce*. Nashville: Thomas Nelson, 2006.

Newheiser, Jim. *Marriage, Divorce, and Remarriage: Critical Questions and Answers*. Phillipsburg, NJ: P&R, 2017.

Rooks, Linda. *Fighting for Your Marriage While Separated: A Practical Guide for the Brokenhearted*. Greensboro, NC: New Growth, 2019.

Smith, Winston. *Divorce Recovery: Growing and Healing God's Way*. Greensboro, NC: New Growth, 2008.

Military Marriages

Green, Rob. *Leaving Your Family Behind: Preparing for Military Deployment*. Greensboro, NC: New Growth, 2011.

———. *Reuniting after Military Deployment: Help for the Transition*. Greensboro, NC: New Growth, 2011.

Biblical Counseling Theology

Adams, Jay. *A Theology of Christian Counseling: More Than Redemption*. Grand Rapids: Zondervan, 1986.

Biblical Counseling Coalition. "BCC Confessional Statement." Updated July 2018, https://biblicalcounselingcoalition.org/about/confessional-statement/.

Kellemen, Bob. *Gospel-Centered Counseling: How Christ Changes Lives*. Grand Rapids: Zondervan, 2014.

Kellemen, Bob, and Steve Viars, eds. *Christ-Centered Biblical Counseling: Changing Lives with God's Changeless Truth*. 2nd ed. Eugene, OR: Harvest House, 2020.

Kellemen, Robert, and Jeff Forrey, eds. *Scripture and Counseling: God's Word for Life in a Broken World*. Grand Rapids: Zondervan, 2014.

Lake, Frank. *Clinical Theology: A Theological and Psychiatric Basis to Clinical Pastoral Care*. London: Darton, Longman, & Todd, 1966.

Lambert, Heath. *A Theology of Biblical Counseling: The Doctrinal Foundations of Counseling Ministry*. Grand Rapids: Zondervan, 2016.

Lelek, Jeremy. *Biblical Counseling Basics: Roots, Beliefs, and Future*. Greensboro, NC: New Growth, 2018.

Powlison, David. *Seeing with New Eyes: Counseling and the Human Condition through the Lens of Scripture*. Greensboro, NC: New Growth, 2003.

Equipping Biblical Counselors

Kellemen, Bob. *Equipping Counselors for Your Church: The 4E Ministry Training Strategy*. Phillipsburg, NJ: P&R, 2011.

————. *Gospel Conversations: How to Care Like Christ*. Grand Rapids: Zondervan, 2015.

Nicewander, Sue. *Building a Church Counseling Ministry Without Killing the Pastor*. Carlisle, PA: Day One, 2012.

Biblical Counseling Methodology and One-Another Ministry

Adams, Jay. *The Christian Counselor's Manual: The Practice of Nouthetic Counseling*. Grand Rapids: Zondervan, 1986.

————. *Competent to Counsel: Introduction to Nouthetic Counseling*. Grand Rapids: Zondervan, 1986.

Emlet, Mike. *CrossTalk: Where Life and Scripture Meet*. Greensboro, NC: New Growth, 2009.

Eyrich, Howard, and William Hines. *Curing the Heart: A Model for Biblical Counseling*. Fearn, Tain: Christian Focus, 2007.

Holmes, Jonathan. *The Company We Keep: In Search of Biblical Friendship*. Minneapolis: Cruciform, 2014.

Kellemen, Bob. *Counseling Under the Cross: How Martin Luther Applied the Gospel to Daily Life*. Greensboro, NC: New Growth, 2017.

Kellemen, Robert, and Kevin Carson, eds. *Biblical Counseling and the Church: God's Care through God's People*. Grand Rapids: Zondervan, 2015.

Kruis, John. *Quick Scripture Reference for Counseling*. Grand Rapids: Baker Books, 2013.

Lane, Tim, and Paul Tripp. *How People Change*. Greensboro, NC: New Growth, 2008.

Powlison, David. *Speaking Truth in Love: Counsel in Community*. Greensboro, NC: New Growth, 2005.

Scott, Stuart, and Heath Lambert, eds. *Counseling the Hard Cases*. Nashville: B&H Academic, 2012.

Tripp, Paul. *Instruments in the Redeemer's Hands: People in Need of Change Helping People in Need of Change*. Phillipsburg, NJ: P&R, 2002.

Welch, Ed. *Caring for One Another: 8 Ways to Cultivate Meaningful Relationships*. Wheaton: Crossway, 2018.

———. *Side by Side: Walking with Others in Wisdom and Love*. Wheaton: Crossway, 2015.

Wiersbe, Warren. *On Being a Servant of God*. Nashville: Thomas Nelson, 1993.

Robert W. Kellemen, PhD, is vice president of strategic development, academic dean, and professor at Faith Bible Seminary in Lafayette, Indiana. The founder of RPM Ministries, he also served as the founding executive director of the Biblical Counseling Coalition and has pastored four churches. He is the author of twenty books, including *Gospel-Centered Counseling*.

Connect with Bob

JOIN THE
Gospel-Centered Biblical Counseling Community on Facebook

Find encouragement and support from fellow counselors and equippers passionate about the sufficiency of Scripture for all of life and ministry.

  BobKellemen

CHANGING LIVES with
CHRIST'S CHANGELESS TRUTH

RPMministries.org

Most Christians care deeply but struggle to speak the truth in love. RPM Ministries exists to equip pastors, lay people, educators, students, and biblical counselors to change lives with Christ's changeless truth.

PROVIDE HOPE AND LOVE
WHEN PEOPLE NEED IT MOST

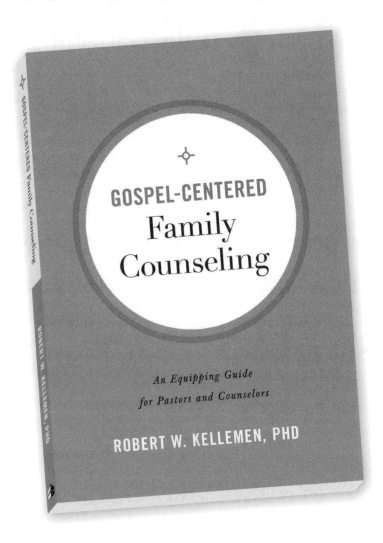

This gospel-centered training manual provides practical, user-friendly guidance that equips pastors, counselors, and lay leaders to help hurting families restore and maintain close, loving relationships.